As a material link between body and culture, self and other, the voice has been endlessly fascinating to artists and critics. Yet it is the voices of women that have inspired the greatest fascination, as well as the deepest ambivalence, because the female voice signifies sexual otherness as well as a source of sexual and cultural power. *Embodied Voices* explores cultural manifestations of female vocality in light of current theories of subjectivity, the body, and sexual difference. The fourteen essays collected here examine a wide spectrum of discourses, including myth, literature, music, film, psychoanalysis, and critical theory. Though diverse in their critical approaches, the essays are united in their attempt to articulate the compelling yet problematic intersections of gender, voice, and embodiment as they have shaped the textual representation of women, and women's self-expression in performance.

New perspectives in music history and criticism

Embodied voices

New perspectives in music history and criticism

GENERAL EDITORS
JEFFREY KALLBERG AND ANTHONY NEWCOMB

This new series explores the conceptual frameworks that shape or have shaped the ways in which we understand music and its history, and seeks to elaborate structures of explanation, interpretation, commentary, and criticism which make music intelligible and which provide a basis for argument about judgments of value. The intellectual scope of the series will be broad. Some investigations will treat, for example, historiographical topics – ideas of music history, the nature of historical change, or problems of periodization. Others will apply cross-disciplinary methods to the criticism of music, such as those involving literature, history, anthropology, linguistics, philosophy, psychoanalysis or gender studies. There will also be studies which consider music in its relation to society, culture, and politics. Overall, the series hopes to create a greater presence of music in the ongoing discourse among the human sciences.

Embodied voices

Representing female vocality in western culture

EDITED BY
LESLIE C. DUNN
AND NANCY A. JONES

CAMBRIDGE
UNIVERSITY PRESS

Published by the Press Syndicate of the University of Cambridge
The Pitt Building, Trumpington Street, Cambridge CB2 1RP
40 West 20th Street, New York, NY 10011–4211, USA
10 Stamford Road, Oakleigh, Melbourne 3166, Australia

First published 1994
First paperback edition 1996

A catalogue record for this book is available from the British Library

Library of Congress cataloguing in publication data

Embodied Voices : representing female vocality in Western culture / edited
by Leslie C. Dunn and Nancy A. Jones.
    p.   cm. – (New perspectives in music history and criticism)
Includes index.
ISBN 0 521 46012 3 (hardback)
1. Voice – Sex differences.   2. Voice – Sociological aspects.
3. Voice – Psychological aspects.   4. Women singers.
I. Dunn, Leslie C.   II. Jones, Nancy A.   III. Series
ML82.E55   1994   93–39496 CIP MN
783.6 – dc20

ISBN 0 521 46012 3 hardback
ISBN 0 521 58583 X paperback

Transferred to digital printing 2001

SN

To our husbands
and to Cora and Leo

CONTENTS

Contents

ILLUSTRATIONS

NOTES ON CONTRIBUTORS

Peter Antelyes is Associate Professor of English at Vassar College, where he also teaches in the American Culture program. He is author of *Tales of Adventurous Enterprise: Washington Irving and the Poetics of Western Expansion* (New York: Columbia University Press, 1990). His current research focuses on ethnicity in American literature, music, and art.

Linda Phyllis Austern, an assistant professor at the University of Notre Dame, has written on music, literature, and culture in sixteenth- and seventeenth-century England. Her work has appeared in Susan C. Cook and Judy S. Tsou, eds., *Cecilia Reclaimed: Feminist Perspectives on Gender and Music* (Urbana: University of Illinois Press, 1994), *The Journal of Musicology*, the *Journal of the American Musicological Society*, the *Journal of the Royal Musical Association*, and *Renaissance Quarterly*. She is also author of *Music in English Children's Drama of the Later Renaissance* (New York and London: Gordon and Breach, 1993), and is presently completing a study of music, culture, and intellectual tradition in late Tudor and early Stuart England.

Janet Beizer is Professor of French at the University of Virginia. Her essay on Louise Colet is part of her book, *Ventriloquized Bodies: Narratives of Hysteria in Nineteenth-Century France* (Ithaca: Cornell University Press, 1994), which details the process whereby hysteria's multiple symptoms become a dictionary of figures from which the writer can profitably draw in a period privileging impersonal or objective styles of narration. She has also published *Family Plots: Balzac's Narrative Generations* (New Haven: Yale University Press, 1986).

Leslie C. Dunn is Associate Professor of English at Vassar College. She has published essays on English Renaissance lyric poetry and music, and on women's song in Shakespeare. Her current project is a book-length study of music, gender, and representation in early modern England.

Barbara Engh is a doctoral candidate in cultural studies and comparative literature at the University of Minnesota. Her work engages questions of music and "the musical" in various critical and theoretical discourses.

xii

Her essay on the musical/maternal in the work of Roland Barthes appears in Ruth A. Solie, ed., *Musicology and Difference: Gender and Sexuality in Music Scholarship* (Berkeley: University of California Press, 1993). Her dissertation is entitled, "After the Master's Voice: Post-Phonographic Aurality."

Sarah Webster Goodwin is Associate Professor of English at Skidmore College in Saratoga Springs, New York. She is author of *Kitsch and Culture: The Dance of Death in Nineteenth-Century Literature and Graphic Arts* (New York: Garland Press, 1988), and co-editor of *Death and Representation* (Baltimore: Johns Hopkins University Press, 1993) and *Feminism, Utopia, and Narrative* (Knoxville: University of Tennessee Press, 1990). Her articles on nineteenth-century fiction and poetry have appeared in *Novel, Tulsa Studies in Women's Literature*, and elsewhere.

Karla F. C. Holloway is Professor of English at Duke University. Her teaching, research, and publications focus on the intersections between linguistics, literary theory, and cultural studies. She is co-author of *New Dimensions of Spirituality* (Westport, CT: Greenwood Press, 1987), and author of *The Character of the Word: The Texts of Zora Neale Hurston* (Westport, CT: Greenwood Press, 1987), and *Moorings and Metaphors* (New Brunswick, NJ: Rutgers University Press, 1992). She is currently working on a book-length study, *Codes of Conduct: Ethics and Ethnicity in Literature.*

Nancy A. Jones has taught French and Comparative Literature at Hobart and William Smith Colleges, in Geneva, New York, Baruch College-City University of New York, and Harvard University. She was a Visiting Scholar in Romance Languages at Duke University and the University of North Carolina at Chapel Hill for the year 1993/94, and is currently a fellow of the Mary I. Bunting Institute of Radcliffe College. She is the author of studies of gender and voice in medieval narrative and lyric poetry, and is writing a book on women, embroidery, and romance in thirteenth-century France.

Amy Lawrence is Assistant Professor of Film Studies at Dartmouth College in Hanover, New Hampshire. She is the author of *Echo and Narcissus: Women's Voices in Classical Hollywood Cinema* (Berkeley: University of California Press, 1991), a study of the way women's voices have been represented in films from the silent era to 1962. Her work has also appeared in *Wide Angle, Film Quarterly*, and *Quarterly Review of Film and Video.*

Rebecca A. Pope teaches courses in nineteenth-century British literature, popular fiction, the theory of gender and sexuality, and the cultural representation of AIDS at Georgetown University. She has published works on British and American Gothic and detective fiction, AIDS in popular fiction, and feminist collaborative scholarship. Her essay in this volume is an early draft of a chapter of a book she is writing with Susan J. Leonardi on fictional and historical divas (*To Have a Voice: The Politics of the Diva*, New Brunswick, NJ: Rutgers University Press, forthcoming).

Charles Segal is Professor of Greek and Latin at Harvard University, a Fellow of the American Academy of Arts and Sciences, and President of the American Philological Association for 1993/94. He was a fellow at the National Humanities Center for 1993/94. His recent books include *Orpheus: The Myth of the Poet* (Baltimore: Johns Hopkins University Press, 1989), *Lucretius on Death and Anxiety* (Princeton University Press, 1990), *Oedipus Tyrannus: Tragic Heroism and the Limits of Knowledge* (New York: Twayne Publishers, 1993), and *Euripides and the Poetics of Sorrow* (Durham: Duke University Press, 1993).

Elizabeth Tolbert is a professor of musicology at the Peabody Institute of the Johns Hopkins University. She has published articles on lament traditions and is at work on a book entitled *Dislocated Voices: Music, Memory, and Gender*.

Edward Baron Turk, who is Professor of French and Film Studies at the Massachusetts Institute of Technology, studied piano at the Juilliard School in New York City. He is author, most recently, of *Child of Paradise: Marcel Carné and the Golden Age of French Cinema* (Cambridge, MA: Harvard University Press, 1990), which won a prize from the Theatre Library Association in 1990. He is currently at work on the biography of Jeanette MacDonald.

Nancy J. Vickers is Professor of Comparative Literature at the University of Southern California. She has written on the works of Dante, Petrarch, and Shakespeare, as well as on the poetic and plastic production of the court of Francis I. Her work in lyric has led to an interest in the relationship of technology and genre, and she is currently at work on a book on music video.

ACKNOWLEDGMENTS

The idea for this book grew out of a 1990 Modern Language Association session entitled "Feminine Figures of Song." We are grateful to the Lyrica Society for Word–Music Relations, whose sponsorship of that session provided the first audience for our explorations of female vocality. We have also benefited from lively exchanges with members of the Vassar College Women's Studies Program, the Gender and Music Group at Harvard University, and participants in the Feminist Theory and Music Conference at the University of Minnesota.

The editors of the New Perspectives in Music History and Criticism series, Jeffrey Kallberg and Anthony Newcomb, were early supporters of a project which might at first have seemed an unlikely candidate for a music series; their enthusiastic engagement with our own perspectives on music was a model for the kind of interdisciplinary dialogue we have tried to foster in the collection itself. We would also like to thank our anonymous reader at Cambridge University Press, whose detailed comments on an early version of the manuscript helped us to refine our conception of the book as a whole and improved many of the individual essays. We thank Penny Souster, our editor at Cambridge University Press, for patiently guiding us through the publication process. We are extremely grateful to our copy-editor, Helen Southall, for a meticulous assistance that helped us to produce a more elegant book.

For intellectual and practical help, we thank Richard Leppert, Susan McClary, Sarah Webster Goodwin, Nancy J. Vickers, Peter Antelyes, and Charles Segal. We also received valuable advice in the early stages of this project from Kaja Silverman, Henry Louis Gates, Jr., Sally McConnell-Ginet, and Ann Morrison.

Our research assistants, Jong Kim at Vassar and Hugh Eakin at Harvard, proved invaluable at several crucial stages in the long process of developing fourteen disparate essays into a collective conversation. Special thanks are due to Vassar's Ford Scholar Program, which provided funding for a summer research assistantship.

We are grateful to the following journals and presses for permission to reprint material that originally appeared in their publications:

"The diva doesn't die: George Eliot's *Armgart*" by Rebecca A. Pope, is reprinted from *Criticism* 32, 4 (1990), by permission of the Wayne State University Press.

Acknowledgments

"Deriding the voice of Jeanette MacDonald: notes on psychoanalysis and the American film musical" by Edward Baron Turk, is reprinted from *Camera Obscura* 25 (1992), by permission of Indiana University Press.

Janet Beizer's article, "Rewriting Ophelia: fluidity, madness, and voice in Louise Colet's *La Servante*," appears, in expanded form, as a chapter in her book, *Ventriloquized Bodies: Narratives of Hysteria in Nineteenth-Century France*, copyright 1994 by Cornell University, and is used by permission of the publisher, Cornell University Press, Ithaca, New York.

Material from Karla F. C. Holloway's article, "The lyrical dimensions of spirituality: music, voice, and language in the novels of Toni Morrison," first appeared in chapters 2, 4, and 8 of *New Dimensions of Spirituality: A BiRacial and BiCultural Reading of the Novels of Toni Morrison*, by Holloway and Stephanie Demetrakopoulous, published by Greenwood Press, 1987, an imprint of Greenwood Publishing Group, Inc., Westport, CT. Reprinted with permission.

The photographs of the three Gorgon figures which appear in Charles Segal's essay were provided by Art Resource, New York. The stills from *Love Me Tonight* and *Rose Marie* which accompany Edward Turk's essay are reproduced by courtesy of Paramount Studios and MGM Studios respectively. They were provided by the Film Stills Archive of the Museum of Modern Art.

The musical transcription of the "Willow Song" in Linda Phyllis Austern's essay is reproduced from *Music in Shakespearean Tragedy* by Frederick W. Sternfeld (London, 1963), by courtesy of Routledge and Kegan Paul.

The lyrics of "You've Got to See Mama Ev'ry Night," words and music by Billy Rose and Con Conrad, copyright © 1923 (Renewed 1931) c/o EMI FEIST CATALOG INC., which appear in Peter Antelyes's essay, are reprinted by permission of CPP Belwin, Inc.

The lyrics of "Like a Prayer," words and music by Madonna Ciccone and Patrick Leonard, and "Promise to Try," words and music by Madonna Ciccone and Patrick Leonard, which appear in the essay by Nancy J. Vickers, are reprinted by permission of Warner-Chappell Music, Inc.:

"LIKE A PRAYER"
(Madonna Ciccone, Patrick Leonard)
© 1989 WB MUSIC CORP., BLEU DISQUE MUSIC CO., INC., WEBO GIRL PUBLISHING, INC. & JOHNNY YUMA MUSIC
All rights on behalf of BLEU DISQUE MUSIC CO., INC. & WEBO GIRL PUBLISHING, INC., administered by WB MUSIC CORP.
All rights on behalf of JOHNNY YUMA MUSIC for the world,

Finally, we would like to thank our contributors, who collectively embodied the voices of this book. Working with them has been an intellectual adventure and a genuine pleasure.

Introduction

LESLIE C. DUNN AND NANCY A. JONES

Feminists have used the word "voice" to refer to a wide range of aspirations: cultural agency, political enfranchisement, sexual autonomy, and expressive freedom, all of which have been historically denied to women. In this context, "voice" has become a metaphor for textual authority, and alludes to the efforts of women to reclaim their own experience through writing ("having a voice") or to the specific qualities of their literary and cultural self-expression ("in a different voice").[1] This metaphor has become so pervasive, so intrinsic to feminist discourse that it makes us too easily forget (or repress) the concrete physical dimensions of the female voice upon which this metaphor was based. *Embodied Voices* returns to the literal, audible voice in an effort to show how it, too, has been a site of women's silencing, as well as an instrument of empowerment.

Our title reflects our desire to avoid the simpler term, "the female voice" and its inevitable metaphorization. By using the terms "embodied voices" and "vocality," we hope to reorient our readers' thinking. We use the word "vocality" to indicate a broader spectrum of utterance. Too often "voice" is conflated with speech, thereby identifying language as the primary carrier of meaning. However, human vocality encompasses all the voice's manifestations (for example, speaking, singing, crying, and laughing), each of which is invested with social meanings not wholly determined by linguistic content. French poststructuralist theorists from Julia Kristeva to Michel Poizat have emphasized the voice's autonomy from language, indeed from signification. To borrow the terminology used by Kristeva and Roland Barthes, the voice can be heard not only in terms of its signified or pheno-song (its verbal or

---

[1] See, for example, such feminist classics as Mary Field Belenky, Blythe McVicker Clinchy, Nancy Rule Goldberger, and Jill Mattuck Tarule, eds., *Women's Ways of Knowing: The Development of Self, Voice and Mind* (New York: Basic Books, 1986) and Carol Gilligan, *In a Different Voice* (Cambridge, MA: Harvard University Press, 1982). For a useful survey of the varied uses of the term "voice" in feminist discourse, see Susan Gal, "Between Speech and Silence: The Problematics of Research on Language and Gender," in Micaela di Leonardo, ed., *Gender at the Crossroads of Knowledge: Feminist Anthropology in the Postmodern Era* (Berkeley and Los Angeles: University of California Press, 1991), pp. 175–203.

Leslie C. Dunn and Nancy A. Jones

cultural content), but also as geno-song, the purely sonorous, bodily element of the vocal utterance.[2] By stressing "vocality" in this sense, we signal our primary concern with the audible female voice, and our desire to focus on the construction of its non-verbal meanings – to attend to, and articulate, what Barthes calls the "grain" of the voice.

"Vocality" also implies an emphasis on the performative dimension of vocal expression, that is on the dynamic, contingent quality of both vocalization and audition, and on their vital interrelationship. The term "vocality" was recently coined by medievalist Paul Zumthor in his polemic against the critical tendency to overlook the primacy of the human voice in medieval poetics.[3] He uses the term to refute what he sees as the excessively literary and text-based conception of medieval verbal art, and to convey more emphatically than does the term "orality" the presence of the human voice in its composition, performance, and reception. We have borrowed his term in order to stress that voices inhabit an intersubjective acoustic space; hence their meanings cannot be recovered without reconstructing the contexts of their hearing.

To move from "voice" to "vocality," then, implies a shift from a concern with the phenomenological roots of voice to a conception of vocality as a cultural construct. By specifying female vocality, we also assert the centrality of gender in shaping that construction. Here our third term, "embodiment," comes into play. As a material link between "inside" and "outside," self and other, the voice is, in Nelly Furman's words, "the locus of articulation of an individual's body to language and society."[4] Since both language and society are structured by codes of sexual difference, both the body and its voice are inescapably gendered. This is not to say that voices possess intrinsically masculine or feminine qualities. Indeed, recent work by feminist anthropologists and socio-linguists has demonstrated that there is no single satisfactory explanation – biological, psychological, or social – for the differences between male and female voices. Rather, vocal gendering appears to be the product of a complex interplay between anatomical differences, socialization into culturally prescribed gender roles, and "the contrasting possibilities for

[2] Kristeva's original terms are "geno-text" and "pheno-text." See *Revolution in Poetic Language*, trans. Margaret Waller, introduction by Leon S. Roudiez (New York: Columbia University Press, 1984), pp. 86–89. By changing "text" to "song," Barthes adapts Kristeva's terminology to chart a similar opposition within vocal music in his essay, "The Grain of the Voice," in *Image, Music, Text*, trans. Stephen Heath (New York: Noonday Press/Farrar, Straus, and Giroux, 1977), pp. 181–83.

[3] Paul Zumthor, *La lettre et la voix: de la "littérature" médiévale* (Paris: Editions du Seuil, 1987), pp. 20–31.

[4] Nelly Furman, "Opera, or the Staging of the Voice," *Cambridge Opera Journal* 3, 3 (1991), 303. Furman is summarizing the approach of Marie-France Castarède in the latter's *La voix et ses sortilèges* (Paris: Les Belles Lettres, 1987).

2

expression for men and women within a given society."[5] In other words, the acoustic and expressive qualities of the voice are as much shaped by an individual's cultural formation as is her or his use of language.

Contributing to this formation are what Furman has called "the many myths that have inflected [the voice's] auditory reception," including myths of vocal gender (303). These range from stereotypes of sexual difference – for example, women's voices are thought to be high and shrill or breathy while men's are low and quiet or harsh – to the social meanings attached to these differences and the specific kinds of power or authority attributed to gendered vocal qualities. Not surprisingly, in Western culture these myths have served to reinforce patriarchal constructions of the feminine. The anchoring of the female voice in the female body confers upon it all the conventional associations of femininity with nature and matter, with emotion and irrationality. More concretely, it leads to associations of the female voice with bodily fluids (milk, menstrual blood) and the consequent devaluation of feminine utterance as formless and free-flowing babble, a sign of uncontrolled female generativity. Such associations further point to the identification of woman's vocality with her sexuality: like the body from which it emanates, the female voice is construed as both a signifier of sexual otherness and a source of sexual power, an object at once of desire and fear.

The archetypal figures of this seductive but dangerous vocality are the Sirens, whose song lures men to their destruction with a false promise of bliss. Yet Odysseus proves able to resist that lure, and in some versions of the story the Sirens must die when their vocal power is "mastered" by a greater masculine power. This narrative pattern, which Catherine Clément, writing about the representation of women singers in nineteenth-century opera, has called "the undoing of women,"[6] recurs throughout the history of Western literary and musical traditions, producing a series of cultural icons that figure the mythic relationship between gender and vocality: Echo and Philomela, the sybil and the hysteric, the diva and the blues queen. Such narratives testify to the persistent desire of male artists to control through representation the anxieties aroused by the female voice, even while they license the display, and the enjoyment, of its powers.

Recently, however, women writers and artists have begun to refigure the relationship between gender and vocality. The idealized figure

---

5 Gal, "Between Speech and Silence," p. 175. For a critical survey of the various approaches used to explain the differences between male and female voices, see David Graddol and Joan Swann, *Gender Voices* (Oxford: Basil Blackwell, 1989), pp. 12–40.
6 Catherine Clément, *Opera, or the Undoing of Women*, trans. Betsy Wing, foreword by Susan McClary (Minneapolis: University of Minnesota Press, 1988). Originally published as *L'Opéra, ou la défaite des femmes* (Paris: Bernard Grasset, 1979).

of the mother, nurturing with the "milk" of her voice, has inspired a contemporary women's poetics of the female body that resists patriarchal devaluation. Texts such as Kristeva's "Stabat Mater" and *The Newly Born Woman* by Hélène Cixous and Catherine Clément are attempts by feminist theorists to reclaim the power of the female voice and give it a new cultural meaning.[7] In another strategy of resistance, contemporary women performance artists deconstruct the traditional paradigms of the voice/body relationship through cross-dressing and technological manipulations of their voices. Performers such as Laurie Anderson and Diamanda Galás also demystify and de-aestheticize the female voice in order to show that women can possess more assertive, less predictable forms of vocality.

Whether approached in terms of theory, fantasy or practice, then, female vocality raises a number of compelling questions for contemporary feminist criticism. How has the relationship between gender, voice, and embodiment been constructed in Western culture? How have these constructions informed the representation of women, and shaped women's own cultural production? Have there been any disruptions or displacements in the representations of female vocality, and if so, what might be their cultural significance?

These are the questions addressed by *Embodied Voices*. Interdisciplinary in conception, it seeks to inaugurate an exploration of the place that the female voice has occupied in the Western cultural imagination. The essays examine the audible voice as it has been represented in a wide spectrum of discourses: myth, drama, prose fiction, poetry, film, opera, ritual lamentation, African American spirituals and blues, popular song, music video, psychoanalysis and critical theory. Each of the authors places her or his object of study within a specific context – social, musicological, historical, literary or cultural.

A number of recent intellectual trends make an investigation into female vocality especially timely. In feminist film criticism, the audible female voice became a major concern with the publication of Kaja Silverman's book, *The Acoustic Mirror*.[8] As the first discipline to apply psychoanalytic theories about voice, music, sexuality, and subjectivity to a specific artistic medium, film studies has taught us to see the audible female voice as a problem of representation. Accordingly, all theoretical discussions of female vocality, including many of those presented here,

---

[7] Julia Kristeva, "Stabat Mater," trans. Leon S. Roudiez, in *Tales of Love* (New York: Columbia University Press, 1987), pp. 234–63; Hélène Cixous and Catherine Clément, *The Newly Born Woman*, trans. Betsy Wing (Minneapolis: University of Minnesota Press, 1986).

[8] Kaja Silverman, *The Acoustic Mirror: The Female Voice in Psychoanalysis and Cinema* (Bloomington: Indiana University Press, 1988).

are indebted to the theoretical formulations and practical criticism provided by Silverman, Mary Ann Doane, Amy Lawrence and others.[9]

In a more general, yet equally important way, this collection responds to an exciting development in musicology, namely the emergence of feminist music criticism. Although the impact of feminist critical theory upon musicology is a belated and, some would argue, controversial development by comparison with other disciplines, it has stimulated influential studies of gender and music, such as Susan McClary's *Feminine Endings*, and an anthology edited by Ruth A. Solie, *Musicology and Difference*.[10] Two successful conferences on feminist theory and music, held at the University of Minnesota in 1991 and the University of Rochester in 1993, are signs of a new critical spirit in musicological studies, which draws on semiotics, film theory, psychoanalysis, and literary criticism to ask new questions about the cultural meanings of music. In Lawrence Kramer's words, the issue is "whether and how to (dis)locate the boundaries between the musical and the 'extramusical.'"[11] By examining representations of the female singing voice in a variety of media, and revealing the embeddedness of those representations in Western discourses of both the musical and the feminine, our anthology also participates in this project.

Much of the new feminist music criticism has been devoted to vocal music, including opera, where the issue of female vocality has been particularly foregrounded. For example, some of the most innovative work in opera studies is being done from the perspective of the listener/fan.[12] For fans/critics such as Marie-France Castarède, Michel Poizat, and Wayne Koestenbaum, opera is above all the experience of listening to the voice, especially that of the diva.[13] From this perspective, listening assumes new importance in critical discourse, for the listener actively engages in the construction of the meaning of a vocal performance. By interpreting opera in terms of their own cultural formation,

---

9   The literature on voice, music, and sound in cinema is vast. See, in particular, Guy Rosolato, "La Voix: entre corps et langage," *Revue française de psychanalyse* 38, 1 (1974), 75–94; Mary Ann Doane, "The Voice in the Cinema: The Articulation of Body and Space," *Yale French Studies* 60 (1980), 47–56; and Amy Lawrence, *Echo and Narcissus: Women's Voices in Classical Hollywood Cinema* (Berkeley and Los Angeles: University of California Press, 1991).

10 Susan McClary, *Feminine Endings: Music, Gender, and Sexuality* (Minneapolis: University of Minnesota Press, 1991); Ruth A. Solie, ed., *Musicology and Difference: Gender and Sexuality in Music Scholarship* (Berkeley and Los Angeles: University of California Press, 1993).

11 Lawrence Kramer, "The Musicology of the Future," *repercussions* 1 (Spring 1992), 18.

12 Furman, "Opera," 303.

13 See Castarède, *La voix*; Michel Poizat, *The Angel's Cry: Beyond the Pleasure Principle in Opera*, trans. Arthur Denner (Ithaca: Cornell University Press, 1992. Originally published as *L'opéra, ou le cri de l'ange, Essai sur la jouissance de l'amateur de l'opéra* [Paris: A. M. Métailié, 1986]); and Wayne Koestenbaum, "Callas and her Fans," *Yale Review* 79, 1 (Autumn 1989), 1–20.

psycho-sexual orientation, and ideological disposition, these writers overturn the traditional hierarchy between work, composer, performer, and listener. Their work thus enacts the poststructuralist challenge to the hermeneutic primacy of the author and the reification of the written text, and develops the "dialogue of listening" which Kramer has called the "aim of musicology, ideally conceived" (17).

The work of Castarède, Poizat, and Koestenbaum (among others) has another relevance to the project of feminist music criticism. Challenging Clément's denunciation of opera in terms of its misogynist plots and libretti, these authors emphasize the performative dimension of the female voice. Thus, while acknowledging what Clément and others have characterized as opera's ultimate will to silence the diva (not to mention the institution's tendency to exploit her sexually), Koestenbaum rejoices in the transgressive vocal interpolations and "will to be heard" of Maria Callas from the perspective of a gay male opera fan.[14] This new body of writing on opera suggests that a multiplicity of responses to the diva's voice is emerging.

Embodied Voices had its genesis in the editors' shared interests in the literary and musical representation of women's song. In our respective research and teaching in medieval and Renaissance literature, we became increasingly fascinated by a persistent tendency on the part of poets and critics to privilege the verbal and textual dimensions of song over the musical and performative. This elision of the vocal was commonly thematized in literary texts as the silencing of a female singer. As we continued to ponder the troubling parallel between the musical "difference" of song and the sexual "difference" of women so often articulated in the Western tradition, we began to reconceptualize the problem of the female literary voice in terms of aural experience as well as textual models. We presented some of this work at the 1990 Modern Language Association Convention, for which we organized a session, sponsored by the Lyrica Society, entitled, "Embodied Voices: Feminine Figures of Song." The revised versions of our papers and those by Sarah Webster Goodwin and Nancy J. Vickers became the nucleus of the present collection. In commissioning further contributions, we have broadened our subject in order to bring out the many resonances between the various, often contradictory, manifestations of the audible female voice.

The essays in this collection not only document the multiplicity of possible responses to female vocality, but also enact it. The editors have made no attempt to impose critical uniformity upon them; we have preferred to let the reader discover and enjoy the individuality of the contributors' approaches. Readers will notice, for example, the contrast

[14] Koestenbaum, "Callas," 8.

between the historicism of Rebecca A. Pope's study of George Eliot's *Armgart* and the psychological approach adopted by Edward Baron Turk in his essay on the film musicals of Jeanette MacDonald. The influence of psychoanalytic theories of the female voice on several essays is evident. Yet, while for some authors, such as Nancy A. Jones, these theories provide an interpretive frame for their readings, for others, including Amy Lawrence, Nancy J. Vickers, and Barbara Engh, they serve merely as a point of departure or as a foil for an alternative approach. The authors also differ in the degree to which they incorporate the voices of their own experience in their writing. The essays by Elizabeth Tolbert and Karla F. C. Holloway both grow directly from the authors' encounters with actual women's voices.

Part I: Vocality, textuality, and the silencing of the female voice

The essays in this section engage with what might be called myths and fantasies of the female voice – narratives through which feminine vocality has been culturally imagined, its powers celebrated and its dangers exorcised. The texts examined are drawn from the canonical Western literary tradition, but the narrative paradigm that they collectively articulate recurs in a range of historical and discursive contexts, from classical myth to nineteenth-century opera to contemporary psychoanalytic theory. It is a fantasy of origins in that it serves to explain and justify the placing, or rather displacing, of the female voice in a patriarchal culture through its alignment with the material, the irrational, the pre-cultural, and the musical. In the works of Pindar, Dante, Shakespeare, and Wordsworth, these forces are projected onto transgressive feminine figures – the Gorgon, the Siren, the madwoman, the prostitute – whose unruly sexuality and disturbing vocalizations threaten to overwhelm the "civilized" order espoused by the text. The mastering of that threat is enacted both thematically, through the defeat or death of the woman character, and discursively, through the containment of her utterance within a textuality identified as masculine, thus opposing her literal, embodied vocality to his metaphorical, disembodied "voice."

Charles Segal's essay examines one of the earliest literary versions of this paradigm, Pindar's Twelfth *Pythian Ode*, which tells how the virgin goddess Athena transforms the Gorgons' wail of mourning at their sister Medusa's death into the artistic flute-song of the Greek polis. Segal reconstructs the complex social imaginary behind the Gorgon, a primordial divinity, both maternal and destructive, who incarnates the ambivalence within ancient Greek culture about the female voice and the maternal body. Athena's transformation of the Gorgons' lament into flute-song brings female musicality into "culture," taming the danger of its physicality and sexuality.

7

The combined themes of violence and transformation are equally prominent in Nancy Jones's reading of female vocality in *Purgatorio XIX*. Here, too, a demonized female voice is brutally cut off and super-seded by a culturally sanctioned male voice. The pilgrim's dream of the Siren in Canto XIX dramatizes his transitory fascination with the pure sonorousness of her singing, a fascination which threatens to delay his spiritual progress. The episode's exposure of the Siren's song as empty babble also reveals Dante's desire to "purge" his *Comedy* of vocal music's destabilizing effects, and to align it instead with the textual tradition of Latin epic.

The gendered opposition between music and language is also the focus of Leslie Dunn's essay on Ophelia's songs in *Hamlet*. Drawing on both Renaissance and contemporary discourses of music, Dunn argues that Shakespeare's dramatic construction of Ophelia as madwoman involves a mapping of her sexual and psychological otherness onto the discursive "difference" of song. The dominance of song in Ophelia's mad scene dramatizes the disruptive power that inheres in her singing voice – a voice at once musical and female, and thus doubly charged with semantic excess and indeterminacy.

The Romantic poet's need to evoke an incoherent, abhorrent female vocality as a foil for his own poetic voice is the subject of Sarah Webster Goodwin's essay. Like Pindar's Athena, the poet brings an inarticulate, feminized Nature into culture by containing it within the linguistic structures of poetry. In Wordsworth's poems "Alice Fell" and "Poor Susan," the poet is haunted, not by nature's music, but by a prostitute's cry which comes to symbolize the frightening effects of a market economy on human relations. By opposing his song to her cry, the poet distances himself from too close an identification with feminine vocality, becoming himself the naturalized singer from whom the woman is alienated.

Part II: Anxieties of audition

Listening is always a cultural act, and it is always mediated by a mode of representation. The essays in Part II deal with listeners' responses to female vocality in three very different contexts: the English Renaissance stage, the American film musical, and Theodor Adorno's writings on phonographic reproduction. Whereas the essays in Part I study the act of listening to the female voice on a thematic level, the essays in Part II focus on the putative role of the female voice in the construction of the listening subject.

Various models of listening to the female voice have emerged, but perhaps none has been as influential as the psychoanalytic theory of auditory *jouissance*. In describing the *jouissance* desired and occasionally experienced by the opera fan in listening to the diva's voice, Michel

Poizat writes: ". . . finally a point is reached where the listener *himself* [our emphasis] is stripped of all possibility of speech."[15] Poizat theorizes that at certain moments of vocal transcendence, when the diva's voice becomes a "voice-object" to the listener, the body's libidinal drives emerge in sound unmediated by language, producing a sensation of radical loss, whereby castration, difference, and subjectivity are annulled. As Poizat's language implies, characterizations of listening as an erotic or infantile experience often assume a male listening subject, whether they take the form of patriarchal myth, psychoanalytic theory, or opera criticism. In this scenario of listening, everything seems to be at stake when women open their mouths, for this experience of loss threatens the stability of the patriarchal order, indeed that of the male subject itself.

For the essays in this section, the female voice, whether it is celebrated, eroticized, demonized, ridiculed or denigrated, is always stigmatized, ideologically "marked," and construed as a "problem" for the (male) social critic/auditor, who demands concern if not control. In inviting us to reflect upon the socio-cultural dimensions of audition, these essays underscore its varied manifestations and complexities within different technologies of representation.

Like the essays by Dunn and Goodwin in Part I, Linda Austern's essay focuses on the scene of a woman's singing. She shows how the seemingly natural relation between voice and body could be unsettled on the English Renaissance stage by the use of boy actors in female roles. The seductive hybridity of the boy actors' artfully feigned feminine voices, which was denounced by Puritan moralists and exploited by dramatists, suggests a specific sexual dynamic of listening that emerged within the intellectual and social worlds of Elizabethan and Jacobean England.

Edward Baron Turk draws on psychoanalytic theory about the sources of auditory pleasure and displeasure to investigate the public hostility to the trained soprano voice in American film musicals. Focusing on the paired voices of Jeanette MacDonald and Nelson Eddy, Turk's essay shows how their vocal symbiosis, enhanced by their film studio's use of sound and visual technology, replaced the traditional phallic eroticism of earlier film musicals with a more feminine, decorporealized eroticism.

Barbara Engh's essay questions the ability of feminist theory to interpret Adorno's notorious claim that a woman's singing voice cannot be recorded well because it demands the presence of her body. Despite its sexist overtones, the passage must be read in the context of Adorno's ongoing meditation on the singing voice – and, by extension, on music – as the site at which, for Adorno, the human and the inhuman are

---

[15] Michel Poizat, "'The Blue Note' and 'The Objectified Voice and the Vocal Object,'" *Cambridge Opera Journal* 3, 3 (1991), 199. This article is derived from *The Angel's Cry*.

distinguished. In Adorno's view, the modern listener's obliviousness to the disembodying of the voice by the nonhuman phonograph prevents him from experiencing the painful feminine hysteria which is the mark of true subjectivity.

Part III: Refigurations: women artists, vocality, and cultural authority

The essays of the two final parts take up the themes of the previous parts: the dynamics of voice and (inter) subjectivity; vocality and textuality; vocal authority and authorial "voice." In many cases they also revisit some of the narratives that preceding essays identify as figuring the female voice's meaning and value in the Western tradition. However, by shifting the focus to the work of women artists, these latter essays reveal the contingency of those narratives, and challenge the masculinist paradigms they serve to legitimize. The texts and performances examined here refute the definition of the embodied voice as a devalued voice. They present us with new figures – the diva, the lamenter, the red hot mama – for whom the very quality of the female voice is, in Rebecca Pope's words, "an empowering difference" that enables women artists to escape containment by the dominant ideology. They also reveal the existence of expressive arenas – some traditionally established, others newly created – in which feminine vocality possesses both cultural authority and creative force.

The essays in Part III offer a prismatic meditation on one of the fundamental questions of this volume: under what cultural conditions, and by what artistic means, can women (re)claim the authority of the female voice? One crucial medium of self-authorization, as we have seen, is that of musical performance. As a more emphatically embodied form of vocality than speaking, the singing voice redefines the issue of authority. No longer is the "grain" or body-in-the-voice a social or aesthetic liability; instead it is a source of power. As Rebecca Pope argues in her essay, the opera diva displays the most elemental and spectacular form of authority through her vocal dominance on stage, which transcends the narrative destruction of the opera heroine so strongly protested by Catherine Clément.[16] Because it literally cannot be usurped or displaced by men, the diva's voice becomes a mode of female redress. It enables her to revise or supplement the male-authored text while freeing her from traditional gender roles. Pope shows how mezzo-soprano Pauline Viardot, by her moving voice and single-minded commitment to her career, inspired George Eliot as a model of the woman artist: Eliot's heroine, Armgart, proclaims, "I carry my revenges in my throat."

[16] Clément, *Opera*.

10

Janet Beizer reads Louise Colet's *La Servante* as a confrontation with traditional models of feminine literary voice. Colet struggled with her lover Flaubert's denigration of her "feminine" style, which he metonymically identified with female bodily fluids. By rewriting the story of Ophelia, Colet worked to resituate this voice, but her attempt was unsuccessful, and her heroine's story ends with her plunge into the "communicative void" of madness. Nevertheless, Colet's challenge to cultural models of feminine expression as unformed and free-flowing, and her refusal to speak in a categorically feminine or masculine voice, make *La Servante* a protofeminist text.

Amy Lawrence's essay focuses on the cinematic convention of direct address, in which the illusion of an unproblematic unity between body and voice invests the speaker with an apparent claim to authenticity. In François Truffaut's *Two English Girls*, the heroine's use of direct address seems to create a voice of "truth" that cannot be assimilated to the male narrator's point of view. Yet this temporary privileging of the female voice is in fact thoroughly contained by a triple layering of masculine authorship. By contrast, in *Surname Viet, Given Name Nam*, Trinh Minh Ha reveals her camera's own "interestedness" and thus reconstructs women's voices, and the feminine subjectivity they represent, as complex, multiple, and fluid.

Like opera, the ritual lament is a cultural form that not only locates power in the embodied voice, but confers that power specifically upon women. In her study of the lamenters of Finnish Karelia, Elizabeth Tolbert identifies the stylized expression of grief, "crying with words," as the source of the woman lamenter's magico-religious power. It is the very quality of the female lamenter's voice that enables her to mediate between personal and collective experiences of grief, and to create a bridge between the worlds of the living and the dead. The lamenter's art thus transforms an expression of emotion that might otherwise be denigrated as "feminine" into an instrument of empowerment for the performer.

Part IV: Maternal voices

The essays in our final section engage in revisionary ways with what is perhaps the primal figure of female vocality – primal because, according to what Silverman has called "a powerful cultural fantasy," the maternal voice is the "first voice of love."[17] This potent dream of maternal presence – a presence that is embodied, literally, in the "bath of sounds" created by the mother's soothing, singing voice – has resonated in

---

[17] Silverman, *The Acoustic Mirror*, p. 72. The phrase "first voice of love" is Hélène Cixous's; see Cixous and Clément, *The Newly Born Woman*, p. 93.

Western literature and music for centuries.[18] But this maternal voice has recently acquired a new prominence through postmodern psychoanalytic and feminist theory. Psychoanalytic theorists have posited acoustic space as the originary psychic space, a "sonorous envelope" in which the infant experiences a primary union with the mother prior to the splitting of subjectivity that marks the child's entry into the symbolic order of language and culture. Reconstruction of this irrecoverable infantile moment gives rise, according to Silverman, to two opposing "fantasies" of the maternal voice: the positive fantasy of blissful union, and the negative fantasy of entrapment.[19]

As mentioned earlier, the positive fantasy of an idealized mother, existing in a kind of prelapsarian immanence outside language, has been a powerful one for many feminist writers. Its most influential theorist, Hélène Cixous, defines femininity-in-writing (*écriture féminine*) as the mark of a privileged relationship to the mother's body, a voice remembered from a time before "the Symbolic took one's breath away." Significantly, Cixous also characterizes this voice as music: "Within each woman the first, nameless love is singing."[20] As a number of critics have pointed out, however, this myth of musical/maternal fullness is precisely that, a myth, and as such does not escape inscription within the very structures of patriarchal thought that it desires to transcend.[21] Nor does it suggest the rich variety of meanings that inhere in the actual voices of women, concretely situated in history and society. Performance artist Diamanda Galás, for example, draws on the traditional dirges of Greek village women to forge her voice into a weapon in the war against AIDS. Her song is a "visceral collage of notes, chants, shrieks, gurgles and hisses" – a far cry, literally, from the comforting acoustic bath of the dream mother of psychoanalytic theory.[22]

The essays in this section are conversant with current theories of the maternal voice, just as the women writers and performers they study are conversant with traditional images of maternal vocality. But the authors of these essays challenge a potentially monolithic discourse of

---

[18] Didier Anzieu, "L'enveloppe sonore du soi," *Nouvelle revue de psychanalyse*, 13 (1976), 173, as cited in Silverman, *The Acoustic Mirror*, p. 72.

[19] Rosolato, "La voix," 81, as cited in Silverman, *The Acoustic Mirror*, p. 72. On the positive and negative fantasies of the maternal voice, see Silverman, *The Acoustic Mirror*, pp. 72–100.

[20] Cixous and Clément, *The Newly Born Woman*, p. 93.

[21] Claire Kahane, "Questioning the Maternal Voice," *Genders* 3, 3 (Fall 1988), 82–91, esp. 83; Toril Moi, *Sexual/Textual Politics* (London and New York: Methuen, 1985), pp. 108–119; Domna C. Stanton, "Difference on Trial: A Critique of the Maternal Metaphor in Cixous, Irigaray, and Kristeva," in Nancy K. Miller, ed., *The Poetics of Gender* (New York: Columbia University Press, 1986), 157–82.

[22] William Harris, "Don't Look to Diamanda Galás for Comfort," *New York Times* July 4, 1993, H20. See also Andrea Juno's interview with Galás in *Angry Women* (San Francisco: Re/Search Publications, 1991), pp. 8–9, 14.

the maternal by revealing the multiplicity of maternal *voices* in women's cultural productions. For women writers and artists, "coming to voice" (to borrow Nancy J. Vickers's term) may entail a confrontation with male-centered myths of the maternal voice, or alternatively, a remembrance of other cultural models of maternal vocality.

Interweaving her own memories with a critical reading of three novels by Toni Morrison, Karla F. C. Holloway explores the ways in which African American women writers' literary voices are "linked to ancestral and modern voices of the black diaspora." She argues that this linking is achieved primarily through memories of music, especially the mother's song. Yet hers is no nostalgic vision of lost plenitude: rather the maternal voice in both Morrison's fiction and Holloway's experience embodies a "(re)creative potential" that actively preserves the continuity of African American cultural traditions.

Peter Antelyes's essay reconstructs the cultural history of the red hot mama, a performing persona of the 1920s epitomized in the careers of Bessie Smith and Sophie Tucker. The "ethnic maternal voice" of his title refers to the ability of the mama, through her artistry of embodiment, to forge a subjectivity out of the racial, ethnic and gendered identities with which she was associated. Focusing on two exemplary performances, Antelyes traces the development of the mama from blues to vaudeville, from black to Jewish musical cultures.

Finally, Nancy J. Vickers's essay brings us to the present moment, and a woman performer who "mothers" herself in an act of vocal self-authorization. In a creative cycle extending from the *Like a Prayer* album to the documentary *Truth or Dare*, Madonna inhabits a succession of maternal images and roles, remaining "in control" throughout. Ironically, however, Madonna's self-mothering is made possible by the absence of her own mother, whose early death freed her to "express herself" by dramatizing a fantasy of empowerment.

While celebrating the diversity of the essays, the editors hasten to acknowledge that they are by no means exhaustive in their discussion of female vocality and representation. We see this collection as a preliminary mapping out of a field rather than as a definitive statement. It is our hope that these essays will stimulate our readers to find other possible subjects and ask other questions. We encourage them to add new voices to the dialogue.

PART I

Vocality, textuality, and the silencing of the female voice

1

The Gorgon and the nightingale: the voice of female lament and Pindar's Twelfth *Pythian Ode*

CHARLES SEGAL

To the memory of Thalia Phillies Feldman

1

The mythologizing and so mystifying of the female voice in the West began with the beginnings of Western culture itself, in ancient Greece. In Pindar's Twelfth *Pythian Ode*, which I take as an exemplary text, the myth of Medusa's death at the hands of Perseus and Athena brings together violence, the female voice, female lament, the origins of an art-form, and the juxtaposition of Athena and the Gorgon. Pindar's myth, like Aeschylus' *Oresteia* on a larger scale, provides a model of the culture's mythopoeic image-world, the social imaginary by which it not only represents basic features of its reality but also holds its more fearful elements in a tolerable, psychological balance.

Throughout archaic and classical Greek literature, the female voice, heard in the singing of the Muses, embodies the beauty of song and its power to immortalize the deeds of men. As the voice of lament, women's ritual chanting is ancient Greek society's instrument for expressing sorrow at the death of kings and heroes in epic and for effecting the separation between the living and the dead that is one of the functions of funerary ritual. In both activities, it has a dangerous side and awakens ambivalence in the male-dominated society of early Greece, in part because women are associated with pollution, corruption, decay, and disorder.[1] In its aural appeal and its power to dispel cares by its "charm," *thelxis*, the female voice also exercises magical power and seduction.[2]

---

[1] Christiane Sourvinou-Inwood, "A Trauma in Flux: Death in the Eighth Century and After," in Robin Hägg, ed., *The Greek Renaissance of the Eighth Century B.C.: Tradition and Innovation* (Skrifter Utgivna av Svenska Institutet i Athen, 1983), series 4, vol. XXX, p. 38.

[2] On this point, see Hugh Parry, *Thelxis: Magic and Imagination in Greek Myth and Poetry* (Lanham, MD: University Press of America, 1992), pp. 24–29.

The songs of the Sirens and of Circe in the *Odyssey* are the earliest and most famous examples. The Sirens would lure Odysseus off his course, end his voyage, and leave him immobilized for death on an island full of the rotting bones and skins of those who succumbed to the magic.[3] The only victims mentioned here are men, *andres*, for whom the voice of the Sirens is apparently irresistible. It is by the beauty of her song, too, that Circe lures the companions of Odysseus into her house before changing them into animals by the magic of her drugs (10.220–43). In both cases, the danger of the female voice is closely associated with its physicality. The Sirens' voice can work only when it is actually heard, and it can be avoided by the simple physical expedient of blocking the organs of hearing. Similarly, the magic of Circe's singing parallels the transformative power of her drugs, and both are neutralized by direct physical means, the plant *moly* and Odysseus' martial and sexual power (10.275–347).

2

Medusa combines many of these ambivalences surrounding the female voice. The name "Gorgon" itself is from the Indo-European root *garj*, denoting a fearful shriek, roar, or shout.[4] The two surviving Gorgons who pursue Perseus in the *Shield of Heracles* attributed to Hesiod have heavily emphasized oral features, licking tongues and gnashing teeth (line 235).[5] In Euripides' *Heracles Mad*, the Gorgon who accompanies the hero's terrible madness has the "hundred-headed shriekings of snakes" (lines 880–84). One of the Graiai, sisters of the Gorgons, is Enyo, the personification of the war-cry (Hesiod, *Theogony*, line 273).[6] These features connect the Gorgons with the fifty-headed Cerberus "of brazen voice" (*Theogony*, lines 311f.); with the chaos-inducing monster, Typhoeus and his 100 serpentine heads, "licking with their dreadful tongues" (*Theogony*, lines 824–26); and with the horrible sounds of the "Gorgon-like" Furies in the *Oresteia*.[7] The visual arts of the seventh and sixth centuries BC show

---

3 Homer, *Odyssey*, 12.45f. See Charles Segal, "Song, Ritual, and Commemoration in Early Greek Poetry and Tragedy," *Oral Tradition* 4 (1989), 332; Jean-Pierre Vernant, *L'individu, La mort, l'amour* (Paris: Gallimard, 1989), pp. 144–46.

4 See Thalia Phillies-Howe (Feldman),"The Origin and Function of the Gorgon-Head," *American Journal of Archeology* 58 (1958), 211f., and "Gorgo and the Origins of Fear," *Arion* 4 (1964), 487; Clark Hopkins, "Assyrian Elements in the Perseus-Gorgon Story," *American Journal of Archeology* 38 (1934), 341; Jean-Pierre Vernant, *La mort dans les yeux* (Paris: Hachette, 1985), pp. 50f.

5 See Hesiod, *Shield of Heracles*, (*c.* 500 BC), trans. Richmond Lattimore (Ann Arbor: University of Michigan Press, 1959), p. 205, lines 233–37.

6 See Ezio Pellizer, "Vedere il volto di Medusa: La storia di Perseo," in his *La peripezia dell'eletto* (Palermo: Sellerio, 1991), p. 83.

7 Aeschylus, *Choephoroe*, lines 835 and 1048–50, and *Eumenides*, lines 48ff., 117ff.

the Gorgon with a huge frontal face, a distended and grimacing mouth, a protruding tongue, and often sharp and prominent teeth. The grotesque face, Thalia Phillies-Howe suggests, "conveys to the spectator the idea of a terrifying roar," while the extended tongue may suggest verbal incoherence, a sub-verbal vocality closer to the bestial than the human.[8]

As Jean-Pierre Vernant has eloquently argued, the awesome frontality of the Gorgon head creates a mask of utter terror. To look into its eyes is to see the visage of death's absolute, terrifying otherness, "the unsayable, unthinkable, pure chaos."[9] In Odysseus' journey to Hades, the Gorgon head appears as the ultimate horror of death, the only thing that inspires fear in him; and the thought of its appearance drives him back to his companions: "Pale green fear seized me, lest mighty Persephone send up from Hades the Gorgon head of the terrible monster" (*Odyssey*, 11.633–36).

The Gorgons' cry may be more animalistic than human, but they also combine this terrifying vocality with a demonic femaleness. In the earliest account of the Perseus-Gorgon episode, Hesiod's *Theogony*, the Gorgon gives birth to the winged horse, Pegasus, from her headless trunk after Perseus decapitates her (lines 280–88). The scene is a nightmare image of birth, which is given an upward displacement that is not uncommon in Greek (and other) myth.[10] The violence, blood, and the snaky hair are all prominent, and they evoke the impurities that the Greeks (like many peoples) associated with birth and the female. The snake-hair calls attention to the "unclean" physical aspects of birth, possibly suggesting both the pubic hair clotted with blood in the process of birth and the visceral depths of the body, usually hidden from view and therefore a potentially fearful sight, as the birth canal dilates in parturition. This bloody birth is the exact antithesis of the bloodless, "male" birth of Athena, Medusa's divine conqueror, from the head of Father Zeus, attended by the male god of craftsmanship, fire, and metals, Hephaestus.[11]

---

[8] Phillies-Howe, "Origin and Function," pp. 211–12; the quotation is from p. 211.

[9] Vernant, *La mort dans les yeux*, p. 12; Phillies-Howe, "Gorgo," pp. 484ff.; also A. David Napier, *Masks, Transformation, and Paradox* (Berkeley and Los Angeles: University of California Press, 1986), pp. 105ff., who further notes the association of the Gorgon head with the otherness of foreign peoples.

[10] See Giulia Sissa, *Greek Virginity*, trans. A. Goldhammer (Cambridge, MA: Harvard University Press, 1990), pp. 59ff. and 166ff.; also Nicole Loraux, *Les expériences de Tirésias: Le féminin et l'homme grec* (Paris: Gallimard, 1989), pp. 139f., with note 103, p. 343. Ovid, *Metamorphoses*, 5.259, explicitly describes the scene as a bloody birth: "I saw Pegasus himself being born from his mother's blood," says Minerva (Athena). Even more vivid is Ovid, *Fasti*, 3.450–52.

[11] See Hesiod, *Theogony*, lines 886ff.; Pindar, *Olympian*, 7; cf. Euripides, *Hippolytus*, lines 616–24, where Hippolytus wishes that children could be obtained by leaving the appropriate precious metals in temples of the gods.

In her own birth from primordial sea-divinities and her resemblance to the hag-like Graiai and to female monsters of the watery abyss (like the serpentine Scylla), Medusa is a version of the terrible Evil Mother and in this respect, too, stands in a contrapuntal relation to the non-maternal, virginal sister-figure, Athena.[12] As Philip Slater suggests in his revisionist critique of Freud's paper on Medusa's head, she is more likely to symbolize a "fear of maternal envelopment" than the fear of castration at the sight of the female genitalia.[13]

As the first mortal creature in the cosmogonic processes of the *Theogony*, Medusa appears among primordial divinities and so, in a sense, stands between mortal and immortal. She can be killed by the male hero, Perseus, whereas her two immortal sisters survive and, in some early versions, like that represented on the so-called Nessus Amphora, they pursue the killer. In Pindar's Twelfth *Pythian Ode*, however, they only mourn their slain sister. Medusa's divine offspring swing back to immortal status and so reveal another area of ambivalence toward Medusa, and indeed toward the maternal female generally: she is a source of life, but is herself associated with blood and violence.

These offspring, though born amid blood and violence, are immediately co-opted into the patriarchal, Olympian order of Zeus. They are associated both with the heavens and with clean, hard metals. Pegasus is subdued and made serviceable for heroic achievements by Athena's gift of the magical bit to Bellerophon (Pindar, *Olympian*, 13). The exploits that follow include victories over the snaky female monster, the Chimaera, and the female warriors, the Amazons. Chrysaor is preemptively purged of his bloody birth, as it were, by his name, "he of the golden sword." Pegasus carries Bellerophon to Olympus and bears Zeus' celestial (and phallic) thunderbolts (*Theogony*, line 284). In contrast to their mother's abode in the shadowy border territory "at the extreme limit of Night" (*Theogony*, line 275), both of Medusa's offspring fly at once to the bright heavens (*Theogony*, lines 284–86). The transposition from the realm of the mother to that of the father is heavily overdetermined. The mother is associated with night, immobility, serpentine monstrosity, and violent, bloody birth; the offspring with sky, mobility, bright metal, and victorious achievement.[14]

[12] On these watery serpentine figures of female monstrosity, see Gilbert Durand, *Les structures anthropologiques de l'imaginaire* (Paris: Bordas, 1969), pp. 104ff.

[13] See Philip E. Slater, *The Glory of Hera* (Boston: Beacon Press, 1968), pp. 17–19, 321f.; the quotation is from p. 18. The coexistence of sexual attractiveness and serpentine horror in Medusa exactly parallels that combination in Ovid's Scylla (*Metamorphoses*, 13.900ff. and 14.50ff.) and Spenser's Duessa in *The Faerie Queene*, Book 1. In both cases, the serpentine horror is associated with the sexual organs and results from a witch's transformation of a desirable young girl, literally by Circe in Ovid, figuratively by Duessa taking the place of Una in Spenser.

[14] Chrysaor, however, passes his Medusan heritage on to the offspring he sires, the

Athena and Medusa occupy the extreme positions possible for the female. Medusa belongs to the older, pre-Olympian order, begotten from the primordial sea-divinities Phorkys and Keto. Placed at "the extreme limit of Night" and between mortality and immortality, death and parturition, she embodies flux, process, and animality, whereas Athena, sprung from the head of Zeus, never bleeds or is wounded, and is the most committed of the gods to the male-dominated order of Olympus.[15] By replacing and displacing the dangerous offspring of Metis, whom Zeus swallows, Athena's birth assures the invincibility of Zeus's patriarchal rule. Whereas Athena never enters a sexual relation or gives birth,[16] Medusa, for all her monstrosity, has an intense sexual vitality, and she has the most physically vivid form of birth possible within the conventions of early Greek literature. Athena's body, covered by masculine armor or her decorous peplos, is always hidden and never obtrusive. Everything about Medusa, however, contributes to the corporealization of her being: the hair with its individualized snaky locks, the protruding teeth and tongue, the bulging eyes, the full, fleshy cheeks, and, of course, the wound, blood, pain, and cry of her fatal parturition.

3

Pindar wrote his Twelfth *Pythian Ode* in 490 BC to celebrate the victory of one Midas of Akragas (modern Agrigento) in the flute contest at Delphi. Viewed in the perspective that we have sketched out above, this occasional text, for all its brevity, takes on significance as one of the founding myths about the female voice. It will be helpful to have a translation of the ode:[17]

Pythian 12

1   Most radiant of mortal cities,
     lady of brightness on the height
     above the sheep-nurturing banks of the Akragas,

---

monstrous three-headed Geryon; cf. also Pindar, *Olympian*, 13.63 on Pegasus as "son of the snaky Gorgon." "Geryon," probably from the same root as "Gorgon," is akin genealogically and typologically to other discordant, multiheaded monsters like Cerberus, Chimaera, and Typhoeus: see *Theogony*, lines 287, 309ff., 321, 825ff.; also Pindar, *Pythian* 1, 15–20 and Aeschylus, *Prometheus Bound*, lines 351–57.

15 In Homer, *Iliad*. 5, for example, Athena remains impenetrable, whereas both Aphrodite and Ares are wounded by the spear of Diomedes when Athena gives him superhuman power.

16 The birth of Erichthonius from the attempted rape by Hephaestus is the exception that proves the rule: see Apollodorus, *The Library*, 3.14.6.

17 Translation by Frank J. Nisetich, *Pindar's Victory Odes* (Baltimore: Johns Hopkins University Press, 1980), with minor modifications. In citing short passages of the ode, I have given my own literal translations in order to stay as close as possible to the original.

among whose lovely buildings
Persephone has her throne –
on you I call:
welcome Midas and his coronal from Pytho.
Grant him the favor of men and of gods,
for he has conquered all Hellas by his skill
in the art Athena once invented,
when she wove
the grim death chant of the cruel Gorgons,   (lines 1–8)

2   which she heard pouring out
in streams of bitter anguish
under the maidens' repulsive serpent heads,
when Perseus cried out in triumph, bringing
the third of the sisters to Seriphos,
death to the people:
he had blinded the weird brood of Phorkys
and now, having despoiled
the head of beautiful Medusa,
he made that banquet a bane to Polydektes,
and made him rue his lust
to rape Danae and keep her in bondage –   (lines 9–16)

3   Perseus, her son, who we say was sired
in a shower of streaming gold.
But when Athena had saved her favorite
from these dangers
she fashioned the music of flutes
to imitate the piercing ululation
that came to her ears
from the fierce jaws of Euryale.
It was the goddess who invented it for mortal men
and called it *the many-headed melody.*
Now it woos
the people to attend the contest   (lines 17–24)

4   when they hear it stream through slender bronze
and through the reeds that have their home
by the city of the Graces,
on ground sacred to the daughter of Kaphisos –
faithful witnesses to the chorus.
If there is any bliss among men,
it does not appear without struggle.
Still, a god may bring it to pass this very day.
No man can avoid his fated end,
and in the time he has,
he will be struck with surprise
when one desire will succeed, but another will fail.   (lines 25–32)

Although music was originally more important than sport at Apollo's festival, *Pythian* 12 is the only surviving ode to celebrate a musical competition. Why, asks Lewis Farnell in his commentary, does Pindar tell a myth about the dirge and wail of death for "the bright festival of a pure god who kept aloof from all association with death and dirges"?[18] Farnell could give no answer; this paper proposes one.

Athena's transformation of the surviving Gorgons' wail of mourning at their sister's death into the flute-song is a cultural act that controls and aestheticizes the mournful wail of woman in her familiar role of lamenting the dead. Medusa's death, as we have seen, also implies the fearfulness and impurity of woman in the act of birth, and Athena's cultural work extends to this area too. Instead of the child emerging from the bloody fluids of the birth canal, and instead of the cry of pain coming out through that so vividly portrayed Gorgonic mouth, a pleasing sound emerges from an artificial channel, the constricted passage of which produces the "many-headed melody" at all-male contests of art and athletics. Athena thus acts out, in the area of the voice, exactly what she does in transforming the impure, plague-bringing, and poison-dripping Furies into beneficent Eumenides at the end of the *Oresteia* and, in a gentler way, in her quasi-parental sponsorship of the earth-born Erichthonius and Athens after Hephaestus attempts to rape her.[19] The ivory figure of the Gorgon's head that Pheidias placed on Athena's breast in his celebrated cult-statue of Athena Parthenos in the Parthenon is a cultural statement parallel to the incorporation of the Erinyes, daughters of Night, into the city of Athens at the end of Aeschylus' *Eumenides*.[20]

However much scholars disagree on the Gorgon's origins, there is wide consensus that she is a form of the Potnia Theron, the Mistress of Animals or Great Mother of the natural world. The literary sources transform the Gorgon's creative power into female monstrosity, but the iconography makes clear her function as a figure of fertility and creation. The most spectacular monument is the huge pediment of the temple of Artemis at Corcyra (Corfu), dating from the early sixth century. The placement of the Gorgon on Artemis' temple is another indication of her fertility functions, for Artemis frequently takes over the role of the ancient Mistress of Animals. This nine-foot-tall winged Gorgon radiates creative energy. She is flanked by her offspring, Pegasus and Chrysaor.

---

[18] See Lewis Richard Farnell, *The Works of Pindar. Critical Commentary* (London: Macmillan, 1932), vol. 2, p. 234, who finds the subject "inexplicable."

[19] For the myth and the iconography, see Nicole Loraux, *Les enfants d'Athéna* (Paris: Maspero, 1981), pp. 35ff.

[20] The Erinyes and the Gorgons are in fact explicitly linked in *Eumenides,* lines 48–51; on this passage and on the association of Gorgons and Erinyes generally, see Elizabeth S. Belfiore, *Tragic Pleasures: Aristotle on Plot and Emotion* (Princeton University Press, 1992), pp. 20ff. For the Gorgon's head on the breastplate of the statue of Athena Parthenos, see Pausanias, *Description of Greece*, 1.24.7; cf. Euripides, *Rhesus*, lines 306–8.

Her snaky hair is kept within decorous bounds and is not especially horrible. The two entwined snakes at the belt suggest a tamer, more tolerable form of her reproductive power than the bloody upward displacement from womb to severed head in the *Theogony*. The belt in early Greek literature has associations with sexuality and reproduction, for young women are said to "loosen the belt" for sexual union or birth. On the other hand, the snakes at the belt still surround female sexuality with a dangerous and demonic quality. The Hesiodic *Shield of Heracles* (sixth century BC) shows an extreme demonization of the snakiness of the Gorgons' belts:

> And on the belts of the Gorgons a pair
> of snakes were suspended,
> and they reared and bent their heads forward
> and flickered with their tongues.
> The teeth for their rage were made jagged
> and their staring fierce,
> and over the dreaded heads of the Gorgons
> was great Panic shivering.[21]

On the Corcyra pediment, the Gorgon dwarfs the small figure of Zeus brandishing a thunderbolt against a fallen giant on her right and the equally small Neoptolemus killing Priam on her left.[22] The Gorgon herself is framed between two lions or panthers, that is in the form of the Mistress of Animals traditional from Minoan and Mycenaean times (figs. 1.1 and 1.2).

The very name "Medusa" signifies power ("she who commands") and has a parallel in the goddess Despoina, "the Mistress," daughter of Poseidon and Black Demeter, worshipped as an awesome, primordial female power of the earth at Lycosura in Arcadia.[23] Despoina, like Medusa, is also associated with the birth of horses. When incorporated into the city, as she is on the Corcyra temple, the Gorgon's demonic energy and creativity are potent apotropaic forces, warding off the evil powers that she herself can embody. Hence she appears frequently on buildings and on the shields of warriors, including the shield of Athena.[24]

---

[21] Hesiod, *Shield of Heracles*, lines 233–37, in the translation of Lattimore, p. 205.

[22] For details, see Reinhard Lullies and Max Hirmer, *Greek Sculpture*, trans. M. Bullock, revised edn. (New York: Harry N. Abrams, 1960), p. 57 with plate 17; Phillies-Howe, "Origin and Function," p. 215; Renate Schlesier, "Das Flötenspiel der Gorgo," *Notizbuch* 5/6 (1982), 22; Napier, *Masks*, pp. 92ff. Also Edouard Will, "La décollation de Méduse," *Revue archéologique* 27 (1947), 60–76, especially 62f.

[23] Ulrich von Wilamowitz-Moellendorff, *Der Glaube der Hellenen*, 3rd edn. (Darmstadt: Wissenschaftliche Buchgesellschaft, 1959), vol. I, pp. 269–70; Walter Burkert, *Structure and History in Greek Mythology* (Berkeley and Los Angeles: University of California Press, 1979), pp. 126–28; see also Phillies-Howe, "Origin and Function," p. 214.

[24] On the apotropaic functions of the Gorgon, see Wilamowitz-Moellendorff, *Der Glaube*, vol. I, pp. 268f.; Will, "La décollation," p. 65; Schlesier, "Das Flötenspiel," p.16 with note 29; Napier, *Masks*, p. 88.

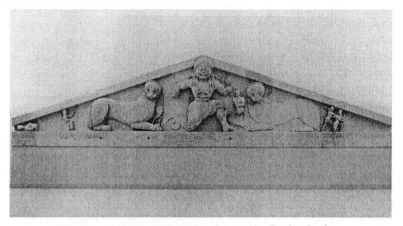

1.1 Pediment, Gorgon, Temple of Artemis, Corfu. Corfu Museum. Early sixth century BC.

1.2 Gorgon Pediment, Corfu. Detail.

Pindar's myth, then, not only reflects this cultural transformation of Medusa but also presents a competition between two images of the female, the maternal and the virginal. Athena takes over the Gorgon's power as serviceable apotropaic energy, and she is regularly attributed Medusa's epithets, "Gorgon-eyed" and "Gorgon-voiced."[25] If Athena

---

[25] See Schlesier, "Das Flötenspiel," p. 13; Napier, *Masks*, p. 91; Loraux, *Les expériences*, pp. 262f.

brings the death-cry surrounding Medusa into the world of art and civic order, her own birth-cry marks the beginning of a new order on Olympus and its extension to the most ancient foundations of power, the elemental divinities, Sky and Earth. When she is born from the head of Zeus, according to another ode of Pindar, she rushes forth with "a most mighty cry, and Ouranos and Mother Earth shudder (in awe)" (Pindar, *Olympian*, 7.37–38).

In another legend, Athena controls the ambiguous power of the Gorgon's blood, of which one drop kills and the other cures (Euripides, *Ion*, 999f.). In a related tale, Apollo's son, Asclepius, "receives from Athena the blood that flowed from the veins of the Gorgon, and he uses the blood that flowed from the veins on the left for the destruction of men, the blood that flowed from those on the right for their salvation, and thus awakened the dead to life" (Apollodorus, 3.10.3). Several stories attribute Medusa's snaky locks to Athena's sexual jealousy (Apollodorus, 2.4.3; Ovid, *Metamorphoses*, 4.793–801). A priestess of Athena, according to Pausanias, is turned to stone for having seen the goddess with her Gorgon-shield in her temple (*Description of Greece*, 9.34.2). Athena not only takes over the Gorgon's head to enhance her masculine force in war, but she also triumphs over her enemies in ways that resemble Gorgonic power: the piercing gaze and the powerful voice.[26] Even if these details are later embellishments, they nevertheless develop a potential that inheres in the dyadic relation between Athena and the Gorgon.

In the logic of the myth, Athena not only acquires Medusa's attributes and transforms her monstrous maternity into a safer form, but she is also the agent of Medusa's death through her aid to the young male hero, Perseus. This role for Athena does not occur in Hesiod, but it is illustrated on a metope from Temple C at Selinus in Sicily, built in the middle of the sixth century BC (fig. 1.3) and, of course, is in Pindar's Tenth and Twelfth *Pythians*, both written at the beginning of the fifth century. The next stage of the myth replicates Perseus' initial victory over the snaky female, except that he now defeats a male serpentine monster and wins a desirable (and totally helpless, dependent) young girl, the princess Andromeda, instead of the monster's head.[27]

Perseus' very origins constitute a neutralization of the bloody birth-amid-death that he inflicts on Medusa. His mother, Danae, has been

---

26 See Marcel Detienne and Jean-Pierre Vernant, *Les ruses de l'intelligence: La métis des Grecs* (Paris: Flammarion, 1974), pp. 173–74; see also Sophocles, *Ajax*, line 450.

27 The story is most familiar from Ovid, *Metamorphoses*, 4.670ff. See Pellizer, "Vedere il volto di Medusa," p. 87. For some of the gender issues in the popularity of the Perseus–Andromeda story, see Joseph Kestner, *Mythology and Misogyny: The Social Discourse of Nineteenth-Century British Classical-Subject Painting* (Madison: University of Wisconsin Press, 1989), pp. 100ff, on Edward Burne-Jones's Perseus cycle.

1.3 Perseus decapitating the Gorgon with the aid of Athena. Metope from Temple C, Selinus (Selinunte), Sicily. Palermo, National Museum. Middle of sixth century BC.

imprisoned in a brazen tower, but Zeus enters in a shower of gold and thus impregnates her with Perseus. The male-centered narrative takes us about as far as possible from the female biological process grimly represented in the *Theogony*. Thanks to Athena, Perseus is the hero most removed from the monstrous form of maternal energy embodied in Medusa, for he not only rescues his mother but manages to keep her for himself in her apparently sex-free life after he wins his own bride,

Andromeda, and defeats Danae's suitor, Polydectes. Thus the neutralization of the female role in conception, and of Danae's sexuality in Zeus's shower of gold, continues into her later life with her adult son.[28] All of these narratives are analogues or allomorphs of Athena's transformation of the Medusa's wail in the Twelfth *Pythian* with which we began.

4

In *Pythian* 12, as often in the *Victory Odes*, Pindar shifts the mood of a myth to suit the occasion. Celebrating the happy victory, he naturally stresses the successful outcome. Hence the triumph of Perseus in the myth is parallel to the victory of Midas of Akragas in the flute contest. But Pindar also depicts the price of winning: the effort, training, expense, the possibility of defeat, and sometimes the actual defeat of the unsuccessful contestants. The death of the Gorgon in *Pythian* 12 is perhaps a mythical way of alluding to the defeat of the unsuccessful contestants, and so the ode depicts the scene more sympathetically than do Hesiod or the early vases. The sympathy is sharpest in the sound of the Gorgons' wail for their sister, "the dirge-cry destructive, which [Athena] heard dripping forth with harshly painful suffering from the maidens' unapproachable heads of snakes" (lines 8–10).[29] Yet the proximity of the dirge to the "heads of snakes" (*kephalais*, line 9) also suggests that their monstrous hissing may accompany the Gorgons' voice, particularly as the music named from the event is called "the *many-headed* melody" (*kephalân pollân nomos*, line 23).

These contrasts run throughout this myth of origins and return in the ode's generalizations near the end on the uncertainties of human happiness and the inescapability of suffering (cf. lines 10 and 28).[30] Medusa herself is "of beautiful cheeks" (line 16), but her severed head will be a "baleful contribution" to Polydectes' banquet (line 14). The wail is not only "heard" (line 10), whether by Athena or Perseus or both, but

[28] See Slater, *The Glory of Hera*, pp. 315ff., who also notes the close and indeed exclusive mother–son relation in the tale of their exposure together on the raft: see Simonides, fragment 543 in D. Campbell, *Greek Lyric*, Loeb Classical Library, (Cambridge, MA: Harvard University Press, 1991), vol. III, pp. 436ff.

[29] Lines 9–12 have been much discussed, and a number of punctuations and translations are possible: see Adolph Köhnken, "Two Notes on Pindar," *Bulletin of the Institute of Classical Studies. University of London* 25 (1978), 92f. and Jenny Strauss Clay, "Pindar's Twelfth *Pythian*: Reed and Bronze," *American Journal of Philology* 113 (1992), 520–23. For reasons that I cannot enter into here, I believe that Nisetich's translation is correct in assigning the "shout" or the "cry" of line 11 to Perseus at the killing of Medusa. Presumably both he and Athena hear the dirge. For further discussion, see Charles Segal, "Perseus and the Gorgon: Pindar, *Pythian* 12.9–12 Reconsidered," *American Journal of Philology* 116 (1995).

[30] See Adolf Köhnken, "Perseus' Kampf und Athenes Erfindung (Bemerkungen zur Pindar, Pythian 12)," *Hermes* 104 (1976), 262, who also calls attention to the *ponoi* ("toils") of line 18. See also Clay, "Pindar's Twelfth *Pythian*," 524f.

also is "dripping forth" (*leibomenon*), like tears or blood.[31] This "dripping" contrasts with the "flowing gold" of the victor's birth (*chrysou autorhytou*, line 17), just as "blinding" or "dimming the race of Gorgons" (line 13) is a foil to the "radiance" of the victory that illuminates the victor's city in the opening line (*philaglaê*).[32] Pindar focuses this mixture of contradictory elements on voice and sound,[33] and he keeps the visual elements, so prominent in the Gorgon legend, in the background.[34]

The ode carefully frames the two descriptions of the Gorgons by the motif of Athena's "inventing" song from the "dirge" or "wail" (*epheure . . . thrênon*, lines 7–8; *goon . . . heuren*, lines 21–22), thereby overdetermining Athena's cultural creation.[35] This formal device of ring-composition verbally enacts the artistic construct of joy and energy enclosing the Gorgons' voice of sorrow and death. In the first passage, Midas "wins by an *art* (*technê*) that Athena invents" as she "weaves" or "entwines" the Gorgons' dirge (line 8). In the second passage, Athena the "maiden" (*parthenos*) "fashioned (*teuche*) a full-voiced tune . . . so that she might imitate with *instruments* the plangent wailing that approached her from Euryale's swift jaws" (lines 19–21; Euryale is one of the surviving sister-Gorgons). The symmetry of verse structure and the syntax reinforce the causal connection between Athena's "full-voiced tune" and the Gorgons' "plangent wailing" (*pamphônon melos*, *eriklanktan goon*, lines 19 and 21).

In an interesting article, Eilhard Schlesinger suggests that Medusa's wail points to the mysterious, elemental forces behind all artistic creativity, citing Rilke's First *Duino Elegy*: "Denn das Schöne ist nichts / als des Schrecklichen Anfang . . ."[36] Such a universalizing, aesthetic

---

[31] Note also the Muses' "pouring forth" of a dirge at the funeral of Achilles in *Isthmian*, 8.63f. Belfiore, *Tragic Pleasures*, pp. 12–14, suggests that *leibomenon* also evokes the libation of wine, which would create another contrast between the violence of the Gorgons' world and the festivity and order created by Perseus' victory under the protection of Athena and Apollo.

[32] For some of these contrasts, see Eilhard Schlesinger, "Pindar, Pyth. 12.," *Hermes* 96 (1968), 283–86; Kevin Crotty, *Song and Action: The Victory Odes of Pindar* (Baltimore: Johns Hopkins University Press, 1982), p. 16; Hubbard, *The Pindaric Mind* (Leiden: Brill), pp. 93–94.

[33] The vocal element is even stronger with the manuscript reading *aüse*, "shouted," in line 11: see Wilamowitz-Moellendorff, *Pindaros* (Berlin: Weidmann, 1922), p. 146 with note l; Schlesinger, "Pindar, Pyth. 12," p. 279 with note 4.1.

[34] See R. W. B. Burton, *Pindar's Pythian Odes* (Oxford: Clarendon Press, 1962), p. 29; Adolf Köhnken, *Die Funktion des Mythos bei Pindar* (Berlin: De Gruyter, 1971), p. 123.

[35] Note also the word order in the last two lines of the first strophe (7–8), *Pallas epheure thraseiân Gorgonôn / oulion thrênon diaplexais' Athana* ("Pallas invented – of the bold Gorgons – / destructive dirge – weaving [it] Athena"), a chiastic alternation of two-word phrases for Athena's creation and the Gorgon's suffering.

[36] Schlesinger, "Pindar, Pyth. 12," p. 281; for criticism, see Köhnken, *Die Funktion des Mythos*, pp. 118f. For some interesting connections of the slaying of the Gorgon with poetic creativity in Ovid and the Renaissance, see Miranda Johnson Haddad, "Ovid's

interpretation has its place, but, as we have seen, the Gorgon has a more culture-specific meaning and cannot be absorbed into Rilke's aestheticized mysticism, however beautiful that is. She is the source of a specifically *female* energy that is both demonic and vital, both creative and destructive. It takes the skill of Athena, the non-threatening female, to transform this power into a manageable cultural product that can adorn Apollo's festival and ennoble the male victor of a proud city.

As Athena mediates between Apollo and the Erinyes (Furies) in Aeschylus' *Eumenides*, so here she mediates between Apollo and the Gorgon. The "many-headed melody" that results from Athena's work is traditionally associated with Apollo;[37] but Pindar here attributes it to Athena in her special role as the one who neutralizes the demonic power of the Great Mother (or chthonic female divinity) and makes it safe and available to the masculine, public activities of the *polis*. In assuring the continuing fame of the male victor in his polis, both her song and Pindar's ode reaffirm civic and panhellenic institutions in the civilized space of human habitation, the *oikoumenê*.

In the myths of Medusa, as we have seen, Athena is regularly paired with the Gorgon as her un-monstrous, non-demonized double. In *Pythian* 12, that neutralizing function is applied to the voice and to song. The horrific cry, one of the essential features of the Gorgon (we recall the root of "Gorgon," *garj*), now becomes the "all-voiced music" of "instruments" (lines 19–21). The bloody birth through the slashed throat is transferred to the dismal dirge of Medusa's sisters, "dripping" amid snakes and pain (line 10), but this now becomes the refined sound of a male artist's breath blown skillfully through a crafted, "fashioned" reed (line 19).[38] An artificial, human, male-controlled throat of bronze (line 25) replaces the monstrously maternal throat/vagina at the edges of "Night". The transformation turns the voice of sorrow and death at the limits of the world into a song of triumph and praise for a Greek city that "love[s] radiance" (line 1) at an orderly festival of the most male of gods, Apollo. All of this is made possible by the "invention" (lines 7 and 22) of the "Maiden" (*parthenos*, line 19), that is by her transformative, civilizing power.

The relation between Athena, the flute, and the Gorgon can be taken a step further. As Vernant and others have suggested, to play the flute is to imitate the Gorgon. This is because flute-playing distorts the face and jaws into an ugly grimace evocative of the Gorgon's grin, and

---

(36 contd.) Medusa in Dante and Ariosto: The Poetics of Self-Confrontation," *Journal of Medieval and Renaissance Studies* 19 (1989), 212ff.

[37] See Pseudo-Plutarch, *De Musica*, 7.1133e, and Burton, *Pindar's Pythian Odes*, p. 26.

[38] On the contrast between the death-cry and the instrumental sound, see Phillies-Howe, "Origin and Function," p. 211, who suggests viewing the reed as a kind of "second throat attached to the real one."

because flute music is associated with wildness, madness, ecstasy, Corybantic revelry, and satyrs, and so is opposed to the order, discipline, and human language of the polis.[39]

Aristotle criticizes flute music as unsuitable for education because it is "not formative of moral character (*êthikon*) but is instead orgiastic and prevents the use of language" (*Politics*, 8.1341a16–25). In this context, he approvingly tells the myth of Athena's rejection of the flute because it made her face ugly. But Aristotle goes on to correct the myth and to suggest that Athena's real reason for throwing it away was that education in the flute does nothing to help thought or intelligence (*dianoia*), whereas Athena is especially associated with scientific knowledge and artistry (*epistêmê* and *technê*, 8.1341b3–9).[40] In the sequel to the myth, the satyr Marsyas takes up the flute that Athena threw away, and is so pleased with the sound that he challenges Apollo and his lyre. The outcome of a contest between the Apollonian lyre and the Gorgonic music of a satyr is predictable, and Marsyas is flayed alive as punishment for his defeat. Here, as in the case of the related instrument, the syrinx or panpipe, the flute not only has its place in the wild but also attracts the more animalistic, disorderly, and uninhibited gods, like Pan, the satyrs, or the impish young Hermes.[41]

To return to *Pythian* 12, the flute's transformation from the Gorgons' wild, death-laden, liquid, and monstrous cry to an instrument of Athena's artistry is a figure for the incorporation of the otherness of female creative energy into the polis. This act of accommodation brings together man and god (line 22), song and the "name" of the new music in human language (line 23), and the celebratory festivals of "contests" at games (line 24). Yet the flute's music, like the female in Greek myth, retains a certain mysterious power in its vacillation between the wild and the city, nature and culture. The ambiguity of flute music, emanating differently from each of the double reeds and stirring unruly emotions, parallels the ambiguities of the Gorgon and, to some degree, even of Athena herself, for the Gorgon is Athena's fearful, demonic side, and, like her, is a *parthenos* ("maiden," lines 9 and 19). These ambiguities

---

[39] See Vernant, *La mort dans les yeux*, pp. 37, 56f., 87ff.; Schlesier, "Das Flötenspiel der Gorgo," 39 with fig. 1; Paul M. Laporte, "The Passing of the Gorgon," *Bucknell Review* 17 (1969), 59ff. On the flute and madness, see Euripides, *Heracles Mad*, lines 871, 1119, and *Orestes* lines 316–20; Sophocles, *Trachiniae*, line 205.

[40] For other versions of this myth, see Apollodorus 1.4.2 and Hyginus 165; see also Schlesier, "Das Flötenspiel der Gorgo," pp. 11ff., 26, 39.

[41] For the syrinx and its association with Pan's violent sexual desire, see Ovid, *Metamorphoses*, 1.689–712. In another, probably much older version, Hermes invents the syrinx but in a context that emphasizes his marginality, rascality, and exuberant, childish playfulness, all in strong contrast to Apollo and his lyre: *Homeric Hymn to Hermes*, lines 496–512. See also Laporte, "The Passing," 57.

are condensed into the figure of sound, the uncanny harmony of snake hiss and Gorgonic dirge that Athena "weaves together" (lines 8–10).[42]

Near the end of the ode, Athena's newly invented flute-song "passes often through the slender bronze and the reeds that grow by the lovely-dancing city of the Graces in the shrine of Cephisus, trusty witnesses of chorus-dancers" (lines 25–27). The reference is to the reedy and marshy area of Boeotia around Orchomenos, the "city of the Graces" and an important place of their cult. The flute consists of "reeds," plants that grow in a marshy and watery place that is evocative of the primitive watery origins of the Gorgon, but these same reeds are also sacred to musical goddesses of a "city." The song "passes frequently" – that is, vibratingly – through a man-made channel that consists of both growing plant and worked metal. The reeds themselves, by the end of the sentence, become "witnesses of chorus dancers," a phrase which balances the preceding figurative description of the flute as the "glorious wooer of people-gathering contests" (line 24). This phrase, in turn, probably refers to the function of flute-song to celebrate athletic victories or "contests," a common use of the flute in Pindar's *Victory Odes*.[43]

Athena's inventive artistry banishes the radical otherness of the Gorgons' wail to a world of pain and suffering far from the city's music, rituals, athletics, and sacred space. Brought within the city, the dirge has, in fact, become the "imitation of a wail" through an instrumental, not a living, voice (lines 19–21). A cry that "drips," like blood, becomes the melodious vibration inside the reeds and metal of the flute (line 25). The instrumental sound from the "slender" or "agile" bronze (*leptou chalkou*) replaces the "trilling" song of mourning from "swift" or "trembling" jaws (line 20). In these details, the flute-song leaves behind traces of its origins in something terrible and monstrously corporeal; through the aid and inventiveness of a virgin goddess these elements have been neutralized as a *mimesis* (line 21) of the pain and the horror. Transformed into the instruments that also celebrate Midas' success when the ode is performed, the growing reeds are fully incorporated into the city as "witnesses" to his achievement (lines 25–27).

This transformation is, in turn, part of a larger figure: Athena's musical invention, "weaving the doom-laden dirge" (line 8), is a trope for the

---

[42] On the dualities involved in both the construction of the flute and the harmonies of its song, see Carl A. P. Ruck and William H. Matheson, *Pindar: Selected Odes* (Ann Arbor: University of Michigan Press, 1968), p. 227, and Clay, "Pindar's Twelfth *Pythian*," 520, 523f., with the further texts there cited.

[43] See, for example, *Olympian*, 7.12 and 10.94; *Isthmian*, 5.27. See also, in general, Köhnken, "Perseus' Kampf und Athenes Erfindung," 246f., and *Die Funktion des Mythos*, pp. 140ff. Whether *mnastêra* in line 24 means "wooer" or "reminder," or both, has been much discussed.

"weaving" of the ode by Pindar as a metaphorical "garland" of victory.[44] Athena "invented" or "fashioned" the art of flute-song from the Gorgons' wail; the makers of the flute fashion an instrument by combining bronze and reed; and Pindar fashions a musical equivalent of the "victory garland" (line 5) which is itself the ode now being sung in Akragas. The poet's art parallels Athena's in bringing into the city, in the transfigured form of the myth that he tells, the fearful and monstrous female cry of birth and death. The contrasts of victory and defeat, Athena and the Gorgon, heroic vitality and death, civic festivity and remote monstrosity all exploit the counterpoint between the musical organization of the ode, with its elaborate metrical and verbal structures, and the unmusical chaos embodied in the Gorgon. The aesthetic form of the ode is itself a victory over Gorgonic dissonance; and the ode, like Athena, absorbs and neutralizes this dissonance by incorporating it into a larger design, much as the total musical and thematic structure of Mozart's *Magic Flute* absorbs and neutralizes the screaming arpeggios of the vengeful Queen of the Night.[45]

Yet the neutralization is not total. In *Pythian* 12, Medusa retains her beauty beside her snaky locks, and the pathos of the wail for her death stands beside the victor's cry of triumph. The city addressed in the opening lines is itself feminine, and is the "seat of Persephone," goddess of fertility and death (lines 1–2). Athena and the Gorgons are joined as "maidens" (lines 9 and 19); and Athena herself "imitates" the Gorgons' monstrosity as the material for her new art (line 21). Pindar is, in turn, "imitating" Athena in reinventing female monstrosity and transforming it into the artistic beauty that surrounds a male heroic act.

By allowing her something that can be transformed into beauty and brought into the city, Pindar grants the Gorgon a partial escape from the total demonization that she receives in most of later Western art and, of course, in Freud.[46] She gives up the invincible otherness of the uncontrolled life-energy embodied in the Mistress of Animals on the pediment at Corfu for a creatureliness that can arouse compassion.

---

[44] For figures of this kind in Pindar, cf. *Olympian*, 7.1–10, *Nemean*, 3.79, 7.77ff.

[45] For Mozart's Queen of the Night and the voice of suppressed femininity, see Catherine Clément, *Opera or the Undoing of Women*, trans. Betsy Wing (Minneapolis: University of Minnesota Press, 1988), p. 73. For Pindar's myths that incorporate dangerous female power into the masculine world of the city, see *Pythian* 4.184–87, 213–23, and Charles Segal, *Pindar's Mythmaking: The Fourth Pythian Ode* (Princeton University Press, 1986), pp. 53f., 62ff., 166ff.

[46] Schlesier, "Das Flötenspiel der Gorgo," 48, observes that Freud's interpretation of Medusa's head makes it impossible to regard her "as a female figure of civilization [*eine weibliche Zivilizationsfigur*] who represents human passions and also the possibility of their sublimation." For a useful survey of feminist and other discussions of Freud's interpretation of Medusa, see Haddad, "Ovid's Medusa," 213f., with the further texts there cited.

Pindar may still be close enough to the archaic worship of the Mistress of Animals (always important in his native Boeotia) to appreciate the Gorgon's vital, creative side and to hold its danger and its power in a kind of balance. Yet when he does let the Gorgon emerge from the veil of demonization that envelops her from Hesiod to Freud, it is only under the sign of the virgin Athena's transformative invention.

The Gorgons' "swift-moving jaws" (line 20), with their ambiguous evocation of both monstrous devouring and pathetic trembling, can refer to the helpless trilling or quivering of the female voice in lament and of the female body in the extreme of suffering. Elsewhere in early Greek literature, such a sound describes the lamenting cry of the nightingale, a traditional figure for the voice of female grieving, especially maternal grieving. Procne, mourning her dead son, is transformed into this bird and forever cries his name, "Itys, Itys," in perpetual sorrow.[47] Both myths emphasize the physical quality of the female voice, the ambiguous maternity of the singer, and her removal from the human to a subhuman world. The poetic elaboration of the Procne–Philomela myth, from Homer on, endows this voice with a lyrical sweetness that seems much closer to poetry and song and very far from the horrors of the Gorgons. Yet in terms of the vocal imagery of the two myths and their underlying narrative structures, the Gorgons are, figuratively speaking, the elder, darker sisters of the plaintive nightingale.

---

[47] For early versions of the myth of Procne, see Homer, *Odyssey* 19.518–23; Aeschylus, *Agamemnon*, lines 1140–48; Sophocles, *Electra*, lines 148f. For the cry, see Euripides, *Phoenician Women* line 1514, and *Helen*, line 1112; in general, see Nicole Loraux, *Les mères en deuil* (Paris: Seuil, 1990), p. 147, note 148; also Hélène Monsacré, *Les larmes d'Achille* (Paris: Albin Michel, 1984), pp. 171, 180; Charles Segal, "The Female Voice and its Contradictions: From Homer to Tragedy," *Grazer Beiträge,* Supplementband 5 (Festschrift W. Pötscher, 1993), 57–75. The association of the nightingale's cry and maternal grief specifically is exploited also by Callimachus, *Hymns*, 5.93–95.

2

Music and the maternal voice in *Purgatorio* XIX

NANCY A. JONES

In a now famous article, French opera enthusiast and psychoanalyst Guy Rosolato coined the term "sonorous envelope" to describe how the maternal voice surrounds and sustains the infant within the womb, creating an illusion of bodily fusion with the mother. The maternal voice, he writes, "is the first model of auditory pleasure and . . . music finds its roots and its nostalgia in [this] original atmosphere, which might be called a sonorous womb, a murmuring house – or *music of the spheres*."[1] The fruitful legacy of Rosolato's ideas for film studies is well known. Few readers have appreciated, however, the medieval resonance of the phrase, "music of the spheres." In fact, Rosolato's characterization of the maternal voice in terms of an enveloping, cosmic music has interesting interpretive implications for some of the musical interludes in the greatest poem of the Middle Ages, Dante's *Divine Comedy*. The image of the infant's bliss evoked in this passage closely resembles that experienced by Dante the pilgrim as he moves from the earthly paradise of *Purgatorio* into the heavens. Turning to *Paradiso* I, we find a grand description of how the harmonious turning of the cosmic wheels fills the sky surrounding the pilgrim with the sweetest music. The third canticle uses the themes of cosmic music and auditory bliss to represent the pilgrim's achievement of complete spiritual concord with the

I wish to acknowledge a fellowship from the American Council of Learned Societies, which enabled me to do much of the research for this essay. I also wish to thank the audiences at the Lyrica Society, New York University, and the University of Oregon for their comments.

[1] Guy Rosolato "La Voix: entre corps et langage," *Revue française de psychanalyse* 38, 1 (1974), 81, as translated by Kaja Silverman, *The Acoustic Mirror: The Female Voice in Psychoanalysis and Cinema* (Bloomington: Indiana University Press,1988), pp. 84–85. Also see Marie-France Castarède, *La voix et ses sortilèges* (Paris: Les Belles Lettres, 1989), pp. 74–100, 125–40.

divine order.[2] In *Paradiso* XXIII, music, voice, and the maternal converge in the extraordinary vision of the Church Triumphant in the sphere of the Fixed Stars. As the pilgrim listens, the Virgin Mother, here evoked as the Mystic Rose, is crowned by Gabriel's torch in the form of a "circling melody":

"I am angelic love, who circle the supreme joy that breathes out from the womb which was the hostelry of our desire; and I shall circle, Lady of Heaven, until thou shalt follow thy Son, and make the supreme sphere more divine by entering it." Thus the circling melody sealed itself, and all the other lights made Mary's name resound.[3]

Dante compares the souls of the redeemed reaching out to Mary to an infant stretching forth its arms toward its mother (lines 121–23). The passage recalls earlier moments of auditory pleasure within the poem.

The advent of the figure "angelic love" caps a series of encounters with singers that articulate the role of vocal music in the salvation quest. The series begins when the pilgrim meets the singer–composer Casella in Ante-Purgatory and includes encounters with three song-stresses, the Siren, the biblical Leah, and finally, in the earthly paradise, Matelda. The pilgrim's responses to their voices clearly demonstrate his spiritual vulnerabilities and progress. Amid all these beautiful voices, the mesmerizing song of the Siren provokes the most divided response on the part of both pilgrim and poet. As an emphatically embodied form of vocality, the Siren's song stands at the opposite extreme from the singing of Angelic Love in *Paradiso* XXIII.[4] Her song's immobilizing effect and its visceral silencing by the pilgrim's guide, Virgil, have psychological and cultural implications which have yet to be fully explored. While not claiming that the Siren is a maternal figure *per se*, I propose to examine this figure in terms of maternal vocality as it has been theorized in recent psychoanalytic theory and to show how the Siren episode manifests the poet's latent anxiety about the musical and vocal elements of his own poem.

[2] Other allusions to the music of the spheres include *Paradiso* VI, 124–26 and XX, 1–12. Amilcare A. Iannucci writes: "In the earthly paradise the pilgrim had, to be sure, a foretaste of this cosmic music, echoed in the 'dolci tempre' ('sweet notes') of the angelic choir (*Purgatorio* XXX: 94). His elevated ontological state now permits him to enjoy the melody in all its glory, because his soul, like that of the blessed, is in tune ('in tempra') with the harmonious order of the created universe." "Casella's Song and the Tuning of the Soul," *Thought* 65 (1990), 28–29.

[3] All citations from the *Comedy* are from the text and translation in the edition of Charles S. Singleton, Bollingen Series LXXX (Princeton University Press, 1970–75).

[4] Both figures introduce themselves with a line beginning with the words "Io son(o)." Similarly, both the Siren and Mary are described in terms of their "ventre" (womb, belly), and this word occupies the same metrical position in each line. In the words of Angelic Love, Mary's womb is "the hostelry of our desire." The Siren's *ventre* has very different connotations, as the discussion below shows.

The dream of the Siren in Canto XIX of *Purgatorio* narrates a crisis at the mid-course of the pilgrim's journey up through the terraced slopes of Mount Purgatory. The second of three purgatorial dreams takes place just before sunrise on the slope between the Cornices of Sloth and Avarice. After contemplating examples of sloth revealed to him by the penitent souls of Canto XVIII, the pilgrim's thoughts wander aimlessly. Closing his eyes, Dante tells us he "transmuted" (*transmutai*) his musing into a dream:

> mi venne in sogno una femmina balba,
> ne li occhi guercia, e sovra i piè distorta,
> con le man monche, e di colore scialba.
> Io la mirava; e come 'l sol conforta
> le fredde membra che la notte aggrava,
> così lo sguardo mio le facea scorta ·
> la lingua, e poscia tutta la drizzava
> in poco d'ora, e lo smarrito volto,
> com' amor vuol, così le colorava.
> Poi ch'ell avea'l parlar così disciolto,
> cominciava a cantar sì, che con pena
> da lei avrei mio intento rivolto.
> "Io son," cantava, "io son dolce serena,
> che ' marinari in mezzo mar dismago;
> tanto son di piacere a sentir piena!
> Io volsi Ulisse del suo cammin vago
> al canto mio; e qual meco s'ausa,
> rado sen parte; sì tutto l'appago!"
> Ancor non era sua bocca richiusa,
> quand' una donna apparve santa e presta
> lunghesso me per far colei confusa.
> "O Virgilio, Virgilio, chi è questa?"
> fieramente dicea; ed el venìa
> con li occhi fitti pur in quella onesta.
> L'altra prendea, e dinanzi l'apria
> fendendo i drappi, e mostravami 'l ventre;
> quel mi svegliò col puzzo che n'uscia.
> Io mossi li occhi, e 'l buon maestro: "Almen tre
> voci t'ho messe!" dicea, "Surgi e vieni;
> troviam l'aperta per la qual tu entre."
>   (*Purgatorio* XIX, lines 7–36)

(there came to me in a dream a woman, stammering, with eyes asquint and crooked on her feet, with maimed hands, and of sallow hue. I gazed upon her: and even as the sun revives cold limbs benumbed by night, so my look made ready her tongue, and then in but little time set her full straight, and colored her pallid face even as love requires. When she had her speech thus unloosed, she began to sing so that it would have been hard for me to turn my attention from her. "I am," she sang, "I am the sweet Siren who leads mariners astray in mid-sea, so full am I of pleasantness to hear. Ulysses, eager to journey on, I turned aside to my song; and whosoever abides with me rarely departs, so wholly do I satisfy him." Her mouth was not yet shut when a lady, holy and alert, appeared close beside me to put her to confusion. "O Virgil, Virgil, what is this?" she said sternly; and he came on with his eyes fixed only on that honest one. He seized the other and laid her bare in front, rending her garments and showing me her belly: this waked me with the stench that issued therefrom. I turned my eyes, and the good master said, "I have called you at least three times: arise and come, let us find the opening by which you may enter.")

All three of Dante's purgatorial dreams depict the metamorphic workings of erotic desire and dramatize the discourse on love and free will pronounced by Marco Lombardo and Virgil at the center of the canticle (and hence of the poem). The moral relapse dramatized by Dante's dream of the Siren has been thoroughly discussed by commentators such as Charles S. Singleton and Robert Hollander, for whom the Siren is a figure of *malo amor* derived from classical and patristic sources.[5]

Dante's Siren combines elements from a host of half-human destructive females from classical myth. Her apparent beauty and powers of entrancement link her with the Homeric Sirens and Circe, while her underlying foul bestiality identifies her with the Harpies.[6] Her mesmerizing song suggests Circe's magic and the Medusa's awful power, and she has been linked with the monstrous women of the *Commedia* – Semiramis, Myrrha, and Pasiphaë – as an icon of transgressive female desire.[7] In accordance with the scheme by which the carnal *femmina* must be rejected in favor of the spiritual *donna*, the Siren is the moral antithesis of Beatrice. Thus Virgil's violent exposure of her belly prefigures the purging of lust in the upper circles of Purgatory.

The Siren episode recapitulates the scene reported by Virgil in *Inferno* II where Beatrice appears to the Roman poet with the request that he succor the wayward pilgrim (put to flight by the ancient she-wolf) by means of his "parola ornata." In *Purgatorio* XIX, Virgil is called forth to break the Siren's spell over the dreamer by an unnamed "lady, holy and alert" (*una donna . . . santa e presta*). The "love triangle" Beatrice-Dante-Siren culminates in Beatrice's reproof of Dante in *Purgatorio*

---

5 Singleton, *Purgatorio, Commentary*, p. 448; Robert Hollander, "*Purgatorio* XIX: Dante's Siren/Harpy," in *Dante, Petrarch, Boccaccio: Studies in the Italian Trecento in Honor of Charles S. Singleton*, Medieval and Renaissance Texts and Studies 22, eds. Aldo S. Bernardo and Anthony L. Pellegrini (Binghamton: Center for Medieval and Renaissance Studies, 1983), pp. 77–88.

6 See Charles Segal's essay in this volume, p. 18.

7 Rachel Jacoff, "Transgression and Transcendence: Figures of Female Desire in Dante's *Commedia*," in Marina S. Brownlee, Kevin Brownlee, and Stephen G. Nichols, eds., *The New Medievalism* (Baltimore: Johns Hopkins University Press, 1991), p. 195. John Freccero also pointed out to me the identical rhyme in -*olto* that links the Siren episode with the figure of Medusa in *Inferno* IX, lines 50–54.

XXXI.[8] Under her sharp questioning, he confesses to having dallied with the false pleasures of feminine beauty in the period following her death ten years before. When Beatrice commands him to listen to her sermon so that he will henceforth be stronger when he hears "the sirens" (*le serene*), we know that the latter's spell has been completely broken. Henceforth Dante the pilgrim will never slide back into sloth or lust.

Such a reading of the Siren episode has great coherence within the wider moral allegory of the poem,[9] but it does not exhaust the rich implications of the episode. The scene from Canto XXXI mentioned above suggests that the Beatrice–Siren conflict releases a charge of affect that exceeds the logic of both the moral allegory of sexual or worldly temptation and conventional medieval misogyny. As his confessor, Beatrice reduces Dante (by his own admission) to the state of a mute, tearful, and downcast child. Her power over him is that of a stern mother over a wayward child, as his shamefaced demeanor reveals. The pilgrim's desire for her is a function of his dependence on her. As the confession scene shows, moreover, it is Beatrice's *voice* that first commands Dante's attention, and the text underscores the specific vocal qualities of her interventions. While the Beatrice of *Paradiso* reveals her grace through her smile, in both *Inferno* and *Purgatorio* her power and authority are made manifest in her voice. *Inferno* II shows her supplicating Virgil: she speaks "sweetly and softly" (*soave e piana*) "with an angelic voice" (*con angellica voce*). *Purgatorio* XIX alludes to an unnamed lady "holy and alert" (*una donna . . . santa e presta*), convincingly identified with Beatrice by Singleton,[10] who speaks angrily when Virgil forgets his charge in the Cornice of Sloth. Finally, in *Purgatorio* XXXI, Beatrice adopts the stern voice of a judge and all but overwhelms the accused sinner Dante with a prepared litany of his shortcomings. Not only does

---

[8] Hollander notes that all three of the purgatorial dreams "centrally reflect what we today might want to call 'love triangles' (IX. Procne–Tereus–Philomela, Juno–Jupiter–Ganymede, Ulysses–Achilles–Thetis; XIX. Beatrice–Dante–Siren; XXVII. Leah–Jacob–Rachel)" "*Purgatorio* XIX," p. 77. For an alternative feminist reading of such female groupings in *Purgatorio*, see Carol Schreier Rupprecht, "Dreams and Dismemberment: Transformations of the Female Body in Dante's 'Purgatorio,'" *Quadrant: The Journal of Contemporary Jungian Thought* 25, 2 (1992), 42–61.

[9] Among the many commentaries on this episode, see: Giorgio Padoan, "Sirene," *Enciclopedia dantesca* (Rome: Istituto dell'Enciclopedia Italiana, 1976), vol. V, p. 269a, and *Il pio Enea, l'empio Ulisse* (Ravenna: Longo, 1977), pp. 200–204; Siegfried de Rachewiltz, *De Sirenibus: An Inquiry into Sirens from Homer to Shakespeare* (New York: Garland Publishing, 1987), pp. 121–44; Giuseppina Mezzadroli, "Dante, Boezio e le sirene," *Lingua e stile* 25, 1 (March 1990), 25–56. On the medieval siren, see Pierre Courcelle, "L'interprétation évhémeriste des Sirènes-courtisanes jusqu'au XIIe siècle," in Karl Bosl, ed., *Gesellschaft.Kultur.Literatur* (Stuttgart: Anton Hiersemann, 1975), pp. 33–48.

[10] Charles S. Singleton, "In Exitu Israel de Aegypto," *78th Annual Report of the Dante Society of America* (Cambridge, Mass., 1960); reprinted in John Freccero, ed., *Dante: A Collection of Critical Essays* (Englewood Cliffs: Prentice-Hall, 1965), p. 119.

each of these episodes connect power with vocality, but the affective power of Beatrice's vocal performance exceeds the moralizing content of her speech.

Characterized by her ability to establish control over the listeners Virgil and Dante through her dynamic vocality, Beatrice stands in a complementary position to the Siren whose song she vocally interrupts. Furthermore, the portrayal of Beatrice as a quasi-maternal intercessor and tutelary figure implies that the allegorical significance of the dream of the Siren and her song is not limited to the theme of sexual temptation. This, combined with the text's emphasis on Beatrice's voice as a counter-weapon to the seductive singing of the Siren, points to a broader concern with the role of maternal intercession and vocal music within the salvation quest. The dream of the Siren, I will argue, portrays a closely intertwined struggle between two forms of music – or song – and between good and bad mothers.

To view music and song as the central theme of the Siren episode accords with the widespread view of *Purgatorio* as the canticle most specifically concerned with art. The long roster of painters and poets, both historical and mythological, encountered in *Purgatorio* underscores Dante's highly self-conscious meditation on the power of his own poem to convert other souls. The ascent of Mount Purgatory represents the spiritual purgation of art where Dante examines and corrects his poetic models, and hence his own career as a poet. Yet *Purgatorio* does not envision this process of poetic self-revision and correction in exclusively verbal and textual terms; it is also a meditation on poetry as a vocalized form of expression that has a special power to affect the soul.[11]

On one level, *Purgatorio* dramatizes an opposition between types of performed song, that is the monodic *canzone* cultivated by secular poets of the *dolce stil nuovo* school and the choral Latin hymns and psalms of the liturgy. The dream of the Siren participates in this opposition between song as an experience which paralyzes a listener's will and song as a participatory act of fellowship and penitence. The Siren's song,

---

[11] Dante's theoretical discussion of music in Book II of the *Convivio* owes much to the Pythagorean tradition known to the Middle Ages through Boethius. Dante's knowledge of Boethius' treatise on music has been studied by numerous scholars: Alessandro Picchi, "La musicalità dantesca nel quadro delle metodologie filsofiche medioevali," *Annai dell-istituto di studi danteschi* 1 (1967), 155–94; Arnaldo Bonaventura, *Dante e la musica* (Livorno: R. Giusti, 1904); Raffaello Monterosso, "Problemi musicali danteschi," *Cultura e Scuola* 4 (1965), 207–12; Nino Pirrotta, "Dante *Musicus*: Gothicism, Scholasticism, and Music," *Speculum* 43 (1968), 245–57; John E. Stevens, "Dante and Music," *Italian Studies* 23 (1968), 1–18. Of the immense critical literature on music in the *Comedy*, two recent articles are particularly pertinent to my discussion. See Amilcare A. Iannucci, "Casella's Song" and Eduoardo Sanguineti, "Infernal Acoustics: Sacred Song and Earthly Song," trans. Adriana De Marchi Gherini, *Lectura Dantis* 6 (Spring 1990), 69–79.

however, is also implicated in a more complex opposition between song as a provider of false plenitude and song as an instrument of spiritual growth.

While song's power is most dramatic in the dream of the Siren, the theme first appears in *Purgatorio* II.[12] In this episode, Dante meets the soul of an old friend, the musician Casella, on the shore of Mount Purgatory, and their meeting demonstrates Dante the pilgrim's misunderstanding of the order of things in this middle realm. First, he attempts to embrace the non-corporeal "shade" of his friend, as if they were meeting on earth, and then Dante asks his friend to console his weary soul with a song – if, Dante adds, "a new law does not take from you memory or practice of the songs of love which used to quiet me in all my longings" ("Se nuova legge non ti toglie / memoria o uso a l'amoroso canto / che mi solea quetar tutte mie voglie" (lines 106–108). Casella complies by intoning one of Dante's own *canzoni*, *Amor che ne la mente mi ragiona* (Love that discourses in my mind). His singing brings the whole assembly – Dante, Virgil, and Casella's companion souls – into a state of rapt attention ("Noi eravam tutti fissi e attenti / a le sue note"). The sudden interruption of Cato's voice – "Che è cio, spiriti lenti?" (a cry to be echoed in Canto XIX by that of the *donna santa e presta*) – breaks the spell of the sweet song and shows that indeed a new law *does* apply in this realm.

The interruption of Casella's singing and the routing of his audience provides a vivid rebuke of the values Dante had espoused when he inserted his *canzone* into his *Convivio*. As commentators point out, Dante had dedicated *Amor che ne la mente mi ragiona* to Lady Philosophy and later cited it as an example of the highest rhetorical eloquence in the *De vulgari eloquentia*.[13] Nevertheless, recent criticism has emphasized the palinodic quality of the scene. Amilcare A. Iannucci writes: "Dante is rejecting not only the text and all that it implies, but also an aesthetic principle . . . His new poetry carries an ethical dimension, and it must

---

[12] The Canto's "pre-eminent musicality" has been emphasized by recent commentators. See also Robert Hollander, "Cato's Rebuke and Dante's *scolgio*," *Italica* 52 (1975), 348–63, and "*Purgatorio* II: The New Song and the Old," *Lectura Dantis* 6 (1990), 28–45; Iannucci, "Casella's Song," 35–44.

[13] Not all critics see the *canzone* strictly in terms of Boethian allegory. In her discussion of Dante's autocitations, Teodolinda Barolini shows how *Amor che ne la mente*, for all its Boethian associations, is presented as a love song in *Purgatorio* II. She also observes how the action of *Purgatorio* II "exactly reproduces the situation of the first stanza of *Amor che ne la mente*, in which the lover is overwhelmed by the sweetness of Love's song . . ." The line, "Lo suo parlar si dolcemente sona" (His speech sounds so sweetly), echoed in *Purgatorio* II by "che la dolcezza ancor dentro mi suona" (so sweetly that the sweetness still within me sounds), conveys the debilitating effect of the sonorous beauty of Dante's poetry. See *Dante's Poets: Textuality and Truth in the Comedy* (Princeton University Press, 1984), pp. 35–40.

produce not a static effect, as Thomistic aesthetics would have it, but a kinetic one. Its function must be to direct the will toward God, not to indulge it in a contemplation of beauty for its own sake."[14] More specifically, the episode may be a correction of the courtly song culture once shared by Dante and his Florentine comrades.[15] In life on earth, love songs may offer consolation, but in the spiritual perspective of Purgatory they are impediments to the soul's progress. Song makes the soul forgetful of its true goal and thus delays repentence and salvation.

The scene in Canto II implies that song, especially in its auditory form, constitutes a form of sloth. Its correction or cure consists in a complementary musical exercise – the choral singing of hymns and psalms. Thus the souls arriving on the shores of Mount Purgatory are heard singing the psalm *In exitu Israel de Aegypto* (When Israel came out of Egypt) and it is their collective, unified (and thus de-individualized and de-gendered) voice as much as the content of their jubilant song that conveys the sense of spiritual progress. Further on, the penitent souls in Purgatory proper are heard performing the familiar and homely hymns *Salve Regina*, the *Te Deum*, the *Te lucis ante*, and numerous psalms and beatitudes as the expression of the newly found spiritual concord between their will and God's.[16] Choral song is an offering to God and a surrendering of personal desire.

The systematic pairing of specific psalms, hymns, and beatitudes with the stages of purgation represents Dante's gloss on the theology of song he inherited from St. Augustine. For Augustine, song is ambiguous: it can "paralyze" the soul by gratifying the senses, but it can also stir the mind to greater religious fervor. Recollecting that the hymns of the Church had been instrumental in his conversion, Augustine concludes that singing in church offers the benefit of inspiring the weaker souls. It is a grievous thing, however, if the singing itself should be more moving than the truth it conveys.[17] Likewise, the ordered integration of liturgical song into the action of *Purgatorio* represents Dante's concerted attempt to purge his song (including church music) of its potential association with sensuality, artifice, and individualistic virtuosity.[18]

---

[14] Iannucci, "Casella's Song," 42–43.

[15] On the moral and aesthetic critique implied by Casella's song, see: John Freccero, "Casella's Song," *Dante Studies* 91 (1973), 73–80; Alan Levitan, "Dante as Listener, Cato's Rebuke, and Virgil's Self-Reproach," *Dante Studies* 103 (1985), 37–55; Iannucci, "Casella's Song," 39–44; Hollander, "*Purgatorio* II"; Sanguineti, "Infernal Acoustics," 73–77.

[16] On the figural meanings of these hymns, see Singleton, "In Exitu Israel de Aegypto," in Freccero, ed., *Dante*, pp. 112–14.

[17] St. Augustine, *Confessions*, Book X, Chapter XXXIII (Cambridge, MA: Harvard University Press, 1977), trans. William Watts, vol. II, pp. 164–69.

[18] See also Sanguineti, "Infernal Acoustics," 77.

The association between vain nostalgia and Dante's earlier culti-
vation of the *canzone* in Canto II signals the psychological dimension of
song's immobilizing power that emerges more fully in the dream of the
Siren. Listening to Casella's musical version of his own poem, Dante
the pilgrim is enraptured and immobilized much as Narcissus was
captivated by his own reflection. Casella's performance is an "aural
evocation" of Dante's "earlier self and art."[19] In one sense, the scene dramatizes a poet's temptation: listening to Casella sing his own words,
Dante succumbs to an infatuation with his own text. The scene may
also allude to the Florentine male coterie of song which Dante had once
enjoyed. Through poetry exchanges, he and his peers reflected each
other's idealizing poetic self-images back upon one another in a form
of ritualized social narcissism.

The Siren episode takes this critique of the abuse of the aesthetic
dimension of music to another level. As noted above, the Siren is a
common figure in patristic and medieval discourses on the effects of
music on the soul. Medieval writers and artists depicted the Siren as a
kind of monster, an allegorized image of *Luxuria*. In manuscript paintings and twelfth- and thirteenth-century bestiaries, the Siren often
appears as a courtesan holding a mirror.[20] Such imagery takes on a
social and polemical dimension in the many clerical denunciations of
minstrelsy dating from this period. In such texts, the term "Siren" has a
more concrete referent, designating the itinerant female performers of
court and town.[21] Thus the term "Siren" belongs to a moralizing discourse in which a wide range of performers and types of performances
are troped as a sexualized voice. Clerical moralists routinely applied this
term to women performers in order to assert the debauchery encouraged
by their music-making. Dante's Siren, therefore, emblematizes not only
the twin dangers of woman and carnal song, but also the indissoluble
link between them.

Purgatorio XIX translates these social and moral critiques of song
into psychological terms. The Siren's song emerges at a moment when

[19] Levitan provides an interesting discussion of the Casella episode as a rewriting of
Ovid's Narcissus episode in *Metamorphoses* III. As befitting the case of a poet, Levitan
writes, "temptation by sound" replaces "temptation by sight." See "Dante as Listener,"
46–47.

[20] John Block Friedman, "L'Iconographie de Vénus et de son miroir à la fin du Moyen
Age," in Bruno Roy, ed., *L'Erotisme au Moyen Age* (Montreal: Aurore, 1977), pp. 53–82;
Jean Gagné, "L'Erotisme dans la musique médiévale," in Roy, ed., *L'Erotisme*, pp.
85–107.

[21] In the medieval vernaculars, the term for woman minstrel was often synonymous with
"prostitute." On clerical attitudes toward minstrels, see Raleigh Morgan, Jr., "Old
French *jogleor* and Kindred Terms: Studies in Mediaeval Romance Lexicology,"
Romance Philology 7 (1954), 279–325, and Carla Casagrande and Silvana Vecchio, "Clercs
et jongleurs dans la société médiévale (XIIe et XIIIe siècles)," *Annales: Economies.
Sociétés. Civilisations* 34 (1979), 913–28.

the pilgrim's physical vulnerability is greatest (he is sleepy at the end of the day) and when the guardian of his will, Virgil, has relaxed his vigilance. Significantly, the Siren's beauty and the sweetness of her song are projections of the dreamer's own desire. Before his gaze, he transforms a stammering, maimed female figure ("una femmina balba, / ne li occhi guercia, e sovra i piè distorta, / con le man monche, e di colora scialba..." lines 7–9) into a lovely songstress. The content of the Siren's song indicates spiritual and psychic regression on Dante's part. When the Siren boasts that she turned Ulysses aside to her song, we are meant to realize that the dreamer has regressed to the condition of *Inferno*'s Ulysses, the evil counselor and exemplar of impious curiosity.

Although the passage conflates the Homeric Siren with Circe, whose allure is more specifically sexual in nature, its verbal music emphasizes the incantatory quality of her song. The line "'Io son,' cantava, 'io son dolce serena'" conveys her seductive powers of voice. It will be echoed and effaced by Beatrice's self-revelation at the top of Mount Purgatory. Beatrice's call to Dante – "Guardaci ben! Ben son, ben son Beatrice!" (*Purgatorio* XXX, line 73) – uses repeated plosives as a hortatory device to break through Dante's grief at the loss of Virgil. It creates a contrast with the euphonious vowels and seductive sibilants of the Siren's song ("'Io son,' cantava, 'io son dolce serena'") and affirms the aptness of her name. She is the blessèd one ("*Benedictus*," [XXX, line 19]) and she, not Virgil, the line tells us, is his true goal.

While the Siren's song will ultimately be redeemed by the vocal beatitudes pronounced by Beatrice, the allusion to Ulysses points to a network of themes peculiar to *Purgatorio*. The Ulysses of *Inferno* was the voyager who listened to the wrong song. *Purgatorio* XIX situates this figure of moral peril between the canticle's great discourses on love and poetry. It is to the second of these discourses that I now wish to turn. In Cantos XXI and XXII, the appearance of the poet Statius builds a set of parallels and antitheses between the poetry of Virgil and the Siren's song. The Statius–Virgil relationship offers a corrective to the legend of Ulysses and the Siren. To support this connection, I would point out that the figure of Statius is closely associated with motifs of song. His advent is heralded in *Purgatorio* XX by an earthquake and a chorus of voices singing the nativity hymn, *Gloria in excelsis Deo*, a sound that leaves Dante and Virgil immobilized in fear and awe (XX, lines 124–38). Later, in Canto XXI, Statius' presentation of his poetic vocation inverts the Siren's song. In his words, *Rome* drew *him* to herself because of his "sweet vocal spirit":

> Tanto fu dolce *mio vocale spirto*
> che, tolosano, a sé mi trasse Roma,
> dove mertai le tempie ornar di mirto.
> (88–90, my emphasis)

(So sweet was my vocal spirit that me, a Toulousan, Rome drew to itself, where I was deemed worthy to have my brows adorned with myrtle.)

Whereas Ulysses was a false counselor who was himself drawn toward his doom by the Sirens of impious curiosity, Statius tells how he looked to Virgil's poetry for nourishment and strength in the course of his own poetic quest. Mixing masculine and feminine metaphors of fertility and nourishment, the poet of the *Thebaid* tells how the "sparks" (*favelle*) from the divine flame of Virgil's poetry became the "seeds" (*seme*) that kindled his own poetic fire. The *Aeneid*, he declares, was both "mother" and "nurse" to his poetry:

> de l'Eneïda dico, la qual mamma
> fummi, e fummi nutrice, poetando
> (97–98)

(I mean the *Aeneid*, which in poetry was both mother and nurse to me . . .)

Unbeknownst to him, of course, "the ancient flame" stands before him. Virgil's humble silence contrasts sharply with that of the Siren, whose boasts about her power to hold men reflect the pagan cult of fame.

This extraordinary passage is often cited to illustrate Dante's privileging of the maternal.[22] In fact, it serves to distinguish two forms of maternal intercession, one good and one bad. Statius' tribute to the maternal power of Virgil's song is meant to reflect back critically on the Siren's song, which can be seen as another form of maternal vocality. The maternal dimension of her song has perhaps been obscured by the (overdetermined) association between female vocality and *Luxuria*. Rather, the Siren's boast that few men leave her abode since she so totally satisfies them – ("sì tutto l'appago" line 24), points toward the problem of male subjectivity explored in psychoanalytic theory.

The mesmerizing sweetness of the Siren's song suggests the fantasy of the maternal voice invoked at the outset of this essay, that is the all-encompassing "blanket of sound" denoting the maternal voice as it is imagined by the infant in the pre-Oedipal phase.[23] In the utopian

---

22 Robert Ball, "Theological Semantics: Virgil's *Pietas* and Dante's *Pietà*," *Stanford Italian Review* 2 (Spring 1981), 59–80; Robert Hollander, *Il Virgilio Dantesco* (Florence: Olschki, 1983); Rachel Jacoff, "Models of Literary Influence in the *Commedia*," in Laurie A. Finke and Martin B. Schichtman, eds., *Medieval Texts and Contemporary Readers* (Ithaca: Cornell University Press, 1987), pp. 165–66. The role of the maternal in the incarnational theology of the *Comedy* is of course extremely complex. For an interesting commentary on the question of female, and by implication, maternal desire, see Jacoff, "Transgression and Transcendence," pp. 194–95.

23 Rosolato, "La Voix," 81; Mary Ann Doane, "The Voice in the Cinema: The Articulation of Body and Space," *Yale French Studies* 60 (1980), 33–60; Didier Anzieu, "L'enveloppe sonore du soi," *Nouvelle revue de psychanalyse* 13 (1976), 173; Michel Chion, *La voix au cinéma* (Paris: Editions de L'Etoile, 1982). An excellent overview appears in Silverman, *The Acoustic Mirror*, pp. 72–100.

version of this fantasy, the infant, unable to distinguish between sounds of its own making and those produced by its environment, experiences a hallucinatory and pleasurable sense of bodily fusion with its mother's body. In another formulation, however, the maternal voice is imagined as engulfing the infant in a kind of primordial chaos. The dream of the Siren closely resembles this second version of the fantasy. Trapped within the net of her song, Dante the pilgrim must be rescued by an outside force.

The *good* mother, Virgil, speaks to the faltering man-child Statius not through pure sound, but rather through the textual medium of the *Aeneid*. The analogy between Statius' (and Dante's) experience and that of *Inferno*'s Ulysses is patent. Unlike the Siren's song, which lures sailors to their doom, Virgil's text (a "song" only in a metaphorical sense) sends the developing child-voyager on his way, thus inverting the image of the evil singer. The Siren's song, on the other hand, leaves the listener completely sated ("sì tutto l'appago"), much as the prostitute was thought to drain the male of his vital sap. The effect of Virgil's song, on the other hand, is to quicken the poet's manly resolve to sing of heroes and gods. Virgil's textual, that is disembodied, voice is seen as an empowering discourse that fosters creativity and zeal. Thus a contrast emerges within the poem between a textualized, metaphoric maternal that circulates between male readers and writers, and an embodied maternal evoked in the Siren's song.

By dramatizing the *Aeneid*'s positive impact on Statius the poet, Dante the poet seeks to justify his own Virgilian cult. Such justification, however, also implies a potential identity between the Siren's song and Virgil's poetry as forms of vain pleasure and knowledge. Dante's enterprise requires a decisive winnowing of good and evil songs and of good and evil mothers as well as fathers. The Statius episode definitively separates Virgil's song from the Siren's. In the world of Dante's poem, Virgil's text is the exemplar of heroic values associated with Empire and the stylistic ideal of the "parola ornata." In order to maintain this opposition between the two songs, Dante must keep Virgilian art pure of the taint (or stench) of the Siren's song.

Such a winnowing takes place in the next Canto. As every commentator remarks, *Purgatorio* XXII shifts the terms of Statius' debt to Virgil from the aesthetic to the spiritual level. Here, again, the worth and significance of Virgil's poetry are conveyed in terms of its effect upon Statius, for Statius reveals that he was converted to Christianity by reading the Fourth Eclogue's prophecy of a Savior's birth:

> Ed elli a lui: "Tu prima m'invïasti
> verso Parnaso a ber ne le sue grotte
> e prima appresso Dio m'alluminasti.

Facesti come quei che va di notte,
    che porta il lume dietro e sé non giova,
    ma dopo sé fa le persone dotte,
quando dicesti: 'Secol si rinova;
    torna giustizia e primo tempo umano,
    e progenïe scende da ciel nova.'
Per te poeta fui, per te cristiano . . .
                    (*Purgatorio* XXII, lines 64–73)

(And he to him, "You it was who first sent me toward Parnassus to drink in its caves, and you who first did light me on to God. You were like one who goes by night and carries the light behind him and profits not himself, but makes those wise who follow him, when you said, 'The ages are renewed; Justice returns and the first age of man, and a new progeny descends from heaven.' Through you I was a poet, through you a Christian . . .")

For Statius, the reading of Virgil's text was like the revelation of a hidden truth. Thus he addresses Virgil as he "that did lift for me the covering that was hiding from me the great good that I can tell of . . ." (XXII, lines 94–95). This traditional motif of rending a veil to reveal a hidden truth echoes Virgil's violent rending of the Siren's garments in Canto XIX, lines 31–33. Statius' metaphorical unveiling of Virgil's poetry exposes a positive good. Virgil's uncovering of the Siren lets loose a foul stench, a metaphor for the female genitals *and* the emptiness of the Siren's song. Again, on a metaphorical level, the Siren's song belongs to the lower material realm, and so it requires a physical force to remove the cover of her disguise and make her song's true meaning clear. Simultaneously, the interpretation of her song requires its destruction. The very literalness of Virgil's gesture shows that the Siren's song has no transcendent meaning. Unlike Virgil's pregnant words of prophecy, her belly (*ventre*) is depicted as sterile; thus there is an opposition between a song-text whose signified (the birth of Christ) exceeds its signifiers, and a vocal song which is *only* signifier. This contrast, in turn, caps a series of hierarchical oppositions between two voices competing for Dante's soul.

The Siren's singing represents song in its embodied form, as a monodic, incantatory performance in which music and sound are privileged over text. Spiritually debilitating in its effect, her singing so sates the senses that a seasoned will is required to break its spell. Virgil's art, on the other hand, represents the textual grounding of song, and song in its epic or prophetic mode. Dante invents the Statius episode to demonstrate the aesthetic and spiritual fertility of Virgilian song, appropriating maternal metaphors of suckling and pregnancy to show that its pleasure is an instrument of a greater good.

To return to the psychoanalytic model, one can observe that the episode of the Siren, presented as a quasi-hallucinatory experience, represents a false dream narrative embedded within a true dream narrative. In narratological terms, the episode is relegated to a secondary level of the poem's diegesis. This positioning of the Siren's song within the text emphasizes its enclosure within the more powerfully signifying voice of the male text, thus reversing the nightmarish fantasy of the infant caught within the net of the maternal voice. This dimension of the episode resembles the discursive strategy identified by Silverman as typical of classical Hollywood cinema and much psychoanalytic theory:

The female voice must be sequestered (if necessary through a *mise-en-abîme* of framing devices) within the heart of the diegesis, so far from the site of enunciation as to be beyond articulation or meaning. It must occupy an "unthinkable point at the interior of thought," an "inexpressible [point] at the interior of the enunciation," an "unrepresentable [point] at the interior of representation." There is, of course, only one group of sounds capable of conforming precisely to these requirements – those emitted by a newborn baby. This, then, is the vocal position which the female subject is called upon to occupy whenever (in film or in theory) she is identified with noise, babble, or the cry.[24]

The diegetic interiority of the Siren's song is further emphasized by its position close to the mid-point of the entire poem, suggesting a kind of psychic blind spot. But even more marked than this structural confinement of the Siren's song to the interior of the diegesis, is Virgil's abrupt and visceral silencing of the Siren, which reduces her to a single body-part, her belly (*ventre*). This burst of violence reveals a defensive mechanism on the part of the poet to disavow his own aural/oral instability by projecting the idea of castration onto the Siren's body through the sudden disclosure of her gaping *ventre*.

As Silverman points out, both the negative and positive versions of the fantasy of the maternal voice perform a distortion of the mother's actual role as linguistic initiator to the child. For Silverman, the tendency to equate the maternal voice with pure sonorousness (or with pure music in Dante's case) is "part of a larger cultural disavowal of the mother's role both as agent of discourse and as a model for linguistic identification."[25] Male discursive potency depends, she argues, upon the "stripping of the female voice of all claim to verbal authority." The Siren, as the figure for an emphatically embodied femininity, functions as a culturally sanctioned target of such abuse.

24 Silverman, *The Acoustic Mirror*, pp. 77–78. Silverman notes that by locating the female voice within the interior of the diegesis, it is associated with an inferior position, meaning that which can be overseen and overheard (p. 69). Similarly, the Siren's voice is presented as being overheard by "una donna . . . santa e presta" and by Virgil himself. The Siren herself seems to have no ability to perceive these figures.

25 Ibid., p. 100. In a very different context, Dante himself pays tribute to the mother's role as linguistic initiator to the child. In *Paradiso* XV, lines 115–26, Cacciaguida nostalgically recalls the voices of virtuous Florentine matrons of old, who would console infants with their babytalk, and recite the patriotic legends of the Trojans, Fiesole, and Rome to their household.

48

The Siren is not the last female singer encountered in the *Purgatorio*, however. The other major figure of female vocality to appear in this canticle is Matelda. Matelda's singing (foreshadowed by the dream figure of Leah in *Purgatorio* XXVII) also transfixes the pilgrim. Initially seen by Dante as he enters the wood of the earthly paradise, she appears as a Persephone-like figure, "singing and culling flower from flower" ("cantando e scegliendo fior da fiore," XXVIII, line 41). Following her along the opposite side of the River Lethe, he describes her as "singing like a lady enamored" ("Cantando come donna innamorata," XXIX, line 1). Like the Siren, Matelda can be viewed in the larger context of *Purgatorio*'s education of the soul's innate impulse to song. However, several elements distinguish the two female singers and their songs. Unlike the invasive, metamorphic Siren, Matelda appears as a figure clearly situated in the main diegesis, becoming one of the pilgrim's crucial interlocutors and guides. Her voice is firmly located at a distance from the pilgrim, on the other side of the River Lethe, in order to lessen what contemporary psychology has labelled boundary anxiety. More-over, in listening to her, Dante the pilgrim holds onto his own voice, and is able to address her, in a clear contrast with the Siren episode. Her song, although initially incomprehensible to the pilgrim, invites him to follow and discern its true meaning which unfolds in a rich sequence of intertextual echoes. As Peter S. Hawkins shows, the pilgrim perceives Matelda as a polysemous text to be read.[26]

Furthermore, she turns out to be another figure of textuality, since her song is revealed to be none other than Psalm 91, a song of praise and thanks for God's works. In performing her song and dance of praise, Matelda is thus finally revealed as a figure for the Psalmist David. Link-ing Matelda's song with Dante's own poem, Hawkins concludes that she "presents us with the possibility that music and lyric – the work of art – can continue to serve as a form of worship."[27] From the perspective of this essay, however, the crucial element distinguishing Matelda's song from that of the Siren is the former's association with male textuality. This move spares the beautiful Matelda from the Siren's ugly fate.

Looking back at Dante's stripped and silenced Siren, we can identify her song and her body as the sacrificial victim of Dante's poetics of tex-tuality. Whereas Virgil simply disappears at the top of Mount Purgatory, the Siren, as the projection onto woman of drives that would jeopardize sublimation (or in psychoanalytic terms, those which might destabilize the male subject), cannot be given such a gentle treatment. For Dante the poet to do so would risk acknowledging a problematic element in his poetics, namely the role of the embodied, audible voice.

---

[26] Peter S. Hawkins, "Watching Matelda," in Rachel Jacoff and Jeffrey T. Schnapp, eds., *The Poetry of Allusion: Virgil and Ovid in Dante's "Commedia,"* (Stanford University Press, 1991), pp. 181–201.

[27] Ibid., p. 200.

3

Ophelia's songs in *Hamlet*: music, madness, and the feminine

LESLIE C. DUNN

In one of the most famous readings of one Shakespearean character by another, Ophelia's brother Laertes calls her a "document in madness."[1] The word "document" is usually glossed with its older etymological sense of "lesson" or "example." In Renaissance terms, Laertes sees Ophelia as an emblem – an image for which he supplies the text, inscribing it with an apparently self-evident, unambiguous cultural meaning. Laertes is not alone in this tendency to emblematize Ophelia: Hamlet also is quick to construe her in terms of cultural stereotypes, as the "Woman" whose name is frailty. And, as Elaine Showalter has shown, the subsequent history of Ophelia's representation, not only on the stage but in the discourses of literary criticism, psychiatry, and the visual arts, has followed these first male readers in constructing her as an archetype of both woman and madness.[2]

In Shakespeare's dramatic construction of Ophelia as madwoman, the discourse of music has a privileged place: Ophelia's songs dominate her mad scene, not only in their profusion, but in their disruptive and invasive power. From her first entrance Ophelia uses singing to command attention and confuse response, frustrating Gertrude's attempts to contain her utterance within the bounds of polite conversation:

Work on this essay was supported by summer fellowships from the National Endowment for the Humanities and the Folger Shakespeare Library. I would also like to thank Richard Leppert, Donald Foster, and Peter Antelyes for their thoughtful comments on early drafts.

1 William Shakespeare, *Hamlet*, ed. Harold Jenkins, The Arden Shakespeare (London and New York: Methuen, 1982), 4.5.176. Subsequent citations will appear in parentheses in the text.
2 Elaine Showalter, "Representing Ophelia: Women, Madness, and the Responsibilities of Feminist Criticism," in Patricia Parker and Geoffrey Hartman, eds., *Shakespeare and the Question of Theory* (New York and London: Methuen, 1985), pp. 77–94.

Oph[elia].	Where is the beauteous Majesty of Denmark?
Queen.	How now, Ophelia?
Oph. (sings)	*How should I your true love know*
	From another one?
	By his cockle hat and staff
	And his sandal shoon.
Queen.	Alas, sweet lady, what imports this song?
Oph.	Say you? Nay, pray you mark.
(sings)	*He is dead and gone, lady,*
	He is dead and gone,
	At his head a grass-green turf,
	At his heels a stone.
O ho!	
Queen.	Nay, but Ophelia –
Oph.	Pray you mark.
[sings]	*White his shroud as the mountain snow –*

(4.5.21–36)

Claudius tries another strategy of containment, attempting to fix the singing's meaning by assigning it a cause: "Conceit upon her father" (4.5.45). But Ophelia again uses music as a means of resistance: "Pray let's have no words of this," she answers, "but when they ask you what it means, say you this" (46–47). What she instructs Claudius to "say" – the St. Valentine's Day ballad – is something that *cannot* be said, both literally (because it is a song) and figuratively (because its sexual content makes it indecorous, inappropriate). Singing, then, functions as a highly theatrical sign of Ophelia's estrangement from "normal" social discourse, as well as from her "normal" self.

This essay explores the role of music, as embodied in a female singing voice, in forging what Showalter has called the "representational bonds" between gender, sexuality and madness in *Hamlet*.[3] Generally speaking, Ophelia's singing has received short shrift in *Hamlet* criticism. Literary critics tend to stress the visual and verbal signs of her distraction – the loose hair, the flowers, the fragmented speech – while about singing they say little more than that it was "a frequent accompaniment of madness" on the Elizabethan stage; by implying that its meaning is obvious and conventional, they give it a Laertes-like emblematic reading.[4] Others, emulating Claudius, reduce Ophelia's singing

---

[3] Showalter, "Representing Ophelia," p. 80.

[4] Maurice and Hannah Charney, "The Language of Madwomen in Shakespeare and His Fellow Dramatists," *Signs: Journal of Women in Culture and Society* 3, 2 (Winter 1977), 453; see also Bridget Gellert Lyons, "The Iconography of Ophelia," *English Literary History* 44 (1977), 60–74. On Ophelia's mad speech, see Sandra K. Fischer, "Hearing Ophelia: Gender and Tragic Discourse in *Hamlet*," *Renaissance and Reformation/*

to a mere "symptom of her pathetic state."[5] The song texts, by contrast, have attracted considerable attention, much of it aimed at identifying to whom or what Ophelia's fragmentary ballad quotations refer, and thereby seeking to establish the causes of her madness.[6] But such an approach, which focuses on the songs' words, assumes that their mode of performance is merely a carrier of meaning rather than a constituent. I wish to argue that Ophelia's singing is full of meaning – indeed, *over*full – which is precisely what makes it such a potent signifier, not only of woman and of madness, but also of music itself.

I would like, then, to propose a new reading of Ophelia as a figure of *song*. My argument is that the representation of Ophelia's madness involves a mapping of her sexual and psychological difference onto the discursive "difference" of music. As female is opposed to male and madness to reason, so song in *Hamlet* is opposed to speech – particularly those modes of speech that serve to defend the patriarchal order from the threat represented by Ophelia's "importunate" (4.5.2) self-expression. Far from being a mere accompaniment of her madness, then, Ophelia's music actively participates in *Hamlet's* larger discourse on gender and sexuality. At the same time, this dramatic use of music reflects the broader discourse of music in early modern English culture, with its persistent associations between music, excess and the feminine.[7]

The discursive status of song in *Hamlet* is grounded in its differentiation from speech, the usual mode of oral communication in Western culture. What distinguishes them is the presence of something "extra" – music – which at once imitates and estranges spoken utterance, shaping it to a different set of rules. At the same time, the singing voice behaves differently from the speaking voice. The very process of vocalization is exaggerated or intensified; the voice seems to have a less mediated

(4 contd.) *Renaissance et Reforme* 26 (1990), 1–11, and David Leverenz, "The Woman in *Hamlet*: An Interpersonal View," in Murray M. Schwartz and Coppelia Kahn, eds., *Representing Shakespeare: New Psychoanalytic Essays* (Baltimore and London: Johns Hopkins University Press, 1980), pp. 119–21.

5 F. W. Sternfeld, *Music in Shakespearean Tragedy* (London: Routledge and Kegan Paul; New York: Dover, 1963), p. 57.

6 See, for example, Carroll Camden, "On Ophelia's Madness," *Shakespeare Quarterly* 15 (1964), 247–55. In a recent article, Carol Thomas Neely has critiqued such attempts to pin down the meaning of Ophelia's songs, arguing that her mad discourse has a "'quoted,' fragmentary, ritualized quality" that is both personal and communal; "'Documents in Madness': Reading Madness and Gender in Shakespeare's Tragedies and Early Modern Culture," *Shakespeare Quarterly* 42 (1991), 323–36. For a survey of commentary on the songs, see Peter Seng, *The Vocal Songs in the Plays of Shakespeare* (Cambridge, MA: Harvard University Press, 1967), pp. 131–56.

7 See Linda Phyllis Austern, "'Sing Againe Syren': The Female Musician and Sexual Enchantment in Elizabethan Life and Literature," *Renaissance Quarterly* 42 (1989), 420–48, and "'Alluring the Auditorie to Effeminacie': Music and the Idea of the Feminine in Early Modern England," *Music and Letters* 74.3 (1993), 343–54.

relationship to the body, perhaps because there is literally more body in the voice – more breath, more diaphragm muscles, a more open mouth.

Along with this greater materiality of language comes a greater indeterminacy of meaning. Kaja Silverman offers a psychoanalytic perspective on this aspect of vocality:

The voice is the site of perhaps the most radical of all subjective divisions – the division between meaning and materiality . . . The sounds the voice makes always exceed signification to some degree, both before the entry into language and after. The voice is never completely standardized, forever retaining an individual flavor or texture – what Barthes calls its "grain."[8]

Silverman is referring here to Barthes' "The Grain of the Voice," an essay in which he explores the dialectic of meaning and materiality in vocal production.[9] Because his subject is song, however, Barthes locates the "grain" more specifically in the voice "when it is in a dual posture, a dual production – of language and of music." He describes this voice-in-music as a space where the normative functionality of language is transcended, where signification gives way to *signifiance*:

[the "grain"] forms a signifying play having nothing to do with communication, representation (of feelings), expression; it is that apex (or depth) of production where the melody really works at the language – not at what it says, but the voluptuousness of its sounds-signifiers, of its letters – where melody explores how the language works and identifies with that work.

According to Barthes, it is this *signifiance* that enables the singing voice to "escape the tyranny of meaning."[10]

As his metaphor suggests, Barthes sees this escape as positive, liberating a suppressed voluptuousness in both language and listener. Through its identification with music in song, the linguistic "body," the materiality of its sound-signifiers, is released from semantic constraint. At the same time, the listener, through his/her identification with music, enters into a relationship with the performer's body that Barthes describes as "erotic."[11] For Barthes, then, music's power lies in its capacity to produce *jouissance*, the intense, ego-fragmenting pleasure that originates in "an excess of the text."[12] Significantly, he associates the excess of the musical text with madness:

---

8   Kaja Silverman, *The Acoustic Mirror: The Female Voice in Psychoanalysis and Cinema* (Bloomington: Indiana University Press, 1988), p. 44.
9   Roland Barthes, "The Grain of the Voice, " in *Image, Music, Text*, trans. Stephen Heath (New York: Noonday Press/Farrar, Strauss and Giroux, 1977), pp. 179–89.
10   Ibid., pp. 181, 182, 185.
11   Ibid., p. 188.
12   Roland Barthes, *The Pleasure of the Text*, trans. Richard Miller (New York: Noonday Press, 1975), p. 19. Although Barthes' notion of *jouissance* originated in his analysis of literary pleasure, "The Grain of the Voice" specifically associates it with musical pleasure, speculating that the threat of loss entailed by *jouissance* is the source of "the old Platonic idea" that "music is dangerous" ("Grain," 179).

The body passes into music without any relay but the signifier. This passage – this transgression – makes music a madness . . . In relation to the writer the composer is always mad (and the writer can never be so, for he is condemned to meaning).[13]

Barthes' concept of musical *signifiance* finds some suggestive parallels in poststructuralist theory, particularly in Kristeva's opposition between the semiotic and the symbolic in language. The semiotic is linked to the pre-Oedipal phase of development, when the child is bound up with the mother's body, communicating with her through gestures, rhythms and nonrepresentational sounds. The sounds of the maternal voice, in particular, are privileged sites of pleasure and identification.[14] This semiotic bond with the mother is shattered with the acquisition of language, which, in Lacanian theory, marks the child's entry into the symbolic order. And just as the child must transfer its identification from mother to father, so the maternal semiotic must be suppressed under the paternal law of the *logos*. According to Kristeva, however, the semiotic survives in language as a "*heterogeneousness* to meaning and signification" which "produces 'musical' but also nonsense effects."[15] Since such effects are ultimately related to the primal "music" of the mother's voice, they represent the return of a repressed maternal realm of linguistic pleasure, a subversive semiotic potential within the symbolic order.[16]

Of course, Kristeva is here using "music" and "musical" metaphorically, to refer to the rhythms and sonorities of language. The metaphor itself is conventional in Western literary criticism, familiar from recurring allusions to the "music of poetry." Kristeva's use of it is also conventional insofar as it articulates what has always been implicit in those allusions, namely the Western tendency to position music among signifying systems not only by analogy with, but also in opposition to language: *melos* vs. *logos*; sound vs. sense; "music" vs. "meaning." Thus such apparently innocent, usually celebratory metaphors of "musical" language reveal how music, whether *as* discourse or *in* discourse, becomes implicated in the binarisms that organize patriarchal thinking,

13 Roland Barthes, "Rasch, " in *The Responsibility of Forms*, trans. Richard Howard (New York: Hill and Wang, 1985), p. 308.

14 On the privileging of the maternal voice in Kristeva and other feminist theorists, see Claire Kahane, "Questioning the Maternal Voice," *Genders* 3 (1988), 82–91, and Domna C. Stanton, "Difference on Trial: A Critique of the Maternal Metaphor in Cixous, Irigaray, and Kristeva," in Nancy K. Miller, ed., *The Poetics of Gender* (New York: Columbia University Press, 1986), pp. 157–82.

15 Julia Kristeva, *Desire in Language: A Semiotic Approach to Literature and Art*, trans. Thomas Gora, Alice Jardine, and Leon S. Roudiez, ed. Leon S. Roudiez (New York: Columbia University Press, 1980), p. 133.

16 Julia Kristeva, *Revolution in Poetic Language*, trans. Margaret Waller, ed. Leon S. Roudiez (New York: Columbia University Press, 1984), p. 63.

and thereby associated with the unconscious and the irrational as well as with the feminine. Kristeva's semiotic encompasses all three; its "music" surfaces in the language of poet and psychotic alike. Other French feminist writers, notably Catherine Clément and Hélène Cixous, have pushed the Kristevan musical metaphor even further by claiming song as the archetypal feminine discourse, "the first music of the voice of love, which every woman keeps alive":

The Voice sings from a time before law, before the Symbolic took one's breath away and reappropriated it into language under its authority of separation . . . Within each woman the first, nameless love is singing.[17]

They have further identified music with madness by linking that song to the hysteric's cry – another form of escape from the tyranny of patri-archal meaning.[18]

It is important to recognize that these theoretical identifications of music with a "mad" or "feminine" discourse, outside the structures of patriarchal signification, themselves remain firmly within those struc-tures. In blurring the distinction between music and musical metaphor, they essentialize music itself; it becomes the discursive "other" through an act of linguistic appropriation. We must therefore be cautious in applying them to the interpretation of music within literary texts, lest our readings reproduce the same binary paradigms. Nonetheless, such theories remain useful in that they reveal how music has been con-structed or, to use Susan McClary's term, "framed" in Western culture. McClary rightly insists that music is more like literature than some literary critics are willing to admit: it too is "condemned to" culturally constructed meanings. Yet she goes on to say that "to the very great extent that Western culture is logocentric, music itself always gives the impression of being in excess, of being mad."[19] In the same way, asso-ciations of music with the feminine are bound up with, and implicated in, ideologies of gender. The writings of Barthes, Kristeva, Cixous, and Clément testify to the power and persistence of these constructions of music, and suggest what can be at stake in maintaining them. As such they offer a point of departure for reading the music, both literal and figurative, in Ophelia's madness.

Though their intellectual context was that of Christian humanism rather than poststructuralist theory, early modern English writers also asso-ciated music with the body and its libidinal energies. Specifically, they

---

17 Hélène Cixous and Catherine Clément, *The Newly Born Woman*, trans. Betsy Wing (Minneapolis: University of Minnesota Press, 1986), p. 93.

18 On music and hysteria, see Cixous and Clément, *The Newly Born Woman*, pp. 19–22, 107; and Catherine Clément, *Opera, or the Undoing of Women*, trans. Betsy Wing (Minneapolis: University of Minnesota Press, 1988), pp. 32–38.

19 Susan McClary, *Feminine Endings: Music, Gender, and Sexuality* (Minneapolis: University of Minnesota Press, 1991), p. 102.

were preoccupied with music's affective power, its capacity to arouse desire. Yet their attitude toward this power, unlike Barthes', was ambivalent, reflecting the conflicting ideologies of music inherited from Platonic and Christian thought.[20] On the one hand, Renaissance humanists saw music as the earthly embodiment of divine order, and believed that its expressive powers could be a positive ethical force, an agent in the formation of both the ideal courtier and the well-ordered state.[21] In post-Reformation England, however, this humanist idealism was qualified by the longstanding Christian distrust of music's sensuousness, its unmediated appeal to the body and the emotions. If music was "so powerful a thing, that it ravisheth the soul, *regina sensum*, the Queene of the senses, by sweete pleasure,"[22] then it could not only distract the mind from higher thoughts, but even unbalance it by arousing excessive and unruly passions. Defenders of music argued that "delight of the eares" might be the means through which "the weak soule may be stirred up into a feeling of godliness."[23] But as Richard Mulcaster observed,

to some [music] seemes offensive, bycause it carrieth away the eare, with the sweetnesse of the melodie, and bewitcheth the mind with a *syrens* sound, pulling it from that delite, wherin of duetie it ought to dwell, unto harmonicall fantasies, and withdrawing it, from the best meditations, and most vertuous thoughtes to forreigne conceites and wandring devises.[24]

The problem lay not only with music's sensuous immediacy but also with its semantic indeterminacy which, combined with the subjective nature of musical response, made music's meaning difficult either to define or to control.[25] The most extreme critics therefore condemned virtually all music as conducive to various forms of psychic, social, and moral excess. In *The Anatomie of Abuses* (1583), Phillip Stubbes warned parents:

if you wold haue your sonne, softe, womannish, vncleane, smoth mouthed, affected to bawdrie, scurrilitie, filthie rimes and vnsemely talking: brifly, if you

---

[20] For an overview of English Renaissance attitudes toward music, see Walter L. Woodfill, *Musicians in English Society from Elizabeth to Charles I* (Princeton University Press, 1953), pp. 201–46.

[21] On Renaissance musical humanism, see D. P. Walker, "Musical Humanism in the Sixteenth and Early Seventeenth Centuries," *The Music Review* 2 (1941), 1–13, 111–21, 220–27, 288–308, and 3 (1942), 55–71; James Winn, *Unsuspected Eloquence: A History of Relations between Poetry and Music* (New Haven and London: Yale University Press, 1981), pp. 163–79; Gary Tomlinson, *Monteverdi and the End of the Renaissance* (Berkeley and Los Angeles: University of California Press, 1987), pp. 3–30.

[22] Robert Burton, *The Anatomy of Melancholy*, 4th edn. (Oxford, 1632), p. 297.

[23] John Case, *The Praise of Musicke* (Oxford, 1586), pp. 70–71.

[24] Richard Mulcaster, *Positions wherein those primitive circumstances be examined, which are necessary for the training up of children* (London, 1581), fol. 29v.

[25] On this point, see Elise Jorgens, "The Singer's Voice in Elizabethan Drama," in Maryanne Cline Horowitz, Anne J. Cruz, and Wendy A. Furman, eds., *Renaissance Rereadings: Intertext and Context* (University of Chicago Press, 1988), p. 35.

56

wold haue him, as it were transnatured into a woman or worse, and inclyned to all kind of whordome and abhomination, let him to dauncing school, and to learn musicke, and than shall you not faile of your purpose. And if you would haue your daughter whorish, bawdie, and vncleane, and a filthie speaker, and such like, bring her up in musick and dauncing, and my life for youres, you haue wun the goale.[26]

Admittedly, Stubbes's attack is more hysterical than most, but it does reflect a widespread cultural anxiety about music, and reveals how that anxiety was rooted in patriarchal constructions of gender and sexuality. As Linda Austern has shown, Renaissance debates over the nature and uses of music bore striking similarities to contemporary debates over the nature and place of women.[27] Like woman, music was associated with the body and female generativity – "as pregnant as *Libia* alwaies breeding some new thing."[28] Like woman, too, music was held to have an essentially changeable nature, unpredictable and sometimes irrational in its behavior. Behind such analogies between music and femininity lay the perception of parallel threats to masculine subjectivity. Music's sensuous beauty gave it power: its sounds could penetrate the ear and so "ravish" the mind. The fear was that masculine autonomy and virtue would be overwhelmed in an abandonment to "sweete pleasure" – that music, in other words, was a Siren.

Given this gendered construction of music, it is not surprising that some Renaissance writers associated musical performance with the transgression of culturally prescribed gender roles. According to Stubbes, men who make music are "transnatured," made "softe" and "womannish," presumably because music encourages them to indulge in "feminine" emotional excess. In women, music mirrors their own inherently excessive feminine nature; their musical pleasure thus generates monsters of unrestrained female desire, "whorish, bawdie, and vncleane." In either case, music produces a breakdown in social order that is expressed, significantly, in unruly utterances: men become "smoth mouthed," women "filthie speaker[s]."[29] Here is the same nexus of associations between music, feminine vocality, and semantic excess that we saw in French feminist theory, viewed from the perspective of male sexual anxiety.

This negative vision of music's power may seem to contradict the more familiar Renaissance image of Pythagorean universal harmony, the "music of the spheres" that epitomized the order of God's creation. But these contradictory images in fact belong to the same discourse;

---

26 Phillip Stubbes, *The Anatomie of Abuses* (London, 1583), sig. D5–D5v.
27 Austern, "'Sing Againe Syren,'" 420–27.
28 Case, *The Praise of Musicke*, p. 4.
29 On the sexualization of the mouth in Renaissance discourses about women, and excessive speech as a sign of sexual transgression, see Karen Newman, *Fashioning Femininity and English Renaissance Drama* (University of Chicago Press, 1991), p. 12.

they are but the two poles of another opposition. Jacques Attali has argued that music, like other signifying systems, is founded upon difference: it is ordered sound that is separated from un-ordered sound, or noise, by both formal and cultural boundaries. As a result, definitions of music are always ideological:

music appears in myth *as an affirmation that society is possible* . . . Its order simulates the social order, and its dissonances express marginalities. *The code of music simulates the accepted rules of society.*[30]

Applying this theory to the Renaissance discourse of music, we might say that Pythagorean harmony is music in its positive or "masculine" aspect: *logos*, reason, order. Its social analogues are those forms of musical practice that are sanctioned by Church and State, and serve the interests of hegemonic groups: the music played at weddings, for example, which symbolizes the containment of sexual desire within the hierarchical "concord" of marriage. Its negative or "feminine" aspect represents all the dis-orderly energies in soul or society, energies that are constantly threatening to escape from patriarchal control, even as musical *signifiance* threatens to escape from signification, or the semiotic to erupt into the symbolic. In this "feminine" aspect, music itself can become – to the ears of anxious male listeners, at least – a cultural dissonance, its "harmonicall fantasies" a kind of madness.

With Attali's opposition between music and noise we can return to Ophelia's mad singing and see how it functions as a discursive dissonance within the play. Paradoxically, Ophelia's music is noise in Attali's sense precisely because it *is* music. As discourse it is radically "other," breaking the "accepted rules" of conversation and hence ambiguous in its meaning. Moreover, when Ophelia sings, she takes on a mask of performance: her personal voice is estranged, filtered through the anonymous voices of the ballads, multiplying and thereby rendering indeterminate the relationships between singer, personae, and audience. At the same time, these voices are doubly embodied in music's materiality – in the melody that "works" at the language, and in the "grain" of Ophelia's own voice – which causes a further surplus, and therefore slippage, of meaning. No wonder Gertrude can only reply to Ophelia's outburst with a bewildered question: "Alas, sweet lady, what imports this song?" (4.5.27).

As social behavior, too, Ophelia's singing is "noisy." It is disruptive, indecorous, defying expectations – particularly the expectation of appropriate feminine behavior implicit in the epithet with which Claudius attempts to stop her: "Pretty Ophelia" (4.5.56). But Ophelia in

---

30 Jacques Attali, *Noise: The Political Economy of Music*, trans. Brian Massumi (Minneapolis: University of Minnesota Press, 1985), p. 29.

her madness refuses to be pretty, as she refuses to be silenced. The ballad that she sings to Claudius tells of a girl's sexual initiation; by the end of the second strophe her lover has "Let in the maid that out a maid / Never departed more" (4.5.54–55). Claudius's discomfiture is obvious from his interruption, but Ophelia is unfazed; she interrupts *him* and finishes her song:

> *By Gis and by Saint Charity,*
> *Alack and fie for shame,*
> *Young men will do't if they come to't –*
> *By Cock, they are to blame.*
> *Quoth she, "Before you tumbled me,*
> *You promis'd me to wed."*

He answers,

> *"So would I a done, by yonder sun,*
> *And thou hadst not come to my bed."*
> (4.5.58–66)

For Ophelia to sing such a lyric, especially in front of her lover's parents, is shocking. My point, however, is that the *fact* that Ophelia sings is just as indecorous as *what* she sings, and in some ways even more disturbing, because of the surplus of meaning that inheres in her singing voice, and the power that voice-in-music gives her.

We are now in a position to understand the cultural resonance that Ophelia's singing might have had for Renaissance audiences. If music arouses excessive "feminine" passions, then it is also an ideal vehicle for representing feminine excess. If its meaning cannot be controlled, then it can signify a loss of control that is perceived as threatening, yet erotically exciting. Music is like the "madwoman" in language, releasing subversive powers of self-expression by embodying them in the expressive powers of the voice. As such it is an apt marker of the mad Ophelia: a frightening figure of female openness, of uncontrolled generativity, whose free-flowing and formless utterance threatens to "strew / Dangerous conjectures in ill-breeding minds" (4.5.14–15).

In singing, then, Ophelia becomes both the literal and the figurative "dissonance" that "expresses marginalities." The question remains: what has been marginalized in Denmark, besides Ophelia herself? The St. Valentine's Day ballad suggests that it is sexuality, particularly female sexuality, and the rest of the play bears this out. At its center is Hamlet, whose tormented awareness of his mother's desire turns him against all women. Laertes, too, is preoccupied with the unruly female body. When Ophelia tells him of Hamlet's love, he warns her to repress her own desires, using a musical image which, in light of Ophelia's fate, seems doubly charged: "Then weigh what loss your honor may sustain / If with too credent ear you list his songs" (1.3.29–30). Peter Seng has argued that Ophelia, in her madness, offers the male characters a dark mirror of their own sexual anxiety: "the heroine of the [St. Valentine's Day Ballad] is not the Ophelia that Hamlet knew, but rather the Ophelia that Polonius and Laertes, without real cause, had feared their daughter and sister might become."[31] I would add that it is not only the ballad's heroine who represents those fears; it is also Ophelia herself, who, in singing, embodies the cultural fantasy of the Siren, woman as eroticized voice-object.[32]

In this respect Shakespeare's representation of Ophelia draws on gender stereotypes of the Elizabethan and Jacobean stage, where the sexually ambiguous eroticism of boy actors was exploited in scenes of feminine musical seduction. When Ophelia sings "*For bonny sweet Robin is all my joy*" (4.5.184), the phallic pun recalls other women characters, many of them Siren figures in the moralized Renaissance sense – seductresses, if not courtesans or bawds – who use song to proclaim their own desires and assert their sexual power over men.[33] But Ophelia's performance dislocates this stereotype: she sings not *as* a seducer but *about* one, reminding us that it was she who "suck'd the honey" of Hamlet's "music vows" and not the other way around (3.1.158). In doing so, she also forces the audience to confront the disjunction between her subjectivity and the "voices" assigned to women in her culture.

These cultural voices are rendered still more problematic by Ophelia's frequent shifts between voices. Not all of her songs are erotic; in fact most of them are laments, expressions of loss and grief:

> And will a not come again?
> And will a not come again?
> No, no, he is dead,
> Go to thy death-bed,
> He never will come again.
> (4.5.187–91)

Here again Ophelia's singing could be construed as reinforcing a gender stereotype, since grief, or indeed any strong emotion, is another

31 Seng, *The Vocal Songs*, p. 148.
32 The Lacanian term "voice-object" is borrowed from Michel Poizat, *The Angel's Cry: Beyond the Pleasure Principle in Opera*, trans. Arthur Denner (Ithaca: Cornell University Press, 1992).
33 For example, Franceschina in Marston's *The Dutch Courtesan* (1605) seduces a customer with a song in the voice of the nightingale, a bird traditionally associated with both women and lust: "My body is but little, / So is the nightingale's. / I love to sleep 'gainst prickle, / So doth the nightingale" (1.2.150–53). For further discussion of musical seduction in English Renaissance drama, see Linda Austern's essay in this volume.

form of excess identified as "feminine" in *Hamlet*. We saw how Stubbes feared that an abandonment to music would render men "softe" and "womannish." The male characters in *Hamlet* express a similar fear of abandoning themselves to the figurative "music" of their emotions. After hearing the Player King describe the grief of Hecuba for her slain husband, Hamlet wonders, "What would he do / Had he the motive and the cue for passion that I have?" (2.2.554–55). Yet, when he does express that passion, he feels effeminized:

> This is most brave,
> That I, the son of a dear father murder'd,
> Prompted to my revenge by heaven and hell,
> Must like a whore unpack my heart with words,
> And fall a-cursing like a very drab,
> A scullion!
>
> (2.2.578–83)

Similarly, when Laertes learns of Ophelia's death, he tries but fails to "forbid" his tears (4.7.185), then rationalizes them as a purging of what Claudius, early in the play, calls "unmanly grief" (1.2.94): "When these are gone, / The woman will be out" (4.7.187–88).

Ophelia's songs might be said to perform a similar function, on both the personal and the cultural level. As Charles Segal and Elizabeth Tolbert observe elsewhere in this volume, the lament is a form of song traditionally associated with women. In mourning the loss of both father and "true love" (4.5.23), Ophelia aligns herself with this tradition, not only through her own singing, but also through her implicit identification with Niobe and Hecuba, the legendary women evoked by Hamlet as icons of mourning. It is as if she is taking on the burden of all the unexpressed grief in the play, becoming the real thing of which the Player King's performance – and, according to Hamlet, Gertrude's – were but imitations, "fiction[s] . . . of passion" (2.2.546).

At the same time, however, the particularities of Ophelia's own performance disrupt this identification. As with her bawdy songs, what is foregrounded is not congruity with conventions but incongruity, not obviousness of meaning but ambiguity. In their fragmentary form, their fictive voices, and their shifts from first to third person, Ophelia's ballads are discursively disjoint; in their inappropriateness to their immediate context, their interruptions of conversation with song, they are both discursively and socially displaced. Moreover, compared to actual lamenting, Ophelia's ballads are emphatically not the real thing. As in the St. Valentine's Day ballad, she does not lament so much as sing *about* lamenting: *"They bore him bare-fac'd on the bier, / And in his grave rain'd many a tear"* (4.5.164–65). Her songs thus become ghostly echoes of rituals that never took place, griefs that were never articulated.

Even in her madness she cannot attain the utter abandonment of Niobe's "all tears" (1.2.149) or Hecuba's "instant burst of clamour" (2.2.511). Far from being an excessive expression of feminine emotion, Ophelia's "broken voice" (2.2.550) is an implicit reproach to the society that has denied her full expression.

If Ophelia's singing lets "the woman" out, then, it does so in such a way as to problematize cultural constructions of women's song, even while containing her within their re-presentation. Her songs are like an inversion of patriarchal speech, a release of repressed psychic energies and unmet emotional needs. But according to the logic of patriarchal narrative, that release can be only temporary: Ophelia's disruptive feminine energy must be reabsorbed into both the social and the discursive orders of the play. The price that Ophelia herself pays is high; her moment of self-expression is, in Showalter's words, "quickly followed, as if in retribution, by her death."[34] Catherine Clément has argued that this narrative pattern is typical of opera, in which heroines are "undone" by a plot that climaxes in "their glorious moment: a sung death."[35] Indeed, Ophelia in her madness resembles another "noisy" heroine, Lucia di Lammermoor, whose mad scene is similarly framed by the reactions of an audience.[36]

Ophelia is unlike those operatic heroines, however, in that her death is not the play's climax. In fact it is not even represented on stage, but rather reported by Gertrude, in one of the play's most lyrical speeches:

> Her clothes spread wide,
> And mermaid-like awhile they bore her up,
> Which time she chanted snatches of old lauds,
> As one incapable of her own distress,
> Or like a creature native and indued
> Unto that element. But long it could not be
> Till that her garments, heavy with their drink,
> Pull'd the poor wretch from her melodious lay
> To muddy death.
>
> (4.7.174–82)

This speech marks a crucial moment in the play's response to the threats of excess and disorder embodied in Ophelia's music. It recapitulates the earlier mad scene in its references to singing and flowers. This time, however, we get only a description of Ophelia's song, rendered in someone else's speech; the "grain" of Ophelia's own voice is inaudible. Moreover, Gertrude now defines her songs as "old lauds" (hymns), a

---

[34] Showalter, "Representing Ophelia," 81.

[35] Clement, *Opera*, p. 45.

[36] My reading of Ophelia's mad scene is indebted to Susan McClary's analysis of the musical representation of madwomen in *Feminine Endings*, pp. 80–111.

lyric genre the cultural connotations of which are very different from those of her earlier ballads and laments. This narrative reframing renders the image of Ophelia singing less immediate, less dangerous: "she chanted snatches of old lauds" is a faint echo of *"By Gis and by Saint Charity."*

But this is only one aspect of the speech's larger project of restoring Ophelia to her original iconic role of modest and delicate virgin. Gertrude's description of Ophelia's drowning aestheticizes her madness, makes it "pretty," and in so doing makes it safe for the easier, distancing responses of pity and compassion; the Siren has become merely "mermaid-like." On the discursive level, too, Gertrude's verbal lyricism performs a crucial function: it re-appropriates Ophelia's music by inscribing it in the containing verbal structures, the metaphorical "music" of poetry. Instead of Ophelia's disjunct fragments of popular song, Gertrude gives us the blank verse of high court culture. Instead of Ophelia's laments, she gives us elegy.

It is fitting, too, that this task is given to Gertrude, who was herself the embodiment of unruly female sexuality earlier in the play. Here, she is merely completing a process that was initiated by Claudius's and Laertes's earlier readings of Ophelia, summed up in Laertes's comment that "Thought and affliction, passion, hell itself / She turns to favour and to prettiness" (4.5.185–86). In telling her "pretty" story of Ophelia's death, Gertrude is implicitly submitting it to patriarchal authority, representing Ophelia the way the men want to see her. This submission is further confirmed at Ophelia's burial, where Gertrude performs a female role that even Hamlet would regard as entirely appropriate. The threateningly eroticized mother-bride is replaced by a mother-lamenter who symbolically places herself outside the sexual arena: "I hop'd thou shouldst have been my Hamlet's wife: / I thought thy bride-bed to have deck'd, sweet maid, / And not have strew'd thy grave" (5.1.237–39). In such mourning, not only Ophelia's "noisy" singing, but also the "music" of Gertrude's own maternal voice are reabsorbed into the symbolic order of speech, even as they are recuperated by the social order.

This final image of Ophelia silenced brings me back to my opening remarks about the tendency to emblematize her, to turn her into a "speaking picture" which, being visual rather than aural, can more easily be read. My own reading views this picturing process as a response to Ophelia's singing, which is perceived by the other characters as dangerous, not only because of the uncontrollable meanings it may suggest to others, but also because of the unruly emotions it provokes in them. Their anxiety is aroused not only because Ophelia is mad, but also because she is a woman, who becomes even more "Woman" when she sings. To draw another analogy from feminist theory, the excess of Ophelia's music intensifies the already excessive femininity of her voice – makes it, in Irigaray's term, even more "fluid."[37] It is as if Ophelia's singing plunges her auditors into the flowing current of a river, and they are desperately afraid of drowning. All their interventions are attempts to "freeze" that flow by containing it within some stable relationship between signifier and signified. Yet it is only when Ophelia herself has drowned that they can at last climb out and dry themselves off, making speeches over her voiceless body.

My own response to Ophelia's songs is to insist that her singing matters, and attend to her music's materiality – the more so because the discourses of criticism have too often written it out of hearing. In those dismissals of singing as a conventional sign of madness I detect a response not unlike those of Claudius and Laertes – an uneasiness when confronted with an alien discursive medium, a resistance to that which is perceived as textual "overflow." Yet I believe it is possible to resist that tendency. We may not be able to avoid converting Ophelia's "noisy" singing into the "music" of our own speech or writing, but by making her singing our subject, we can at least acknowledge its significance. In doing so, we will move toward a critical language that can not only put singing back into the "picture" of Ophelia's madness, but also the voice back into the singing, and the body back into the voice.

---

[37] Luce Irigaray, "The 'Mechanics' of Fluids," in *This Sex Which Is Not One*, trans. Catherine Porter (Ithaca: Cornell University Press, 1985), pp. 106–118. For a fuller discussion of voice, fluidity, and madness, see Janet Beizer's essay in this volume.

4

Wordsworth and Romantic voice: the poet's song and the prostitute's cry

SARAH WEBSTER GOODWIN

The male Romantic poet's problem, crudely stated, is to bridge the gap between an inarticulate, pre-verbal nature and the linguistic utterances of the poem. Located squarely in language, the poem must nevertheless partake of and convey the visceral experience of the non-linguistic. This much has long been recognized as a distinguishing feature of Romanticism, whatever the vocabulary of subjectivity used to describe it. However, the problem has a gendered aspect that has been less commonly remarked. Because the non-linguistic and pre-verbal are associated in our culture with femininity, the challenge for the masculine poet, overt or tacit, is often to effect an appropriation of the feminine.[1]

Another major cultural locus of the non-linguistic is music, itself

Work on this essay was supported by a grant from the American Council of Learned Societies. An earlier version was read at the Lyrica Society Session at the 1990 Modern Language Association convention. Thanks also to Susannah Harris, Douglas Wilson, and Nancy Jones, who read and commented on the earlier version.

[1] Hélène Cixous and Catherine Clément in *La jeune née* (Paris: Union Générale d'Edition, 10/18, 1975), and Julia Kristeva in *La révolution du langage poétique* (Paris: Seuil, Collection "Tel Quel," 1974), among others, argue for femininity as a cultural construct aligned with the pre-verbal and with the body more generally. For the implications of that construct in Romantic literature, see Margaret Homans, *Bearing the Word* (University of Chicago Press, 1986).

A seminal text for my argument here is Nancy A. Jones's "The Rape of the Rural Muse: Wordsworth's 'The Solitary Reaper' as a Version of *Pastourelle*," in Lynn A. Higgins and Brenda R. Silver, eds., *Rape and Representation* (New York: Columbia University Press, 1991), a suggestive discussion of Wordsworth's "The Solitary Reaper" in the context of the medieval *pastourelle*: as she puts it, "To an earlier generation of scholars, equating masculinity with culture and femininity with nature, it seemed obvious that 'masculine Art-Poetry' gradually emerged from 'feminine Folk-Song' during the Middle Ages. This view is itself part of a deep-seated tendency to subsume a female voice of the folk, the earth, or nature into a masculine voice of artfully shaped, controlling song" (p. 263).

often associated with femininity.[2] That association rests primarily upon the emergence of the voice from the body: the pre-articulate voice seems infantile, animal-like, un-self-conscious, and primitive. Song, combining words and music in a controlled way, returns the voice to its pre-verbal origins. Lawrence Kramer presents this view of song suggestively: he argues that "song is a partial dissociation of speech: a loosening of phonetic and syntactic articulation and a dissolving of language into its physical origin, vocalization. If speech is taken as a norm, song is a regressive form of utterance, and its linguistic regressiveness seems to have a psychosexual dimension."[3] Speech would thus evolve from music – would be indeed a more differentiated, sublimated form of music. Kramer goes on to quote the following cogent lines from Wordsworth's "Michael," without considering the gendered cultural constructs implicit in them:

> Never to living ear came sweeter sounds
> Than when I heard thee at our fire-side
> First uttering, without words, a natural tune;
> While thou, a feeding babe, didst in thy joy
> Sing at thy Mother's breast.[4]

The "natural tune" emerges here in direct response to the "Mother's breast," within the benign domestic space of the hearth, in an image of infantile bonding with the feminine body. There is an implicit hierarchy here, from the pure body of the mother's breast to the babe's primitive utterance in song to, finally, the articulated poem. Thus the power of such song is the power the poet seeks literally to incorporate into his poem, rendering its pre-Oedipal body verbal.

It is no accident that Kramer's example comes from Wordsworth. The juncture of music and the feminine is common in cultural representations during the Romantic period, and especially so in Wordsworth's poetry. In such texts, the poet responds to music by modeling his poetic utterance on the physicality of song, and aligning song with the woman. He thus encounters and subsumes the feminine voice. Repeatedly, for the male Romantic writer, to appropriate femininity is also to appropriate the woman's embodied voice, itself often represented as more

---

[2] Kristeva articulates this association, which she does not invent but discovers – for example in citing Mallarmé, she writes, "Nous pourrions citer à l'appui tout le texte du 'Mystère dans les lettres.' Evoquons seulement, en ce lieu, les passages qui apparentent le fonctionnement de cet 'air ou chant sous le texte' à la femme . . ." *La révolution*, p. 29. ("As evidence, we could cite 'The Mystery in Literature' in its entirety. For now, however, we shall quote only those passages that ally the functioning of that 'air or song beneath the text' with woman . . ." [trans. Toril Moi, *The Kristeva Reader*, New York: Columbia University Press, p. 97]). Kristeva's notion of the *chora* emerges from that association.

[3] See Lawrence Kramer, *Music and Poetry: The Nineteenth Century and After* (Berkeley: University of California Press, 1984), p. 130.

[4] Lines 345–49, cited in Kramer, *Music and Poetry*, p. 130.

physical than verbal, as ecstatic, dangerous, seductive, and mysterious – and in need of a mastering vehicle.

There seem to have been two major ways to effect this appropriation. One was to celebrate "feminine" utterance and its links with music, and to represent the ways the masculine poet first encounters, then internalizes it. The celebration of femininity is one of the major impulses in Romantic literature, and it has been traced and analyzed.[5] Less attention has been paid to the association between femininity and the folk song out of which the lyrical ballad emerges, and from which it seeks to distinguish itself. As Nancy Jones has pointed out, this is an essential theme of Wordsworth's poem "The Solitary Reaper," which exemplifies the ways the male poet appropriates feminine song. The reaper speaks in a language the speaker does not understand, and he becomes her translator, occupying the place of her song but also giving it comprehensible language.[6]

The reaper is just one of countless singing women in Romantic literature, including such notable figures as the Abyssinian maid in Coleridge's "Kubla Khan," who plays her dulcimer and sings of Mount Abora; Keats's "Belle Dame sans Merci," who sings a faery song; and Goethe's Gretchen, whose song at the spinning wheel became one of the most memorable moments from *Faust*. (The gallery expands rapidly if we consider the feminine attributes of Romantic songbirds.)[7] In each case, the woman's song is implicitly eroticized by its connection with the sensual female body. The woman singing invokes, simply by her bodily presence, an illicit and seductive sexuality. An embodied feminine voice in song has a particular kind of power: that of nature, the material world – and more, that of the mother, whose body and voice assimilate to the undisclosed meanings of the pre-symbolic. Encountering that power, the poet makes it his own, giving it in return a disembodied and transcribed voice, symbolic functions, contingent status.

[5] See, for example: Michael Cooke, *Acts of Inclusion* (New Haven: Yale University Press, 1979); Sarah Webster Goodwin, "Romanticism and the Ghost of Prostitution: Freud, Maria and 'Alice Fell,'" in Sarah Webster Goodwin and Elizabeth Bronfen, eds., *Death and Representation* (Baltimore: Johns Hopkins University Press, 1993); Karen Swann, "Harassing the Muse," in Anne K. Mellor, ed., *Romanticism and Feminism* (Bloomington: Indiana University Press, 1988), pp. 81–92; Alan Richardson, "Romanticism and the Colonization of the Feminine," in Mellor, *Romanticism*, pp. 13–25.

[6] Kramer, *Music and Poetry*, p. 140, describes this process in his interpretation of the poem: "As he [the poet/speaker] listens, he improvises a poetic text to replace that of the reaper's song." For Kramer, the poem's act of "replacement" does no violence to the feminine, "indecipherable music," because it celebrates that music's power. Jones, in "The Rape of the Rural Muse," argues for just such a violence.

[7] Kramer, *Music and Poetry*, p. 140, is surely not alone in seeing a direct echo of "The Solitary Reaper" in the voice of Keats's nightingale, who sings with "full-throated ease" – an adjective that could hardly foreground the voice's body more evocatively.

A second possibility for the male poet, however, is to relocate the woman's song, displace it and occupy its position, on the sly as it were. This is a rather less overt and more complex move, and the primary figure for effecting it, I will argue here, is the prostitute, a figure culturally only two steps removed from the woman singing. Singers, like other female performers, have historically been associated with courtesans; and the women represented as singing in Romantic poetry generally are sexually accessible by virtue not only of gender but also of lower social class and/or foreignness.[8] Not all women who sing in early nineteenth-century literature are sexually suspect, of course; there is a tradition of social song in the drawing room. But even someone as proper as Jane Austen's Elizabeth Bennett knows that when she sings she is participating in one aspect of the courtship ritual, presenting herself to a masculine audience for assessment as attractively as possible. Her performance at the keyboard has a direct corollary in the posturing promenade around the room, in which the woman presents her body's attractions. Elizabeth Bennett ultimately refuses both forms of self-marketing, and in Austen's text more power accrues to her because of her refusal.

The woman who sings displays herself, in an art-form that – discreetly or indiscreetly – calls attention to the body. Reviews of women singers during the Romantic period often allude both to the performance's physicality and to its effects on the listener. In a monthly profile of women performers and writers in the *Ladies' Monthly Museum*, for example, the magazine's writers strain to strike a balance between propriety and enthusiasm: of one singer it is written, in 1817,

Miss Lydia Ellen Merry . . . was received with rapturous and enthusiastic applause by a crowded audience: her diffidence and native modesty was with difficulty so far surmounted as to enable her to display the sweetness and extent of her voice, but applause revived her confidence, and when restored to sufficient self-possession, she warbled her songs in the most enchanting-style [*sic*]; and while the amateur was captivated with her science and voice, others were enraptured with her voice, manner, and a pleasure inexpressible.[9]

Rapture, enchantment, sweetness and inexpressible pleasure are terms here of aesthetic experience borrowed from Eros. Small wonder that the profile's first paragraph opens by stressing Miss Merry's "private worth," "modest demeanour" (metonymy of the former), "innate virtue," and command of respect. All of these are qualities that seemingly threaten to evaporate the moment they are put on display. "Private worth" cannot comfortably be warbled on a public stage.

---

[8] Here again, Jones's reading of "The Solitary Reaper" pertains, and that poem seems exemplary. She notes, in "The Rape of the Rural Muse," p. 273, that such poems tend to underscore the various kinds of power in the poets' positions, including socioeconomic power.

[9] "Miss Lydia Ellen Merry," *The Ladies' Monthly Museum*, vol. 6 (August 1817), pp. 61–62.

As a result of that overt element of display, professional women singers of the period occupy the margins of courtship, marriage and controlled exchange as practiced by the middle class. Their body has inserted itself too prominently into the relation with the male audience, such that they become figurative cultural courtesans even if they are not actual ones. As another profile in the *Ladies' Monthly Museum* notes, women who perform on stage are, "from the profession they have . . . made choice of, more than ordinarily exposed to the shafts of slander."[10] The consequences are clear. In the case in question, the actress's female relations have also been in the theater, but they have been the exceptions that prove the rule: "they have ever sustained a most unblemished reputation; and some of them in consequence formed alliances with gentlemen of the first rank and of the highest respectability in society." It is not surprising that the middle-class ladies' magazine, with its need to obey the strictures of propriety, stresses a fantasy respectability over the social marginalization of women performers. Here, the direct consequence of propriety is marriage into the social and economic hierarchy. It is clear what the consequence of a "blemished" reputation would be: banishment from middle-class marriage, in which rank and property are acquired and exchanged.[11]

In contrast to such performers, the prostitute represents the other possibility latent in the woman as a singer: she is the woman whose very sexuality, her link to nature, becomes the means by which she inserts herself into an "unnatural" economy of abstract exchange. Observing her with horror, the poet distances himself from her position. Far from trying to internalize her song, as he does that of the reaper or the Abyssinian maid, he transforms her utterances into something denaturalized and abhorrent, and becomes in the process himself the natural singer from whom she is alienated. As I have argued elsewhere, Romantic texts are haunted by the ghost of prostitution; the figure of the prostitute hovers about a number of key texts, signifying the poets' fear of the market economy and its seductions, pressures, and compromises.[12] I will propose here that this ghostly prostitute is an inarticulate one, whose voice is heard not in song but in cries, curses, moans, and coughs – if it is heard at all.[13] Like song, these utterances are aspects of

10 "Miss Eliza Brunton," *The Ladies' Monthly Museum*, vol. 6 (August 1817), p. 242.
11 For a much more detailed treatment of the woman performer's social identity in nineteenth-century Britain, see Tracy C. Davis, *Actresses as Working Women: Their Social Identity in Victorian Culture* (London: Routledge, 1991). Davis is concerned with Victorian culture, but some of her sources are earlier, and much of her study corroborates the evidence I have noted here.
12 See Goodwin, "Romanticism and the Ghost of Prostitution," *passim.*
13 Perhaps the most famous of all Romantic prostitutes is the young girl Ann in De Quincey's *Confessions of an English Opium Eater*; her deathly cough echoes menacingly in his book. Theirs is a relationship whose complexity requires lengthier treatment than space here allows.

the embodied voice that foreground materiality in all its undisclosed meanings. However, in another sense, the curses and moans are the exact inverse of song, lacking all pretense of or aspiration to beauty or discipline, and signifying instead disease, hatred or suffering. The poet's culture aligns all that the prostitute represents in a figured other, a woman whose seductiveness vanishes when her diseased face emerges from the mask.

And yet the poet is haunted by an uncanny sense of identity, of sharing her position. Poetry is, after all, a discourse of seduction, at this historical moment more than ever before functioning in a marketplace of commodities.[14] The language of poetry is an embodied language, one that uses its music to seduce the reader, to be "felt in the blood, and felt along the heart," in Wordsworth's phrase, and thus to touch the reader viscerally. One way for the poet to draw an emphatic line of distinction between himself and the prostitute is to silence her, or to stress all the ways her vocality is fragmentary and inadequate. In such representations, she retains, like the songstress, the power of the body. But by contrasting with her different vocality the poet augments his power of articulation.

The prostitute as a Romantic figure seems somewhat shadowy. There are prostitutes all over Victorian literature; the whore, the courtesan, and the fallen woman of the streets are among the pervasive stock figures of the realist novel, not just in Britain but on the Continent as well. However, those figures of realist narrative emerge most clearly after the urban governments had established the surveillance and regulation of prostitute culture, so that such women had been entered into an official and public discourse. In the earlier part of the century (and the late eighteenth century), the prostitute is a more marginal and ill-defined figure, in both public discourse and literature.[15] Her very indistinctness allows her to represent that much more potently the frightening effects of a market economy on human relations and on the practice of literature.

Thus the Romantic prostitute, in her rare appearances, seems half-submerged in the text, as if her full significance had not yet revealed itself. The striking exception is the powerfully-present harlot in Blake's "London," whose voice concludes the poem:

[14] There is a growing literature on this subject. See, for example, Sonia Hofkosh, "The Writer's Ravishment: Women and the Romantic Author – The Example of Byron," in Mellor, *Romanticism*, pp. 93–114, and Julie Ellison, "Rousseau in the Text of Coleridge: The Ghost-Dance of History," *Studies in Romanticism* 28 (1989), 417–37.

[15] On the history of prostitution in Western culture, and the discourses surrounding it, see Charles Bernheimer, *Figures of Ill Repute: Representing Prostitution in Nineteenth-Century France* (Cambridge, MA: Harvard University Press, 1989); Judith R. Walkowitz, *Prostitution and Victorian Society: Women, Class, and the State* (Cambridge University Press, 1980); Alain Corbin, *Les filles de noce: misère sexuelle et prostitution: (19e siècle)* (Paris: Flammarion, 1982).

> But most thro' midnight streets I hear
> How the youthful Harlots curse
> Blasts the new-born Infants tear
> And blights with plagues the Marriage hearse[16]

Her curse not only provides closure but in some sense is the very type of verbal expression in the city Blake wants to represent: London *is* the whore of Babylon, and the poem presents a demonic revelation. This prostitute may be clearly drawn, but she is also dream-like in the dark nightmare world of the poem. Her voice is powerful, but her curse brings disease, not cure. More than any other aspect of Blake's London, the city of the damned, her voice haunts the poem, with a power to "blast" and to "blight," but not to envision and articulate another possible world. Hearing her and inscribing her, the poet establishes an authority for himself outside of her world, marked by but distinct from it.

A much more elliptically rendered Romantic prostitute-figure is Wordsworth's Alice Fell, the little orphan girl who, in the poem of the same name, weeps over her torn cloak, and accepts the offer of a new one from a stranger. Written in the voice of the stranger, the poem recounts how, riding in a coach, he first hears her passionate cry, then finally finds her weeping over her cloak, which is caught in a wheel and torn to shreds. She tells him she is an orphan, and he impulsively arranges for a new cloak to be bought for her, then applauds his own charity: "Proud creature was she the next day / The little orphan, Alice Fell!"[17]

Alice Fell is just a child, too young to be a prostitute, and yet everywhere in the poem there lurks the potentiality of prostitution, from the pun in her name (not, to my knowledge, ever remarked, so clearly innocent does she seem) to the transaction that placates her and concludes the poem. Alice Fell is just a few years away from the age at which an orphan might have to fend for herself as best she could, rather than rely on public charity for bread. Blake's harlot's curse echoes in midnight streets, joining other cries of fear and suffering; Alice Fell's voice, too, echoes through the night, a mysterious moan that frightens and puzzles the speaker at first, then occasions his response. In their exchange, fully recounted in the poem, her body all but subsumes her voice. The poet establishes his voice as its translator, in a gesture that conveys but also controls the various kinds of power for which she is a vehicle.

---

16 William Blake, *The Poetry and Prose of William Blake*, ed. David Erdman (Garden City, NY: Doubleday, 1970), p. 26.

17 William Wordsworth, *Poetical Works*, eds. Thomas Hutchinson and Ernest de Selincourt (Oxford University Press, 1981), p. 65. All further quotations in the text from Wordsworth's poems are taken from this edition. I have developed this interpretation more completely in my essay [Goodwin], "Romanticism and the Ghost of Prostitution." Much of what I say here about "Alice Fell" is also taken up there, though in a markedly different context. In that essay I also work out some biographical parallels between the poet and Alice Fell.

Fully a third of Wordsworth's fifteen-stanza poem is given over to describing the girl's cry. In fact, her voice is arguably the primary subject of the poem, which opens with four stanzas describing the mystery of her voice when the speaker first hears it:

> The post-boy drove with fierce career,
> For threatening clouds the moon had drowned;
> When as we hurried on, my ear
> Was smitten with a startling sound
>
> As if the wind blew many ways,
> I heard the sound, – and more and more;
> It seemed to follow with the chaise,
> And still I heard it as before.
>
> At length I to the boy called out;
> He stopped his horses at the word,
> But neither cry, nor voice, nor shout,
> Nor aught else like it, could be heard.
>
> The boy then smacked his whip, and fast
> The horses scampered through the rain;
> But, hearing soon upon the blast
> The cry, I bade him halt again.

Her cry is a lament that not only is not verbal, but also, we learn, threatens repeatedly to slip off into silence. The cry occasions the poem, but remains inarticulate. Still, even translated by a suspect speaker, it retains its power to convey suffering. It represents both what the poet's voice aspires to – the power to stop the reader dead in her tracks – and what it fears. The power of affect here, of suffering, comes close to psychosis.

Alice Fell suffers, we understand, because her body is exposed. Not in any crude sense because she is cold or wants protection from the rain, but because the shredded cloak has become a metonymy of her (and our) physical vulnerability. Each time the carriage rolls, the speaker hears her mysterious cry; it is as though the violence done to the cloak were done to her own body:

> "What ails you, child?" – she sobbed, "Look here!"
> I saw it in the wheel entangled,
> A weather-beaten rag as e'er
> From any garden scare-crow dangled.
>
> There, twisted between nave and spoke,
> It hung, nor could at once be freed;
> But our joint pains unloosed the cloak,
> A miserable rag indeed!

Nowhere is there direct mention here of her body, and yet the threat to it pervades these lines. The dangling, the twisting, the pains, all seem mobile references alluding in context to one thing but threatening (like the "threatening clouds" that have "drowned" the moon in the poem's first stanza) to shift referents and inflict physical suffering on her. The coach in which they are riding, the stormy night they are riding through, pose dangers that are real – in the sense that the body is real – and that Alice Fell gives voice to. The poem, then, represents her knowledge in her terms, and we are challenged to understand it more fully than the speaker, who registers its effects without becoming fully conscious of its significance. He simply thinks she is hysterical.

> Again, as if the thought would choke
> Her very heart, her grief grew strong;
> And all was for her tattered cloak!

Here, he recognizes her pain, but refuses to hear her right: clearly, he implies, she is unreasonable, pathetic, excessive. If we have not been suspicious before, these lines should make us pause. He mistakes the cloak for the referent, when it is instead the signifier.

For the speaker, it should be clear by now, is not fully reliable, despite the tendency of most readers to assume he is. "Alice Fell" has posed an interpretive conundrum. It is one familiar from others of Wordsworth's narrative poems, and it has to do with the relation between the speaker and the poet. The speaker congratulates himself for having solved the orphan's problem by buying her a cloak, and most of the handful of commentaries on the poem assume that the poet sympathizes with the speaker. At its most astute, this interpretation sees the poem as a political argument in favor of an immediate and material response to poverty.[18] And yet there is much that such a reading fails to consider, including Wordsworth's generally ironic distance from his narrators, who so often fail to see the import of their story. Their voice is rarely his.

More subtle, and more telling, is the complex relation the poet wants to establish between his own voice and the orphan's. It is clear from the five opening stanzas that her voice has the power to arrest the listener, to grip him irresistibly. When we are first told about it, the speaker says, "as we hurried on, my ear / Was smitten with a startling sound": here, her voice quite literally has a physical power to strike the listener. The poem seeks to replicate, indeed to appropriate that power, to make it its own by arresting our attention with it; we are driven into the poem by its mystery in those opening stanzas. It is a power in distinct contrast to that of the speaker, whose ways are more mundane. His power

---

[18]   David Simpson, *Wordsworth's Historical Imagination: The Poetry of Displacement* (New York: Methuen, 1987), develops this reading most consistently.

is defined by his gender – and by the possession of money, which she of course lacks. The poet thus seeks access to both positions, that of the inarticulate, primitive but mysteriously potent child and that of the narrator, possessed of money, position, and moral. And, we may as well say, of phallic power. The poem allows him to have it both ways.

One aspect of Alice Fell's position that seems peculiarly treacherous in its appeal is the threat of prostitution that lurks in it. When we view the poet metaphorically in the orphan's place, we see him as an innocent youth who is about to be corrupted by a cultural system of exchange that he hesitates to enter. Alice Fell's inarticulate horror over the loss of her cloak may be read as signifying a semi-conscious awareness of her vulnerability in that system, just as we may interpret the poet's veiled identification with her voice as a way of representing thoughts about himself that cannot be expressed, indeed that threaten verbal expression. Wordsworth makes it amply clear in his *oeuvre* that for him poetry is a vocation, quasi-religious in its intensity and its mission. If writing poetry is not always glorious, it is in the service of glory. The identification with Alice Fell's powerful but incoherent voice must be muted, just as her position on the brink of falling – socially, sexually and morally – must be intimated and at the same time erased.

It is Wordsworth who has most effectively defined the difficult ambiguities of a Romantic masculine voice that speaks for the marginalized female, and translates her utterance. "Alice Fell" is not an isolated example, of course; the vulnerable female is one of his major subjects. Wordsworth's poem "The Reverie of Poor Susan" returns us to the relation between silenced prostitute and powerful poet-singer. Like Alice Fell, Susan is a figure of potent imagination. Where the first poem arises from a ghostly cry, this one is located within a silent "reverie," a dream-state akin to the poetic imagination in its power to bring a virtual or remembered world into being. Like the "little orphan, Alice Fell," poor Susan represents a mental life that is intense and meaningful, but also threatening in its primitive, raw affect. The cry and the reverie are both *chora*-like, agents of dissolution, and the poem's anapestic music is an ordering answer to their agency.

"Poor Susan" recounts a moment in the life of a woman who lives in London and dreams of the countryside. It is a familiar Wordsworthian moment: the city is inadequate to all that is noble and lovely, and the city-dweller must have recourse to memories of other places, where there is a more unmediated relation to nature. Here the city-dweller is not the poet himself, however, but a woman who regularly walks the streets of Cheapside when daylight appears. I am not the first to notice how the poem implicitly defines her.[19] The innocence she has lost is not

---

[19] In "Placing Poor Susan: Wordsworth and the New Historicism," *Studies in Romanticism* 25 (1986), 351–69, Peter J. Manning builds a careful case, and sees Susan's ambiguity

only that of the green pastures and small cottage she remembers, but also, we infer, her own sexual innocence. Indeed, the two cannot be distinguished, as the sexual fall is metonymically connected to her social fall, and both are signified by the move from country to city.

What prompts Susan's reverie of lost pastoral innocence is a thrush's song:

> At the corner of Wood Street, when daylight appears,
> Hangs a Thrush that sings loud, it has sung for three years:
> Poor Susan has passed by the spot, and has heard
> In the silence of morning the song of the Bird.
>
> 'Tis a note of enchantment; what ails her? She sees
> A mountain ascending, a vision of trees;
> Bright volumes of vapour through Lothbury glide,
> And a river flows on through the vale of Cheapside.
>
> (*Works*, p. 149)

The thrush's song is a "note of enchantment" that not only inspires Susan's reverie but also occasions the poem, much as Alice Fell's mysterious cry occasions that poem. The difference here is that the poem even more pointedly occupies the position of the thrush; Susan is struck dumb by his song – invoked three times in the first stanza – and by the vision it brings her. She is also something of a poet-figure in her visionary powers, and in her position as city-dweller who, like the poet in such poems as "Tintern Abbey," can recall and draw on the natural scenes he once frequented. To go one step further, the poet sympathizes with "poor" Susan both in her poverty and in her need to compromise herself and to sell her favors. But that sympathy stops short of identification, as the poem adopts the power of the bird to sing and to transfigure: "And a river flows on through the vale of Cheapside." Seemingly concerned with her memory, in fact this line bespeaks the power of the bird's song to redeem the fallen consciousness by generating a visionary, even baptismal recollection. There is nevertheless an undecidable question here: we cannot say that the bird "creates" this vision any more than that Susan does. She is the visionary – but his is the voice.

In the edition of his poems published in 1849/50, Wordsworth chose a significant placement for "The Reverie of Poor Susan." The poem

as the poem's central, though repressed, concern: "A reader would not be wholly unjustified who saw in Susan the country girl gone wrong, perhaps even become one of the many prostitutes to be found in the windings and alleys of the City" (362); and again, "The speaker's meeting with Susan occurs within that structure of social power in eighteenth-century London which makes girls in the streets in the early morning a subject for male explanation" (367). Manning goes on to compare Susan to the woman in "The Solitary Reaper": "Both poems present a male speaker, arrested for a moment of erotically charged contemplation by the sight of a woman of a lower class" (369).

immediately preceding it is "I wandered lonely as a cloud," which describes an enchanted moment of his own, but without the intrusion of the world of Cheapside. The points of similarity between the two poems are as clear as their differences: Wordsworth as first-person speaker comes up smelling like a rose, because he is better able to bridge the gap between city and country, corruption and experience. "I wandered lonely as a cloud" has a light-hearted ending, in which the poet's "heart with pleasure fills / And dances with the daffodils"; it is a celebratory poem, a success story. Thus the poem adjacent to "Poor Susan," featuring the masculine voice directly, effects a multi-media performance, in which hearts and daffodils alike take to an immense, seemingly orchestrated but also spontaneous and natural dance. It is a perfect metaphor for the harmony between body and mind, voice and poem.[20]

The contrast with poor Susan is striking. Her reverie ends with failure: "And the colours have all passed away from her eyes!"[21] Not only does the bird stop singing, the voice cease, but also the vision goes dark. Her place is not the poet's place, whatever his sympathy; on the contrary, her place defines his by its very difference. Streetwalker, denatured, bereft, mute, she represents a displacement of his own poetic voice. Even in the city and enmeshed in its transactions, he is not of it any more than the thrush could be said to be.

The poem does not, however, present a simple dichotomy between urban, corrupt Susan and rural, righteous poet. The crux that undoes the dichotomy is her vision, whose reality the poem's syntax stubbornly leaves in doubt, as Manning has persuasively argued. Susan's vision, like Alice Fell's cry, represents a power akin to that of poetry (and, on several levels, to that of the thrush). It is a transformative power, and for Wordsworth probably, too, a redemptive one. It seems also, finally, to be a feminine one, where the reverie and the river add their "Bright volumes of vapour" and their "flow," potent forces of fluidity and dispersion, subsuming the streets' grid and their marketplace in an image that recalls the rivers in the *Prelude*, Book I, and the opening stanza of "Tintern Abbey." Susan and the thrush return us, in other words, not just to a rural place but to a more primitive mental one, not unlike the place of music described at the outset of this essay.

---

[20] The poem after "Poor Susan" is equally significant in its contrasts. Entitled, "The Power of Music," it is a little-known sentimental ballad describing a (male) street-singer in London on Oxford Street – the same street haunted by De Quincey's prostitute. This poem celebrates the singer's extraordinary power to arrest and hold his audience, and it, too, contrasts starkly with the impotence represented in "Poor Susan."

[21] The first published version of the poem has one more stanza (see below), but Wordsworth omitted it from all subsequent publications (Manning, "Placing Poor Susan," 361; Manning shows, however, that much of the best critical commentary on the poem has addressed the five-stanza 1800 version).

The poem's fifth stanza, generally omitted by Wordsworth, makes a rhetorical turn as if to contain precisely that kind of power:

> Poor Outcast! return – to receive thee once more
> The house of thy Father will open its door,
> And thou once again, in thy plain russet gown,
> May'st hear the thrush sing from a tree of its own.[22]

Here "the house of [her] Father" is being offered as an alternative to this kind of suffering – but not very convincingly. That is, the Father's forgiveness may suffice to bring Susan back from the city, but it cannot restore to her the unmediated pleasure in the rural landscape that we sense is definitively lost for her. Instead, it frames her experience with an allusion to her Father, the person whose authority she has violated, in a way that cannot be reversed. (And it *is* just an allusion: the Father doesn't open the door, the house does.) That curious final line represents her difficulty: what would it mean for a thrush to "sing from a tree of its own"? In what sense would the rural tree be that bird's own any more than an urban one? To speak in these terms is already to speak with a vocabulary of property (and loss) that opposes both the mentality of reverie and the "nature" represented by the bird. Alone the reverie/river offers a cognitive alternative to that mercenary vocabulary, however temporary, and the mute vision is hers. The poem takes the reverie as its subject, translating its power in a gesture that at once conveys and contains it. As a visionary, however, Susan remains mute, no prophet. She sees, and hears, but does not speak.

Curse, cry, silence: all are forms of expression that signify through indirection, and that, like song, inhabit the body without fully leaving it, in contrast to the "voice" of the written word. What we see here then is a pattern: male poet/female prostitute, with the prostitute's cry of pain, or her silence, occasioning the poet's voice. The poems leave all sorts of indications that the poet identifies with the prostitute, not the least of them being the ways her identity is left in shadowy outline, suggested but not pressed forward. Still, it is also clear that he fears her vocality and wishes to displace her, to locate her elsewhere. Whatever sympathy he feels blends with a need to draw distinctions.

In "The Reverie of Poor Susan," the thrush's song is a "note of enchantment." Wordsworth has chosen the word closest at hand to describe the song: it is a veritable cliché in the contemporary reviews of female singers. I noted above that a reviewer in 1817 wrote of the singer, Miss Lydia Ellen Merry, "she warbled her songs in the most enchanting-style," so that the audience was "captivated" and "enraptured." The bird accomplishes, then, precisely what the performing

---

[22] Quoted in Manning, "Placing Poor Susan," 356.

artist – and the poet – sets out to do: to enchant, captivate, enrapture. "Enchant" refers directly to the power of song, of chant or incantation, to overcome the listener and submerge the critical intellect in a power that is clearly erotic – ravishing, enrapturing – and, on some level, threatening. The ability to respond in one's own voice enables one to counter the *chora*-like power of song's enchantment.

I opened this essay with a claim about Romanticism as a whole. It is of course risky to do that; even the carefully pruned masculine canon embraces significant variety. A more detailed treatment of my subject would explore the differences among them, and their significance. My point here, however, is that Wordsworth reflects the dominant culture of his time in the significance he assigns to masculine and feminine vocalities. A minor poem by Coleridge – "minor" in part because he tips his hand too far in his irritability – rehearses the scene in terms that are by now quite familiar. It is entitled "Lines Composed in a Concert-Room," and it opens with a comment on a female singer and her audience:

> Nor cold, nor stern, my soul! yet I detest
> These scented Rooms, where, to a gaudy throng,
> Heaves the proud Harlot her distended breast,
> In intricacies of laborious song.
>
> These feel not Music's genuine power, nor deign
> To melt at Nature's passion-warbled plaint;
> But when the long-breathed singer's uptrilled strain
> Bursts in a squall – they gape for wonderment.[23]

All the elements are there: the singer is a Harlot, largely by virtue of her public performance before a "gaudy throng"; the poet despises her hold on the crowd; and her song helps to define, by contrast, the "genuine power" that the poet seeks to make his own, the power of "Nature's passion-warbled plaint."[24]

---

[23] Samuel Taylor Coleridge, *The Portable Coleridge*, ed. A. Richards (New York: Viking Press, 1950), pp. 164–65.

[24] The Harlot is also described as proud, clearly part of her sinfulness. In this context, it bears mentioning that Alice Fell, too, is described as proud, though for entirely different reasons ("Proud creature was she the next day / The little orphan, Alice Fell"). Still, the reader knows what pride goeth before.

A note is in order on the word "harlot." By 1799, when Coleridge's poem was written, it had long been a synonym for prostitute, though it is certainly more pejorative. In its earliest usages – even as late as the seventeenth century – it referred not to a woman but to a man, a ruffian or a rogue. Milton, in a key passage in *Paradise Lost*, uses it in Coleridge's sense here. He is contrasting Adam and Eve's paradisal sexual pleasure, innocent in its bliss, with "the bought smile / Of Harlots, loveless, joyless, unindear'd . . . Or Serenate, which the starv'd Lover sings / To his proud fair, best quitted with disdain" (IV. 765–70).

The body of the poem presents three other musicians who differ from the Harlot in that their performances are private and spontaneous. The first two are men, but the final one is a woman, addressed intimately as Anne, and he praises her performance of a traditional ballad:

> Thee, gentle woman, for thy voice remeasures
> Whatever tones and melancholy pleasures
>   The things of Nature utter; birds or trees,
> Or moan of ocean-gale in weedy caves,
> Or where the stiff grass mid the heath-plant waves,
>   Murmur and music thin of sudden breeze.

This stanza returns us to the alternative model with which I opened this essay: here the poet admires a woman's song, aligns it with a non-verbal but signifying nature, and makes its voice his own. In a word, *he* remeasures *her* voice, into the measure of poetry. The "Harlot's" song evidently lacks "Music's genuine power" for three reasons: it is intricate artifice; it is laborious, revealing evidence of her work, her employment, and her marketplace; and it intrudes the female body into the performance: she "Heaves . . . her distended breast" as she sings. In fact, that bodily movement precedes her song in his perception of her.

The alternative Coleridge presents – an alternative that pervades the Romantic canon – is a song that is as disembodied and incoherent as a murmuring breeze. The breeze as song has distinct advantages for the poet. It is untainted by any economic transaction or public performance; more, it needs a translator, an articulate voice. The Harlot, in contrast, is too reminiscent of himself, body-bound, on the market, laboring, seeking an audience. Thus her wordlessness, her dangerous and illicit body – and his song.

PART II

Anxieties of audition

5

"No women are indeed": the boy actor as vocal seductress in late sixteenth- and early seventeenth-century English drama

LINDA PHYLLIS AUSTERN

A central aspect of the late Renaissance and early Baroque theater that has finally begun to attract scholarly attention is the fluidity with which many characters' gender was reconstructed, often against what modern viewers would consider inalterable physical evidence. The same conventions that permitted actors and actresses to belong convincingly to a variety of social classes, times, and places also permitted them to spend all or part of their time on stage as members of either sex. Nowhere is this self-consciously reflexive attitude toward gender more obvious than in the late sixteenth- and early seventeenth-century English theater. For this theatrical tradition employed no women to act its many roles, but instead relied entirely on men and boys. The resulting recognition of female characters completely by conduct and outward appearance, separated by established convention from physical reality, permitted a unique vision of women's behavior that could be shattered or re-created through a single word or gesture.

Since many sixteenth- and early seventeenth-century English actors were highly trained musicians, since many of the era's plays integrate music into their plots, and since music occupied a central place in the actual lives of men and women, it is not surprising to find musical characters of both sexes on the stage. However, as ethnomusicologist Ellen Koskoff points out, musical performance provides an excellent context for observing and understanding any society's gender structure because similar notions of power and control often lie at the heart of both gender and musical/social dynamics.[1] This is especially true of

A shorter version of this paper was read at the Durham Conference on Baroque Music, Durham, England, July 1992.

[1] Ellen Koskoff, ed., *Women and Music in Cross-Cultural Perspective* (Westport, CT: Greenwood Press, 1987), Introduction, p. 10.

late-Renaissance England, and makes staged representations of men and women all the more important because they represent fictive stereotypes and cultural ideals. It was a culture in which the cardinal virtue of public female silence was so firmly entrenched that the soprano and alto voices of the church choir belonged exclusively to males, lest the sound of Eve's descendants lure Adam's fallen sons from their devotion to God. Numerous conduct manuals and private diaries of the time go to great lengths to explain the differences between socially acceptable musical behavior for men and women in all contexts, and warn of the unnatural consequences of deviating from the established norms.[2] In most plays that feature singing women, playwrights either slyly emphasize the singer-actor's underlying maleness or carefully construct masculine frames around their songs; or they present women's musical utterances as part of a glimpse into the private world of feminine confidence and contemplation from which men were normally excluded. In this manner, actors' and characters' voices are used independently to reinforce the dominant social mores of musical performance.

Centuries of Western thought have made the body itself as much an intellectual as a physical construct, continually re-articulated and assembled to conform to subtly changing concepts of gender.[3] Ideas of maleness and femaleness, from the time of Aristotle onward, have been formed within intellectual and social hierarchies that necessarily yield a superior and inferior, positive and negative, and essential and complementary. The resultant duality has served as an expression of value as much as a descriptive principle.[4] As Denise Riley remarks in her landmark study of feminism and the category of women,

[2] See Linda Phyllis Austern, "'Alluring the Auditorie to Effeminacie': Music and the Idea of the Feminine in Early Modern England," *Music and Letters* 74.3 (1993), 349–51, and "'Sing Againe Syren': The Female Musician and Sexual Enchantment in Elizabethan Life and Literature," *Renaissance Quarterly* 42 (1989), 420–48.

[3] Denise Riley, *"Am I That Name?" Feminism and the Category of "Women" in History* (Minneapolis: University of Minnesota Press, 1988), pp. 96–114. See also Katherine Usher Henderson and Barbara F. McManus, eds., *Half Humankind: Contexts and Texts of the Controversy About Women in England, 1540–1640* (Urbana and Chicago: University of Illinois Press, 1985), pp. 11–19 and 99–130; Suzanne Hull, *Chaste, Silent, and Obedient: English Books for Women 1475–1640* (San Marino: The Huntington Library, 1982), pp. 117–19; Sherry B. Ortner and Harriet Whitehead, eds., *Sexual Meanings: The Cultural Construction of Gender and Sexuality* (Cambridge University Press, 1981), pp. 6–26; Francis Lee Utley, *The Crooked Rib: An Analytical Index to the Argument About Women in English and Scots Literature to the End of the Year 1568* (Columbus, OH: Ohio State University Press, 1944); and Linda Woodbridge, *Women and the Renaissance: Literature and the Nature of Womankind* (Urbana and Chicago: University of Illinois Press, 1984), pp. 13–17.

[4] Genevieve Lloyd, *The Man of Reason: "Male" and "Female" in Western Philosophy* (Minneapolis: University of Minnesota Press, 1984), pp. 103–104. See also, for example, Jean Bethke Elshtain, *Public Man, Private Woman: Women in Social and Political Thought* (Princeton University Press, 1981), pp. 15–16; Carol Gilligan, *In a Different Voice: Psychological Theory and Women's Development* (Cambridge, MA: Harvard University

anyone's body is – the classifications of anatomy apart – only periodically either lived in or treated as sexed, therefore the gendered division of human life into bodily life cannot be adequate or absolute. Only at times will the body impose itself or be arranged as that of a woman or a man.[5]

The acceptance of boys as imitation women on the Elizabethan and Jacobean stage was an extension of inherited attitudes toward gender, sexuality, and physiological development which held all norms to be both male and adult. Literary critics and social historians such as Natalie Zemon Davis, Stephen Greenblatt, Thomas Laqueur, and Stephen Orgel have pointed out that the sixteenth and early seventeenth centuries did not recognize the clear, enduring genetic distinctions between the sexes that inform our own attitudes.[6] Instead, based on longstanding ideas of developmental physiology, the female was considered an incomplete, imperfect male, lacking only the heat, from the moment of conception onward, that would transform her into the superior sex.[7] The actual physical metamorphosis from female to male had been documented by late-Renaissance physicians, which meant, as certain English Puritan divines warned, that the opposite, less natural transformation remained frighteningly possible throughout life if a man should behave in an inappropriately effeminate fashion.[8]

At the most basic levels of psychology and physiology, a large number of Renaissance thinkers noted specific similarities between boys' and women's underdeveloped masculinity, for the true distinction in

Press, 1982), pp. 1–6; Ortner and Whitehead, eds., *Sexual Meanings*, Introduction, pp. 6–26; and Joan W. Scott, "Gender: A Useful Category of Historical Analysis," *The American Historical Review* 91 (1986), 1054–66.

5 Riley, "*Am I That Name?*," p. 103.

6 See, for example, Natalie Zemon Davis, "Women on Top," in *Society and Culture in Early Modern France* (Stanford University Press, 1975), pp. 127–29; Stephen Greenblatt, "Fiction and Friction," in Thomas C. Heller, Morton Sosna, and David E. Wellbery, eds., *Reconstructing Individualism: Autonomy, Individuality, and the Self in Western Thought* (Stanford University Press, 1986), p. 35; Ann Rosalind Jones and Peter Stallybrass, "Fetishizing Gender: Constructing the Hermaphrodite in Renaissance Europe," in Julia Epstein and Kristina Straub, eds., *Body Guards: The Cultural Politics of Gender Ambiguity* (New York and London: Routledge, 1991), pp. 80–85; Thomas Laqueur, *Making Sex: Body and Gender from the Greeks to Freud* (Cambridge, MA: Harvard University Press, 1990), pp. 122–40; Laura Levine, "Men in Women's Clothing: Anti-Theatricality and Effeminization from 1579 to 1642," *Criticism* 28 (1986), 121–22 and 126–27; and Stephen Orgel, "Nobody's Perfect: or, Why Did the English Stage Take Boys for Women?," *The South Atlantic Quarterly* 88 (1989), 13.

7 See Stephen Greenblatt, "Fiction and Friction," pp. 38 and 40; Jones and Stallybrass, "Fetishizing Gender," pp. 81 and 84; Thomas Laqueur, "Orgasm, Generation, and the Politics of Reproductive Biology," *Representations* 4 (Spring 1986), 4–12; and Orgel, "Nobody's Perfect," 13.

8 See Davis, "Women on Top," pp. 127–29; Greenblatt, "Fiction and Friction," pp. 30–41; Laqueur, *Making Sex*, p. 123, and "Orgasm," 12–14; Levine, "Men in Women's Clothing," 121 and 131; and Orgel, "Nobody's Perfect," 13–15.

this patriarchal society was not between the sexes, but between fathers and children.[9] One Elizabethan collection of epigrams, for instance, likens woman to a weak, pliant vessel,[10] while another applies a similar metaphor to youth,[11] for both required adult male guidance in order to become proper, productive members of their culture. In addition, Jacobean anthologist Thomas Gainesford combines several contemporary commonplaces to define woman as

faire, and proude, and wanting wisdome: . . . a looking-glasse of vanitie, and a miror of inconstancy, idle fantastick, desirous of novelties, disdainfull, changeable, a daintie feeder, a gadder, a talker, and every way irregular.[12]

This description is remarkably similar to William Shakespeare's list of characteristics common to boys and women in *As You Like It*, one of the most famous dramatic works of the era, which explores the inconstant relationship between gender identity and biophysical reality:

Rosalind [as Ganimede] . . . I set him everie day to woe me At which time would I, being but a moonish youth, greeve, be effeminate, longing, and liking, proud, fantastical, apish, shallow, inconstant, ful of teares, full of smiles: for everie passion something, and for no passion truly any thing, as boyes and women are for the most part, cattle of this colour[.][13]

Since femininity was so easily reducible to a set of actions and responses, especially when set against a masculine norm, it was easily reproducible by an actor whose natural tendencies were believed to be effeminate and whose additional training specialized in close mimicry. In the Elizabethan and Jacobean theater, gender became a topsy-turvy game in which illusion and reality continually merged, only to be shattered into kaleidoscopic fragments by a single word or gesture.[14] It

---

[9] See Stephen Greenblatt, *Shakespearean Negotiations: The Circulation of Social Energy in Renaissance England* (Berkeley and Los Angeles: University of California Press, 1988), p. 78, and "Fiction and Friction," p. 35; Louis Adrian Montrose, "'Shaping Fantasies': Figurations of Gender and Power in Elizabethan Culture," *Representations* 1 (1983), 73; Stephen Orgel, "Nobody's Perfect," 10; Riley, "*Am I That Name?*," p. 24; and Lawrence Stone, *The Family, Sex and Marriage in England, 1500–1800* (New York: Harper and Row, 1977), p. 201.

[10] Thomas Gainesford, *The Rich Cabinet Furnished with Varietie of Excellent Discriptions, Exquisite Characters, Witty Discourses, and Delightful Histories, Devine and Morall* (London, 1615), fols. 163v–164.

[11] Francis Meres, *Palladis Tamia. Wits Treasury* (London, 1598), fol. 65.

[12] Gainesford, *The Rich Cabinet*, fol. 164.

[13] William Shakespeare, *As You Like It*, in Shakespeare, *Comedies, Histories & Tragedies* (London: Isaac Jaggard and Ed[ward] Blount, 1623), 3.2 (p. 197).

[14] For more information on the use of gender and its constructional ambiguities in the English Renaissance theater, see, for example, Juliet Dusinberre, *Shakespeare and the Nature of Women* (London: Macmillan, 1975), pp. 231–71; Robert Kimbrough, "Androgyny Seen Through Shakespeare's Disguise," *Shakespeare Quarterly* 33 (1982), 17–33; and Phyllis Rackin, "Androgyny, Mimesis, and the Marriage of the Boy Heroine on the English Renaissance Stage," *Proceedings of the Modern Language Association* 102 (1987), 29–41.

has, in fact, been suggested that the English Renaissance conception of Woman specifically transcended even this fluid biophysical reality to become a purely cultural and political construct, a text onto which men could project their own desires.[15] The Elizabethan or Jacobean actor, then, simply conveyed a male or female bodily image by literally giving life to the strongly dualistic ideas codified by gender theorists. He made good use of the costumes, properties, and gestures through which each gender was identified until the clothes almost literally made the man or woman. Thus Shakespeare's sham Ganymede, disguising the equally sham Rosalind, tells us in *As You Like It*,

I could finde in my heart to disgrace my mans apparell, and cry like a woman: but I must comfort the weaker vessell, as doublet and hose ought to show it selfe coragious to petty-coate.[16]

Through its clever reference to the actual hidden body, the same passage also reminds us how easily an actor could redirect audience attention to what lay just beneath the visible surface. Shakespeare's contemporary and fellow playwright George Chapman writes tongue-in-cheek about similar boy actresses as they enter the stage to sing in his comedy *The Gentleman Usher*:

> And women will ensue
> Which I must tell you true
> No women are indeed
> But pages made for need
> To fill up womens places
> By vertue of their faces
> And other hidden graces
> A hall, a hall; whist, still, be mum
> For now with silver song they come.[17]

Chapman's equal emphasis on the visual and auditory beauty of these sham women is neither coincidental nor unique. Many Renaissance writers praise the extraordinary versatility and mimetic ability of the professional player far beyond his ability to wear the garments of either gender with equal grace. Gainesford, for example, tells us that

Player hath many times, many excellent qualities: as dancing, activitie, musicke, song, elloqution, ability of body, memory, vigilancy, skill of weapon, pregnancy of wit, and such like: in all which hee resembleth an excellent spring of water, which growes the more sweeter, and the more plentiful by the often drawing out of it: so are all these the more perfect and plausible by the often practise.[18]

---

15 Virginia Mason Vaughan, "Daughters of the Game: *Troilus and Cressida* and the Sexual Discourse of Sixteenth–Century England," *Women's Studies International Forum* 13 (1990), 209–11.
16 William Shakespeare, *As You Like It*, 2.4 (p. 191),
17 George Chapman, *The Gentleman Usher*, 1.2.
18 Gainesford, *The Rich Cabinet*, fol. 118.

To the Renaissance actor belonged

the Arte of *Imitation and Demonstration*, expressinge the thinges conceaved in the minde . . . for it doth so aptly represent with pleasant gesture an olde man, a boye, a woman, a servaunt, a handmaide, a drunkarde, an angrie person, and the differences and passions of all persons, that also the beholder standing aloofe of, not hearinge the Enterlude maie perceave the argument thereof by the onely motions of the Plaier.[19]

Of the stage-player's many capabilities, the one most frequently discussed, especially by the most virulent detractors from the theater, was the uncanny realism with which the youngest "put on the attyre, the gesture, the passions of a woman."[20] As Stephen Gosson informs us with obvious fascination in his raving diatribe, *Playes Confuted in Five Actions*, "If it shoulde bee Plaied, one must learne to tripp it like a Lady in the finest fashion . . . that he may give life to the picture hee presenteth."[21] The same author further states that

Whatsoever he be that looketh narrowly into our Stage Playes, or considereth how, and which waye they are represented, shall finde more fithines in them, the[n] Players dreame off. The Law of God very straightly forbids men to put on wome[n]s garments . . .

All that do so are abhominations on the Lord, which way I beseech you shall they bee excused, that put on, not the apparell onely, but the gate, the gestures, the voyce, the passions of a woman?[22]

The strength of Gosson's language demonstrates the attractive qualities and utterly convincing mannerisms of these boy actresses, which clearly went far beyond costume and simple gesture to the most basic questions of gender and sexuality. Modern scholarship is only just beginning to rediscover that the late sixteenth- and seventeenth-century English theater was perceived by its detractors and more neutral observers alike to be a sexually charged arena in which prostitution and adulterous liaisons of all sorts flourished off stage as well as on, and in which the bodies of the actors fed the erotic imaginations of the spectators.[23] Most English Renaissance theatergoers could sustain a dual

[19] Henry Cornelius Agrippa von Nettesheim, *Of the Vanitie and Uncertaintie of Arts and Science*, trans. Ja[mes] Sa[nford] (London, 1575), fol. 32. See also Abraham Fraunce, *The Arcadian Rhetorick* (London, 1577), sig. 17v.

[20] Stephen Gosson, *Playes Confuted in Five Actions* (London, [1582]), sig. E5. See also Anthony Munday, *A Second and Third Blast of Retrait From Plaies and Theaters* (London, 1586), pp. 110–11; William Prynne, *Histrio-Mastix or the Players Scourge* (London, 1633), p. 420; and Phillip Stubbes, *The Anatomy of Abuses* (London, 1583), sig. D3.

[21] Gosson, *Playes Confuted*, sig. E6.

[22] Ibid., sig. E3v.

[23] See Alan Bray, *Homosexuality in Renaissance England* (London: Gay Men's Press, 1982; 2nd edn. Boston: Gay Men's Press, 1988), pp. 54–55; Gordon Lell, "'Ganymede' on the Elizabethan Stage: Homosexual Implications of the Use of Boy-Actors," *Aegis* 1 (1973), 7–11; and Orgel, "Nobody's Perfect," 15–17.

consciousness of actor and character that enabled them to be especially aware of the contrast between the boy player and his female role.[24] It seems apparent that the sumptuous display of female dress on young men's bodies was perceived to be a stimulus to the forbidden, but not uncommon, fruit of homosexuality.[25] Indeed, Marjorie Garber considers these convincingly cross-dressed actors, clearly homoerotically attractive to male spectators and capable of affecting a complete range of feminine passions, to constitute a complete "third sex."[26]

Given the emphasis on passion and sensual response in eyewitness accounts of the theater and its attractive female impersonators, it is hardly surprising that music, an indispensable component of Renaissance drama with its own recognizably sexual, effeminate, and repulsively attractive aspect, elicited similar comments from the same group of writers. The seventeenth-century Puritan divine, William Prynne, for instance, specifically considers what he labels "effeminate, delicate, lust-provoking music" to be among the principal "unlawfull Concomitants of Stage-playes."[27] A great admirer of boys' voices in a cappella sacred music, Prynne explains that it was the combination of boy actresses' erotic, costumed beauty with the seductive love-songs that their roles often required which made theatrical music so dangerous to the listener, their songs the deadly songs of Sirens.[28] Elsewhere, Prynne writes with disgusted fascination about these hybrid creatures:

From these songs of Harlots a very flame of lust doth presently set the Auditors on fire, and as if the sight and face of a woman were not sufficient to inflame the minde, they have found out the plague of the voyce too. But by the singing of our holy men, if any such disease doth vex the minde, it is presently extinguished. And not onely the voyce and face of a woman, but the apparell doth much more trouble the Spectators.[29]

Although the distinctive clarity and penetrating sweetness of a boy's voice is difficult to mistake for the richer complexity of most adult women's, Prynne makes it abundantly clear that text and costume serve to magnify and contextualize the power of sound itself, as if even the voice must be dressed for a given occasion. The difference between cassock and erotic female costume, godly and lust-provoking text, or holiness and profanity of occasion is for Prynne the ultimate way of distinguishing between positive and negative uses of the male voice.

24 Michael Shapiro, "Lady Mary Wroth Describes a 'Boy Actress,'" *Medieval and Renaissance Drama in England* 4 (1989), 189.
25 See Levine, "Men in Women's Clothing," 131; and Orgel, "Nobody's Perfect," 16.
26 Marjorie Garber, *Vested Interests: Cross-Dressing and Cultural Anxiety* (New York and London: Routledge, 1992), p. 10
27 Prynne, *Histrio-Mastix*, pp. 273–74
28 Ibid., p. 275.
29 Ibid., p. 420.

On stage or off, through the voice of an apparent man, woman, or artificial instrument, music was perceived to have the capacity to arouse the senses with a rhetoric far more powerful than speech alone, and in a more lingering manner than vision.[30] Fear of emasculation through uncontrolled musical ravishment clearly informed a number of sixteenth- and seventeenth-century English treatises on music and evidently influenced attitudes toward musical practice in life and on the stage.[31] The late sixteenth-century Puritan writer Phillip Stubbes, for example, not only speaks against the unmanly effect of listening too closely to secular music, but warns, as had many before him, that the intensive study of practical music would effectively transnature young men into women – which was, of course, the very illusion aimed for by the musical boy-actresses of his time.[32] William Prynne specifically attacks what he perceives as the emasculating qualities of the sort of love-music frequently presented in plays, in particular its use of chromaticism and vocal ornamentation, which he calls "whorish music crowned with flowers."[33] He labels such music deceptive, dishonest, sorcerous, and effeminate, and warns that it corrupts the masculine strength and cogitation of its listeners, leading to a "delicate and slothful kind of life" – the kind women were perceived to enjoy.[34] Prynne especially considers the use of a high vocal register will damage the masculinity of performer and auditor alike, although such is most natural for boys.[35]

Other writers commented that music's capacity for sexual arousal and weakening of masculine vigor made it even more unsuitable for *women's* performance, especially in front of a male audience.[36] One popular seventeenth-century aphorism, for instance, claims that "there could be smal agreement" between music and women's chastity.[37] Conduct manuals, sermons, and the diaries and private accounts of noble-women, from the time of Queen Elizabeth I to that of King Charles I, make it clear that the most respectable high-born ladies did indeed reserve their own musical performances for private moments, and that those who did not were morally suspect.[38]

[30] See Austern, "'Sing Againe Syren,'" 424–27.
[31] See Austern, "'Alluring the Auditorie to Effeminacie,'" 350–51, and "'Sing Againe Syren,'" 420–48.
[32] Stubbes, *The Anatomy of Abuses*, sigs. D5–D5v. See also Roger Ascham, *Toxophilus, The Schole, or Partitions of Shooting* (London, 1571), fol. 7v.
[33] Prynne, *Histrio-Mastix*, p. 275.
[34] Ibid., pp. 275 and 287.
[35] Ibid., p. 280.
[36] See Austern, "'Sing Againe Syren,'" 431–32.
[37] Robert Allott, *Wits Theater of the Little World* (London: J. R. for N. L., 1599), fol. 98. See also Austern, "'Sing Againe Syren,'" 431–32; and Koskoff, ed., *Women and Music*, Introduction, p. 3, where it is shown that many cultures associate women's music with licentious sexual behavior or real or implied prostitution.
[38] See Austern, "'Sing Againe Syren,'" 434–35.

Condemnations and limitations of music were far from universal, but late sixteenth- and early seventeenth-century English attitudes toward the art, especially in relation to gender and performance practice, were contextually determined to maintain appropriate "masculine" control over a potentially overpowering, sense-altering force. On stage it was especially important that musical performance be given an appropriate frame through which audience arousal and response could be manipulated, for the theater was already a world rife with ambiguity that could be directed, dispelled, or further emphasized through the words and actions of its performers.

.In keeping with strongly gendered attitudes toward music itself, and toward a drama that literally re-presents social and intellectual reality from a biologically male perspective, the musical women of the later English Renaissance stage are invariably presented in relation to masculine ideas and ideals of feminine musical performance. The same duality that influenced attitudes toward men's and women's music, which worried about loss of control and restricted professional performance, composition, and military music to men, while recommending private chamber performances to women, translated into the theater as a contrasting pair of conventional female musicians who represent absolute moral extremes, if only the most common dramatic stereotypes of musical women: those whose sexuality is heightened through music, and those whose sexuality is restricted through the same.[39] On the one hand, and by far the most prevalent, are the immoral stage sirens who use music as a means to pursue their own sexual pleasure, often to the utter destruction of any men who become caught in their webs of enchantment. On the other hand, are those women who use music as a private source of moral strength, most often at moments of emotional stress, generally in the intimate presence of trusted confidants, or spilling into the public domain as a clear indication of insanity. Verbal comments or the music itself often let us know that the former rely on effeminate artifice, the latter on simplicity and directness, to achieve their ends and move other characters and audience alike toward revulsion or genuine approbation.

The figure of the attractively amoral or absolutely deadly woman who is ruled by her insatiable sexual appetite and who attracts men through a glittering web of lies, deceit, and musical artifice is a stock archetype of English Renaissance fiction whose foremothers are the Sirens themselves.[40] Her presentation on stage ranges from the benign

---

[39] Ibid., 431–36. Ellen Koskoff also points out that this dual treatment of musical women is prevalent and widespread throughout human culture in general (*Women and Music*, Introduction, p. 6).

[40] See Austern, "'Sing Againe Syren,'" 441–48; Angela J. C. Ingram, *In the Posture of a Whore* (Salzburg: Institut für Anglistik und Amerikkanistik, Universität Salzburg, 1984),

"bawds" and servants of Elizabethan comedy to the fatally attractive courtesans of Jacobean and Caroline drama whose glances are poison and whose voices are death.[41] Of the "million of prostitute countenances and enticements"[42] she uses to trap men, the love-songs that she repeats with feigned sincerity to each new conquest are perhaps the most dangerous and certainly the most effective. As Prynne raves about such "ribaldrous, lascivious songs,"

such Songs, such Poems as these [are] abundantly condemned as *filthy, and unchristian defilements, which contaminate the soules, effeminate the mindes, deprave the manners, of those that heere or sing them, exciting, entising them to lust, to whoredome, adultery, prophanes, wantonnesse, scurility, luxury, drunkennesse, excesse: alienating their mindes from God, from grace and heavenly things: and Syren like, with their sweet enchantments entrap, ensnare, destroy mens soules, proving bitter portions to them at the last, though they seeme sweet and pleasant for the present.*[43]

Imperia, the Venetian courtesan and brothel-keeper of Thomas Dekker's *Blurt, Master-Constable* is quite typical of the lascivious musical women of English Renaissance drama. Everything about her is demonstrably fraudulent: her love, her promises, her goodness, the virginity that she sells repeatedly, and, as the audience must have been patently aware, even her womanly sexual appetite. In fact, by placing her in a masculine frame and emphasizing her complete falseness, the author further affirms the unnaturalness of the sexually aggressive woman. In this case, the character borrows the boy actor's prerogative and moves fluidly between the world of feminine sexuality and male homoeroticism as both kinds of male-oriented sexual attractiveness and power blend to create an impossible but irresistible conglomeration of erotic magnetism.[44]

To an English audience of Dekker's time, Imperia represented a specific kind of sexual exotic, the learned Venetian courtesan, famous throughout Europe for accomplishment in and out of the bedchamber. She was a particularly appropriate figure for a boy actress to imitate in a scene that calls attention to gender ambiguity and to the erotic tension between the concealed male body and the revealed female one, for Venetian courtesans often wore breeches beneath their skirts and

(40 contd.) especially pp. 1–60; Paul Vernon Kreider, *Elizabethan Comic Character Conventions* (Ann Arbor: University of Michigan Press, 1935), pp. 51–52; and Alexander Leggatt, *Citizen Comedy in the Age of Shakespeare* (University of Toronto Press, 1973), pp. 99–124.

41 For more information on the connection between such courtesan characters and practitioners of the occult sciences, see Linda Phyllis Austern, "'Art to Enchant': Musical Magic and its Practitioners in England Renaissance Drama," *Journal of the Royal Musical Association* 115 (1990), 199–206.

42 Thomas Overbury, *New and Choise Characters* (London, 1615), sig. E3.

43 Prynne, *Histrio-Mastix*, p. 267.

44 The boy actor was not infrequently used in such plays specifically for his homoerotic potential; see Lell, "'Ganymede' on the Elizabethan Stage," 5–15.

presented themselves as enticing hybrids of boy and woman.[45] As to another of her most renowned skills, the famous Jacobean traveller to Italy, Thomas Coryat, remarks that

shee will endeavour to enchant thee partly with her melodious notes that shee warbles out upon her lute, which shee fingers with as laudable a stroake as many men that are excellent professors in the noble science of Musicke: and partly with the heart-tempting harmony of her voice.[46]

By specifically comparing the Venetian courtesan to an unusually skill-ful male professional, Coryat connects her uncanny musical ability to the negation of natural femininity. He also thereby removes her from the passive world of women and places her into the masculine realm of power, perhaps as a way of absolving men of responsibility for their liaisons with her.

In Dekker's play, Imperia sings quite frequently, often as a metaphor for her lasciviousness or for the sexual consummation that a boy actor could not render graphically on stage. Act V, scene ii opens with her smooth seduction of the French prisoner Fontinell, during which she takes the stereotypically male role of sexual aggressor. During the process, she refers to his beardless, effeminate beauty, which, from an audience perspective, would have drawn attention to her similar youth-ful androgyny. She thus sets up a masculine standard of appearance against which she can be judged, and continues to behave in a manner that belies her feminine garments:

Imperia. Ah you little effeminate sweete *Cheveleere*, why dost thou not get a loose Periwig of haire on thy chinne, set thy French face off: by the panting pulse of *Venus*, thou art welcome a thou-sand degrees beyond the reach of Arithmeticke: Good, good, good, your lip is moiste and mooving; it hath the truest French close, even like *Mapew*; [she begins to sing] *la, la, la,* etc.

She continues to toy with him, swears by her virginity, and, after expressing her hope that he is not a Puritan, calls for music. Following a stage direction for music, she offers to entertain him with "a poore Italian Song" even as she apologizes for the equally poor voice that will strug-gle to keep up with the accompaniment that has already begun to play.

Her song, identified almost certainly as an extant composition by Edward Pearce,[47] renders her introductory remarks untrue. Far from

---

[45] See Garber, *Vested Interests*, pp. 86–87.

[46] [Thomas Coryat], *Coryats Crudities* (London, 1611), p. 267.

[47] The song, whose text appears in somewhat garbled form in the quarto publication of the play, *Blurt, Master-Constable, or, The Spaniards Night-Walke* (London, 1602), is pub-lished in Thomas Ravenscroft, *A Briefe Discourse of the True (but Neglected) Use of Charact'ring the Degrees* (London, 1614), sigs. E4v–f. For more information, see Linda

belonging to any of the Italian musical genres popular in Dekker's and Pearce's England, Imperia's song is an almost archetypal representative of the native English consort song. And far from having a poor voice that needed to "wrastle with this Musicke and catch a straine," as she puts it, the actor who played the original Imperia was a member of the Children of Paul's, famous throughout England for their excellent musical training, exquisite voices, and, in some cases, membership of the legendary choir of London's St. Paul's Cathedral.[48] The song's text, in a complete inversion of feminine modesty and the serenade tradition, expresses the sexual desire of male and female classical deities for such beautiful boys as the comely young Fontinell. By extension, the similar actor beneath Imperia's clothes becomes an identical object of this omnivorous desire, even as the text equates Ganymede with Adonis, and Jove with Venus. To further emphasize the attractiveness of Imperia's voice and her falsely modest lie about her musical ability, Fontinell praises her vocal beauty between stanzas, and begs her to sing again. Dialogue makes clear that it is specifically her music that enchants the young Frenchman, making him her Ganymede and her Adonis, clearly the inferior in their erotic encounter:[49]

[*Imperia.*]　　*Song.*
　　　　　　Love for such a cherrie lip,
　　　　　　Would be glad to pawne his arrows:
　　　　　　Venus heere to take a Sip,
　　　　　　Would sell her Doves and teeme of Sparrows.
　　　　　　But they shall not so,
　　　　　　Hey nony nony no:
　　　　　　None but I this lip must owe,
　　　　　　hey nony nony no.

(47 contd.) Phyllis Austern, "Thomas Ravenscroft: Musical Chronicler of an Elizabethan Theater Company," *Journal of the American Musicological Society* 38 (1985), 238–63; and Andrew J. Sabol, "Two Songs with Accompaniment for an Elizabethan Choirboy Play," *Studies in the Renaissance* 5 (1958), 149–54.

48 See Linda Phyllis Austern, *Music in English Children's Drama of the Later Renaissance* (New York and London: Gordon and Breach, 1993), pp. 4–7 and 19–21; Roma Ball, "The Choirboy Actors of St. Paul's Cathedral," *Emporia State Research Studies* 10 (June 1962), 5–16; Reavley Gair, *The Children of Paul's: The Story of a Theatre Company, 1553–1608* (Cambridge University Press, 1982), pp. 140–41 and 167–69, and "Second Paul's: Its Theatre and Personnel: Its Later Repertoire and Audience (1602–6)," *The Elizabethan Theatre* 7 (1977), 21–43; and Michael Shapiro, *Children of the Revels: The Boy Companies of Shakespeare's Time and their Plays* (New York: Columbia University Press, 1977), pp. 18–22.

49 Aside from the obvious mythological meaning of these names, the term "Ganymede" was English Renaissance slang for a male prostitute or servant kept for sexual purposes; see Bray, *Homosexuality in Renaissance England*, p. 65; and Garber, *Vested Interests*, p. 77. Furthermore, as Natalie Zemon Davis points out, female disguise drew on the contemporary belief that woman was the lustier sex, ("Women on Top," 138).

1. Love   for   such a
2. Did   love   see   this

cher - ry lip,   would be glad   to   pawne his   ar - rowes,
wan - ton eye,   Gan - i - med   should wayte no   lon - ger:

Ve - nus here   to   take   a sip,   would sell   her doves   and teeme   of
Phe - be heere one   night   to lye,   would change her face,   and looke   much

5.1 Imperia's Song from *Blurt, Master-Constable* by Thomas Dekker (London, 1602).

Fontinell.	Your voice does teach the Musicke.
Imperia.	No, no, no.
Fontinell.	Againe, deare Love.
Imperia.	*Hey nony nony no.*
	Did Jove *see this wanton eye,*
	Ganymede would waite no longer:
	Phoebe *heere one night to lye,*
	Would change her face and looke much younger.
	But they shall not so,
	Hey nony nony no:
	None but I this lip must owe,
	Hey nony nony no.

The song (Example 5.1) is written in the key of G major for solo voice with the accompaniment of three viols. The vocal part lies comfortably low in the soprano range, and the viol parts are full of the graceful idioms associated with contemporary English writing for that instrument. The continuous and mostly stepwise motion of the viols provides rich harmonic support for a piece that is punctuated by unexpected rests, changes in direction, syncopation, harmonic alteration, and sudden shifts in rhythm that finally collapse into a slow cadential suspension and resolution. Aside from the clear musical presentation of foreplay, climax, and release, this song not only epitomizes Prynne's effeminate "whorish musicke," but belongs to an entire English Renaissance convention of representing the feminine through musical syntax, as described by Thomas Morley and Charles Butler among others.[50] These structural features not only give the song appropriate aesthetic meaning, but also place it into the most practical possible theatrical context. Its limited vocal range is not atypical of English solo song at the close of the sixteenth century, but the single octave, short phrases, and simple, stepwise motion that dominates Imperia's part make this piece an especially excellent vehicle for a younger or newly trained voice.

Throughout Dekker's scene, Imperia's voice belongs to the same high register as Fontinell's, resulting from the same common developmental physiology as their effeminate beauty and beardless chins. Imperia's apparent womanliness is completely artificial, a learned set of musical, sartorial, and behavioral gestures, that, combined with her spoken web of lies, draw attention to the underlying reality of opposition. The courtesan and her conquest, then, are revealed as similarly boyish creatures, equally attractive to an audience not unfamiliar with homosexual literary allusions.[51] And this audience is drawn at once

---

[50] See Austern, "'Alluring the Auditorie to Effeminacie'," 352–53.

[51] Gordon Lell and Stephen Orgel both demonstrate how common explicitly homosexual erotic literature was in Renaissance England; see Lell, "'Ganymede' on the Elizabethan Stage," 7–10; and Orgel, "Nobody's Perfect," 22–26.

into the world of homoeroticism and the dramatic world of unnatural women through the courtesan's song.

At the opposite end of the English Renaissance moral spectrum was the chaste wife or daughter who remained silent and all but invisible in the public world of men, whose sexuality and public utterances were completely controlled by her closest male relative. However, in spite of strong patriarchal regulation and the perceived bond between music and uncontrollable sexuality, music was not denied her in life or in the reflected stage-play world as long as it was performed in private and for spiritual, not carnal, purposes.[52] What the Puritan extremist Phillip Stubbes says clearly applies to women as well as to men:

> But [music] being used in publique assemblies . . . estrangeth ye mine[,] stirreth up filthy lust, womanish ye mind, ravisheth ye heart, enflameth concupiscence and bringeth in uncleanes. But if Musick openly were used (as I have said) to ye praise and glory of God as our Fathers used it, and was intended by it at the first, or privately in a mans secret Chamber of house for his own solace or to drive away the fantasies of idle thoughts, solicitude, care, sorowe, and such other perturbations and molestations of the minde, the only ends whereto true Musick tends, it were very commendable and tollerable. If Musick were thus used it would comfort man wonderfully, and moove his hart to serve God the better.[53]

One of the most poignant uses of private reflective song to drive away the perturbations and molestations of the mind in all of English Renaissance drama is Desdemona's "Willow Song" in Act IV, scene iii of Shakespeare's *Othello*. Desdemona is an unusual character who has long puzzled critics, for while she is a chaste, obedient wife who would ultimately rather die silently than accuse her husband of brutality and murder, she is also a headstrong, outspoken young woman who defies her father and too often speaks her mind.[54] However, in spite of a morally

---

52 Austern, "'Sign Againe Syren,'" 428–38.

53 Stubbes, *The Anatomie of Abuses*, sig. D4. See also Stephen Gosson, *The Schoole of Abuse* (London, 1579), sigs. A8v-B3; Anonymous, *The Praise of Musicke* (Oxford: Joseph Barnes, 1586), pp. 30, 58, and 66–67; Prynne, *Histrio-Mastix*, pp. 273–90; and Stubbes, *The Anatomie of Abuses*, sigs. O3v-O6.

54 See, for example, W. D. Adamson, "Unpinned or Undone?: Desdemona's Critics and the Problems of Sexual Innocence," *Shakespeare Studies* 13 (1980), 169–86; Joan Montgomery Byles, "The Problem of the Self and the Other in the Language of Ophelia, Desdemona, and Cordelia," *American Imago* 46 (1989), 37–59; Dympna Callaghan, *Women and Gender in Renaissance Tragedy* (Atlantic Highlands, NJ: Humanities Press, 1989), pp. 74–86; Ann Jennalie Cook, "The Design of Desdemona: Doubt Raised and Resolved," *Shakespeare Studies* 13 (1980), 187–96; Gayle Green, "'This That You Call Love': Sexual and Social Tragedy in *Othello*," *Journal of Women's Studies in Literature* 1 (1979), 16–32; Eamon Grennan, "Women's voices in *Othello*: Speech, Song, Silence," *Shakespeare Quarterly* 38 (1987), 275–303; Margaret Lenta, "*Othello* and the Tragic Heroine," *Crux* 21 (1987), 26–35; Carol Thomas Neely, "Women and Men in *Othello*: 'What should such a fool / Do with so good a woman?,'" in Carolyn Ruth Swift Lenz, Gayle Greene and Carol Thomas Neely, eds., *The Woman's Part: Feminist Criticism of*

mixed presence and ambiguously gendered behavior throughout much of the play, in this pivotal scene her admirable femininity is restored within the private world of women. It is significant that her only song belongs to the most intimate feminine action of the play, a scene from which the entire public world of men is banished along with the literal and metaphorical male voice.[55] The only visible or audible point of comparison for Desdemona is her maid and confidante, Emilia, who, like her, behaves naturally within this exclusionary female realm. The audience is given a keyhole view of relaxed feminine intimacy with its confidential chatter and familiar removal of the garments worn in public to the point that any male intrusion, from within or without, would seem jarringly out of place. It is only in this environment, in which Desdemona's femininity is utterly unquestionable and the only sound at all is the female voice expressing feminine concerns, that she is allowed to sing, in spite of numerous references to her musical ability throughout the play. Here Desdemona has gone from likening herself to the trumpet, public instrument of masculine proclamation, in Act I, scene iii, to becoming the singing voice, the Renaissance emblem of the soul itself.[56]

Unlike Imperia, who gives a virtuous performance to an enraptured audience of one, and whose song is broken only between stanzas for Fontinell to beg for continuance, Desdemona's song is punctuated irregularly by snatches of dialogue between herself and Emilia that prevent the audience from becoming completely drawn into its performance. Unlike Imperia, whose song is introduced by an off-stage consort of viols, Desdemona passes unannounced and unprepared from speech

Shakespeare (Urbana and Chicago: University of Illinois Press, 1980), pp. 211–39; Bernard J. Paris, "'His Scorn I Approve': The Self Effacing Desdemona," *American Journal of Psychoanalysis* 44 (1984), 413–24.

[55] Previous studies that focus on this scene include Byles, "The Problem of the Self and the Other," 52; Grennan, "Women's Voices in *Othello*," 277–82; Rosalind King, "'Then Murder's Out of Tune': The Music and Structure of *Othello*," *Shakespeare Survey* 39 (1987), 157–58; John H. Long, *Shakespeare's Use of Music* (Gainesville: University of Florida Press, 1961), vol. III, pp. 153–61; Richmond Noble, *Shakespeare's Use of Song* (Oxford, 1923), pp. 123–26; Peter J. Seng, *The Vocal Songs in the Plays of Shakespeare* (Cambridge, MA: Harvard University Press, 1967), pp. 191–99; and Frederick W. Sternfeld, *Music in Shakespearean Tragedy* (London: Routledge and Kegan Paul, 1963), pp. 23–52.

[56] See Austern, "'Art to Enchant,'" 194–99; Gretchen L. Finney, "Ecstasy and Music in Seventeenth-Century England," *Journal of the History of Ideas* 8 (1947), 157 and 176–86; Wayne Shumaker, *The Occult Sciences in the Renaissance: A Study in Intellectual Patterns* (Berkeley and Los Angeles: University of California Press, 1972), pp. 123–33; Gary Tomlinson, "Preliminary Thoughts on the Relations of Magic and Music in the Renaissance," in Fabrizio Della Seta and Franco Piperno, eds., *In Cantu et in Sermone: For Nino Pirrotta on his 80th Birthday* (Florence: Leo S. Olschki, 1989), pp. 125–28; and D. P. Walker, *Spiritual and Demonic Magic* (London: Warburg Institute, 1958, reprinted in Notre Dame, IN: University of Notre Dame Press, 1975), pp. 8–9.

to song. Unlike Dekker's play, Shakespeare's includes no stage directions necessitating the instrumental accompaniment that would raise the song from the play's constructed world of private intimacy to that of public performance. Desdemona's performance is an unrehearsed, heartfelt cry, taking place between spoken directions ("Lay by these") and expressions of fear ("Harke, who is't that knocks?") to Emilia. Her song is introduced as the simple song of an abandoned servant, linking her not only with another woman whose love turned to tragedy, but to a woman of a lower social order through their shared suffering, rather than to the lofty artifice of classical gods, omnivorous sexuality, and the stylistic subtleties of the consort song.

Like "Love For Such a Cherry Lip," this "Willow Song" also remains extant, but in a number of versions that are difficult to connect specifically to the play.[57] However, the melodic line, that which would actually be sung, is nearly identical in all, transcribed as for the play by Frederick W. Sternfeld (Example 5.2).[58] Like Imperia's song, Desdemona's is apparently for low soprano voice, is limited to the same d' to d" octave, is comprised of short, simple phrases, and includes numerous rests. But here the rests occur only between phrases or to illustrate sighs in the text, never in a novel, teasing manner to retain interest. The key is a much darker d minor, and nearly all phrases end at a lower pitch than they begin, as if to indicate that even music cannot heal the singer's failing psychological strength. Any breathlessness that might occur in a continuous performance is negated by Desdemona's singing in snatches between spoken lines, more indicative of her fragile, shattered state of mind than of an aggressive sexual artifice. What remains is a careful, restrained series of independent musical phrases, each one simple, direct, smooth, and oriented toward a specific melodic goal.

In addition, by placing even these melodically uncomplicated phrases of music at irregular intervals between spoken lines, and by allowing Desdemona to pass gently from speech to simple, unaccompanied song, Shakespeare cleverly prevents the audience from being seduced by the music or the artificial beauty of her singing voice; this voice is never prepared, or heard long enough for such an effect on the auditors. No instrumental introduction permits the audience to prepare to judge the power of her song, or the beauty of her voice. No unexpected harmonic or melodic shifts maintain a state of excitement, and, whenever a familiar snatch of melody returns in a stanzaic repetition, it may be cut off at any moment. It is undoubtedly significant that Henry Jackson,

---

57 See John P. Cutts, "A Reconsideration of the Willow Song," *Journal of the American Musicological Society* 10 (1957), 14–24; Long, *Shakespeare's Use of Music*, vol. III, pp. 153–61; Seng, *The Vocal Songs in the Plays of Shakespeare*, pp. 191–99; and Sternfeld, *Music in Shakespearean Tragedy*, pp. 23–52.

58 Sternfeld, *Music in Shakespearean Tragedy*, pp. 43–44.

1. [stanza 2, bar 16, singing interrupted:]
   Lay by these.

2. [stanza 2, bar 24, singing interrupted:]
   Prithee, hie thee; he'll come anon.

3. [stanza 3, bar 6, singing stops here:]
   Nay, that's not next. Hark! who is't that knocks? It is the wind.

4. [stanza 4, bar 14, singing stops here:]
   So get thee gone; good night. Mine eyes do itch. Doth that bode weeping?

5.2 Desdemona's "Willow Song" from Shakespeare's *Othello*.

who saw the original dramatic company, The King's Men, perform *Othello* at Oxford in September of 1610, lavished praise on the boy who played Desdemona for "her" ability to evoke pathos in the murder scene through the use of facial expression; not only does Jackson respond to Desdemona as if she was entirely believable, but music, always exceptional in spoken drama, is never even mentioned.[59] Through her song, Desdemona transcends the whoredom of Othello's earlier accusations and the indecisive, immature, negatively feminine aspects of her persona. Through its interrupted, unaccompanied performance and simple style, all trace of seduction is eradicated and Desdemona becomes an object of pity and noble femininity. By placing her within a completely feminine frame and allowing her a seemly hesitancy of performance, Shakespeare allows Desdemona's vocality to seem a genuine and admirable feminine product.

In conclusion, English Renassiance gender theory equated boys and women on many levels, including outward physical characteristics and a shrillness of voice that enabled the former to imitate the latter in the theater in a highly convincing manner. In addition, both groups, perceived as morally and spiritually undeveloped, required adult male control and gentle guidance toward properly restrained behavior. The issue of sexual control was strongly reflected in attitudes toward musical performance, since music itself was perceived as the most powerfully sensual of the arts, and, in the theoretical language of the era, was regarded as an overwhelmingly feminine force unless strictly regulated in terms of time, place, audience, performer, and purpose. As part of a stock repertory of techniques used to draw attention to either an actor's or character's sometimes opposite gender, playwrights were able to construct masculine or feminine frames around singers that emphasized or de-emphasized their physiological and vocal similarities to other characters in the same scene, "dressing" their voices as well as their bodies for the necessary context. In so doing, the underlying masculinity and unnaturalness of the woman who imitated male musical behavior could be exhibited and ultimately punished or ridiculed, while greater sympathy or even pathos could be directed toward the more proper female singer.

[59] Shapiro, "Lady Mary Wroth Describes a 'Boy Actress,'" 189–90.

6

Deriding the voice of Jeanette MacDonald: notes on psychoanalysis and the American film musical

EDWARD BARON TURK

What is there about screen sopranos that so often elicits derisive laughter in men? How is it that the trained soprano voice, when recorded on film, has the potential to evoke both intensely strong pleasure and equally intense displeasure? Why is it that Hollywood's most successful soprano, Jeanette MacDonald, continues to generate visceral responses so ardent as to impede measured critical evaluation of her persona and films?

The odd reception history of the MGM Jeanette MacDonald–Nelson Eddy operetta series (1935–42) signals the pertinence of such questions for these films: after an initial period of mass adulation, the series found itself subject to virtually unparalleled extremes of parody and disparagement, and, in recent years, it has been relegated by most critics and historians to near oblivion. A full understanding of these critical vicissitudes would require a multitude of considerations, including but not limited to the history of American popular vocal music and its uneasy relations with the so-called semi-classical repertoire; the changing character of aspirations to cultural gentility among the lower and middle classes during the Great Depression and beyond; the impact of World War II and the cold war on reassessments of singing performance styles, especially those associated with Central Europe; and changes in the technology and economics of vocal music's dissemination, such as the advent of high-fidelity recording for home use and the decline in sheet music consumption during the postwar era. Since matters of individual and collective pleasure subtend all of these considerations, psychoanalytic theory may serve as a fruitful first approach to the issue of aggressively negative responses to cinematic sopranos. Given the

This essay is an abridged version of an essay that originally appeared in *Camera Obscura* 25 (1991), 225–49. Reprinted by permission of the publisher.

scant attention which musicals have received from psychoanalytically oriented film critics, this approach may also suggest fresh perspectives for addressing the genre more generally.

My attempt to elucidate the visceral character of the negativity and dismissiveness that have become attached to Jeanette MacDonald's later films will begin with general observations on the status of gender and voice in the MacDonald–Eddy movies, and will conclude with commentary on *I Married an Angel* (1942), the eighth and final picture in the cycle. A lavish dream comedy scripted by Anita Loos and directed by Woody Van Dyke, this adaptation of Rodgers and Hart's 1938 Broadway musical is noteworthy as the MacDonald–Eddy picture that most approximates a continuous integration of vocal line, orchestral music, and drama. More important, however, is the fact that *I Married an Angel* gently parodies the element which, I believe, has most determined audience response to Jeanette MacDonald: the deployment of a cinematically powerful soprano voice. Presenting MacDonald as both an operatically voiced angel and a husky-toned sophisticate, the film self-consciously explores the American public's and, more precisely, the American *male* public's ambivalence toward the trained female voice.

Christian Metz has identified two psychic triggers of filmic displeasure: on one hand, instinctual frustration of the id, and, on the other, "an intervention of the super-ego and the defenses of the ego, which are frightened and counter-attack when the satisfaction of the id has, on the contrary, been too intense."[1] In the following sections I hope to establish that the animosity evinced toward the MacDonald–Eddy cycle, and particularly *I Married an Angel*, is in large part a defense against exorbitant satisfactions of the id, and that the source of this excess resides in MacDonald's singing voice. At issue is viewer response to the acoustic authority which MacDonald exerts within a cinematic environment that privileges maternal incantation over male logocentrism.

I: Psyche and Euterpe

The film musical may be, as Alain Masson suggests, "the theatrical unconscious of comedy."[2] Nevertheless, it has attracted minimal attention from psychoanalytically oriented commentators who tend to be drawn to specimens dating from the 1940s and 1950s, to the near exclusion of those made in the 1930s. This preference may relate, firstly, to the fact that while the musical's conventions were more or less in place during the latter decades, they were still being invented during much of the 1930s: applied psychoanalysis lends itself to examination of

---

[1] Christian Metz, *The Imaginary Signifier: Psychoanalysis and the Cinema* (Bloomington: Indiana University Press, 1982), pp. 111–13.

[2] Alain Masson, "George Sidney: Artificial Brilliance/The Brilliance of Artifice," in R. Altman, ed., *Genre: The Musical* (London: Routledge & Kegan Paul, 1981), p. 4.

repeated and varied schemas more readily than it does to the seemingly idiosyncratic. Secondly, psychoanalytically oriented film critics have proffered highly suggestive insights into the thematic, narrative, and ideological structure of musicals, but they have virtually ignored or, perhaps more accurately, they have resisted attending to that which is most constitutive of the film musical – music.

The widespread critical bias toward the visual rather than the aural may partly explain why, irrespective of method, scholars of the 1930s' film musical (not to mention exhibitors and anthologizers) have been drawn to *song-and-dance* comedies (Warners' *Gold Diggers* pictures, RKO's Astaire–Rogers cycle) while scrupulously avoiding in-depth treatment of the (mainly) all-singing MacDonald–Eddy series.[3] Similarly, the limited attention to psychoanalysis in Rick Altman's magisterial *The American Film Musical* leads him to see the American film musical as *romantic comedy*, a genre whose subject is heterosexual courtship, whose narrative outcome is socially sanctified marriage, and whose telos is cultural normalization.[4]

Romantic comedy reaffirms phallic authority. Such is the case in the risqué, pre-Production Code MacDonald–Chevalier films. Designed to showcase his Continental charm, sexual appetite, and success at womanizing, the Chevalier–MacDonald comedies made at Paramount granted top billing and most of the songs to the Frenchman. Delivering bouncy lyrics and jaunty dialogue in seductively accented English, the Gallic *diseur* evinced a stunning mastery of verbal discourse perhaps best epitomized during those frequent moments when, overstepping expected bounds, he would look directly at the camera and address the audience, as if capable of taking each viewer into his personal confidence. Within this exceedingly male-dominated, logocentric world, MacDonald's vocal solos articulated female desire through a delicate lyricism that was invariably overpowered by Chevalier's showstoppers. In her typically playful duets with Chevalier, MacDonald's lyric capacities were of necessity restrained in order to accommodate Chevalier's raspy untrained voice.

---

[3] Critical resistance to song, especially from a psychoanalytic perspective, is all the more remarkable (and perhaps understandable) inasmuch as the film that inaugurated the musical, *The Jazz Singer* (1927), is not simply an Oedipally inflected tale of a son's love for his mother and his expiation for having betrayed his dead father, but it also takes the male singing voice as the medium *par excellence* for establishing child–parent–lover ties. The extraordinary relations among song, sentiment, and intense child–parent bonding in Jolson's early features (*The Singing Fool, Say It With Songs, Mammy, Big Boy*) expose primal gender-linked aspects of the film musical, many of which have been suppressed, masked, or displaced in the course of the genre's subsequent development.

[4] Rick Altman, *The American Film Musical* (Bloomington: Indiana University Press, 1987), pp. 76, 81, 143–47, 194.

The politics and erotics of gender and voice are markedly transformed in the MacDonald–Eddy movies. With boudoir operettas losing
their appeal, MGM envisioned *Naughty Marietta* (1935) as effecting the
rebirth of film operetta with an unmistakably American, that is, *whole-
some* character. Consequently, a new type of leading man was needed,
and the studio's search led them to baritone Nelson Eddy. An ascen-
dant figure in the concert and opera worlds (his operatic roles included
Amonasro in *Aida*, Tonio in *I Pagliacci* and Wolfram in *Tannhäuser*),
Nelson Eddy had accrued a mere seven minutes of screen time in his
three pictures prior to *Naughty Marietta*. Louis B. Mayer knew the risk
his studio was taking – not only because of Eddy's inexperience, but
also because of a persistent strain in post-Civil War American ideology
which maintained that music is not a man's domain and that classical
singing by males is especially suspect, undermining accepted standards
of native manliness.[5] Indeed, Hollywood had proved far more receptive
to the unschooled, "natural" voices of Jolson, Astaire, and Crosby than to
the more operatic talents of Dennis King, Lawrence Tibbett, and John
McCormack. But Eddy managed to allay potential viewer discomfort.

Eddy's inexperience and awkwardness as a dramatic actor, his projection of arrested adolescence, and his uncommon vocal talent all
contributed to revising and extending MacDonald's persona and career.
Taking on the task of eroticizing her nonvocal interactions with Eddy,
MacDonald became the active, determining agent in a new scheme of
male–female relations. No longer locked into playing sex kitten to
Chevalier's tomcat, she found herself empowered, through Eddy's relative passivity, to project genuine warmth, commitment, and sentiment.
The conjunction of Eddy and MacDonald inaugurated a libidinal enterprise whereby, for male and female protagonist alike, the locus of
sexual expression became displaced from the genitals to the larynx.
The allure of the MacDonald–Chevalier comedies resulted in large
measure from mismatched voices; the sweet mystery of the MacDonald–
Eddy movies would stem from vocal symbiosis.

The boudoir antics associated with the earlier cycle are perhaps best
emblematized by the mischievous episode from *Love Me Tonight* in
which Maurice, discovered embracing the lingerie-clad Princess Jeanette,
proceeds to take her measurements with the ostensible goal of making
her a custom-tailored riding habit (fig. 6.1). By contrast, the decorpore-
alization inherent in the later cycle is most manifest in the repeated
mise en scène that finds Nelson, frame left, and Jeanette, frame right,
both virtually immobile as he serenades her and as the rest of the world
seems to vanish (fig. 6.2). (Eddy sings "I'm Falling in Love with Some-

5 See Stuart Feder, "Charles and George Ives: The Veneration of Boyhood," in *The Annual of Psychoanalysis: A Publication of the Chicago Institute for Psychoanalysis* 9 (New York: International Universities Press, 1981), pp. 276–77.

6.1 Maurice Chevalier with Jeanette MacDonald in *Love Me Tonight*. Paramount Pictures, 1932.

one" in a boat drifting on the bayou in *Naughty Marietta*, "Indian Love Call" at the edge of a mountain lake in *Rose Marie* [1936], and "Who Are We To Say?" beside a stream in *Girl of the Golden West* [1938].)

Gerald Mast aptly notes that while Rogers and Astaire "project the abstract idea of love" through dance, MacDonald and Eddy do so through "vocal harmony."[6] But it is important to add that where dance functions to *clinch* the mutual physical attraction of Rogers and Astaire, song operates in the MacDonald–Eddy pictures to *defer* physical consummation indefinitely. "Change Partners" (*Carefree*), "Night and Day" (*The Gay Divorcee*), and "Cheek to Cheek" (*Top Hat*) are indeed "private" dances that have much in common with the duets of MacDonald and Eddy. But, when Astaire lays Rogers back at the conclusion of "Night and Day" or slings her into in a reclining position at the climax of "Cheek to Cheek," he exhibits what commentators have rightly emphasized as his "phallic power."[7] There is no such equivalent in MacDonald–Eddy. The most intriguing element in the *mise en scène* of their love songs is *the space that separates them*, the volume of air which ostensibly yet invisibly conveys the sound waves uniting them.

6 Gerald Mast, *Can't Help Singin': The American Musical on Stage and Screen* (Woodstock, NY: Overlook Press, 1987), p. 234.
7 Jim Collins, "Toward Defining a Matrix of the Musical Comedy: The Place of the Spectator Within the Textual Mechanisms," in Altman, ed., *Genre: The Musical*, p. 144.

6.2 Nelson Eddy with Jeanette MacDonald in *Rose Marie*.
MGM Pictures, 1936.

In MacDonald–Eddy, where climaxes are acoustic, not orgasmic, libidinal excitations are virtually limitless. Pointedly demonstrated by the inconclusive denouement of *Rose Marie*, in which Sergeant Bruce reappears after months of separation to rejoin Marie in reprising "Indian Love Call," erotic gratification for MacDonald and Eddy inheres in its ever-renewable postponement. As *Maytime* (1937), *Girl of the Golden West* (1938), and *Sweethearts* (1938) confirm, the MacDonald–Eddy pictures are propelled not by the norms of romantic comedy (courtship battles culminating in marriage) but by a willing relinquishment of conventional consummation and by a compulsive need to repeat erotic rituals that activate throbbing and pulsating singing voices, not genitalia. Much of the critical negativity attached to the cycle marks a defensive maneuver designed to avoid acknowledging that the vocal and acoustic apparatus may function as powerful erogenous zones.

II: Sopranos and authority

To what extent do psychoanalysis and psychoanalytic film theory elucidate what is at stake in the rejection of this brand of auditory pleasure?

Two strains of current cinema research offer suggestive clues. The first addresses background music in classical narrative film, and is perhaps best exemplified by Claudia Gorbman's *Unheard Melodies*. For Gorbman, underscoring "greases the wheels of the cinematic pleasure machine by easing the spectator's passage into subjectivity." Taking on the character of an invisible, transparent, and, in a certain sense, inaudible "bath" or "gel" of affect, background music functions like a "hypnotic voice" because it "bypasses the usual censors of the preconscious." Gorbman's theses are not meant to apply to musicals, where vocal and orchestral tracks are so emphatically foregrounded that they constitute, in themselves, main narrative events. But her line of argument invokes psychoanalytic references that are relevant to the issue of auditory pleasure in the MacDonald–Eddy cycle.

Following Jean-Louis Baudry, Gorbman views the classical cinema as fostering regression to a simulated infantile state of sensory hyper-receptivity and primitive narcissism whereby boundaries between active and passive, body and environment, self and other, perception and representation become blurred. Drawing on the work of such French psychoanalysts as Guy Rosolato, Didier Anzieu, and Dominique Avron, Gorbman examines the ramifications of positing auditory space as the first psychic space. If sounds such as the mother's heartbeat, digestion, and voice constitute a sonic environment even for the fetus, and if the neonate exists within a sonorous envelope that promotes a sense of auditory omnipotence because the infant is as yet unaware of distinctions between sounds emanating from itself and from its surroundings, then adult pleasure in musical listening may represent an imaginary longing for bodily fusion with the mother. Moreover, if the rise and fall of the mother's voice, its rhythm, timbre, pitch, tempo, and intensity, represent a "good object" for the child as yet uninitiated into language, and if these very same qualities become tinged with anxiety, doubt, and confusion as the child begins to learn that words have reference, then music, as contrasted with language, may remain a "good" acoustic object to be introjected with gusto. These views lead Gorbman to conclude that "the underlying pleasure of music can be traced to originary hallucinations of bodily fusion with the mother, of non-separation prior to the Oedipal crisis of language and interdiction."[8]

Although insufficient to illuminate precisely what generates pleasure and displeasure in the MacDonald–Eddy movies, the foregoing

---

[8] Claudia Gorbman, *Unheard Melodies: Narrative Film Music* (Bloomington: Indiana University Press, 1987), pp. 5, 63, 64, 69. See also Guy Rosolato, "La Voix: entre corps et langage," *Revue française de psychanalyse* 1 (1974), 75–94; Didier Anzieu, "The Sound Image of the Self," *International Review of Psychoanalysis* 6, 23 (1979), 23–26; and Dominique Avron, "Notes pour introduire une métapsychologie de la musique," *Musique en jeu* 9 (1976), 92–110.

remarks suggest a psychoanalytic context capable of accommodating traits that distinguish these films from the Chevalier–MacDonald comedies: MacDonald's enhanced capacity to control her environment; her greater opportunity to project deep emotion; Eddy's relative passivity and boyishness; the centrality of their matched voices and their many duets; and their shared disengagement from the hegemony of the spoken word.

A second pertinent field of research addresses cinematic sound and, more specifically, the female voice as conceived from feminist perspectives. Many theorists maintain that Hollywood sound editing and mixing practices virtually fetishize synchronization, or the inseparability of human sound and image, and thereby reinforce spectator confidence in speech as an individual property right.[9] But in activating nostalgia for the infant's imaginary sonorous unity with the maternal voice, the cinematic experience evokes simultaneously a prelinguistic, pre-Oedipal phantasm of corporeal plenitude *and* a premonition of potential division, dispersal, and dismemberment as symbolized by the primordial, traumatic intervention of the father's voice into the infant's auditory environment. For Kaja Silverman in *The Acoustic Mirror*, this line of theoretical speculation is a manifestation of film theory's overall obsession with threats to the stability and coherence of male subjectivity. Film theorists' insistent recourse to psychoanalytic notions of loss, castration, disavowal, and fetishism, as well as the prominent view that "woman's desire is subjected to her image as bearer of the bleeding wound," are, for Silverman, in woeful conformity with Freud's own defensive need to place maximal distance between the male subject and his early experience of bodily lack (loss of feces, of the mother's breast, of the mother's gaze, etc.) – a lack stubbornly and exclusively projected onto the female. Hollywood film practice has proved complicitous in this phallocentric, self-deluding stratagem insofar as it massively "orchestrates the burdensome transfer of male lack to the female subject by projecting the projections upon which our current notions of gender depend."[10]

With respect to cinema's vocal and auditory regimes, the nub of this transfer entails an exaggerated relegation of the female voice to the narrative's interior, where it is typically deprived of verbal potency, and the male voice's assumption of a position of apparent discursive

---

9 See, for example, John Belton, "Technology and Aesthetics of Film Sound," in E. Weis and J. Belton, eds., *Film Sound: Theory and Practice* (New York: Columbia University Press, 1985), pp. 63–72; Michel Chion, *La voix au cinéma* (Paris: Editions de l'Etoile, 1982), *passim*; Mary Ann Doane, "Ideology and the Practice of Sound Editing and Mixing," in Weis and Belton, eds., *Film Sound*, pp. 54–62; and Steve Neale, *Cinema and Technology: Image, Sound, Colour* (Bloomington: Indiana University Press, 1985), *passim*.

10 Kaja Silverman, *The Acoustic Mirror: The Female Voice in Psychoanalysis and Cinema* (Bloomington: Indiana University Press, 1988), p. 24; Laura Mulvey, "Visual Pleasure and Narrative Cinema," *Screen* 16, 3 (1975), 7.

exteriority, whereby he acquires the authority to determine and constrain her vocalizations. Principal contrivances for ensuring woman's vocal inferiority are, following Silverman's nomenclature, the "folding" of the female voice into an overtly spectacularized inner textual space and the "depositing" of the female body into the female voice (in the guise of a heavily marked accent, impediment, timbre, or grain) – operations that emphatically situate the female subject on the side of what can readily be heard, overheard, and eavesdropped upon.[11]

I would claim that by shifting emphasis from the logocentric to the incantatory, the MacDonald–Eddy pictures unsettle these gender-based norms. Even in terms of verbal dexterity, it is Eddy whose capacities appear as partial, flawed, and self-entrapping, whereas MacDonald wields sufficient authority to regulate (and enhance) enunciative acts. But with song assuming primacy over dialogue, these films intimate notions of subjectivity that confound mainstream assumptions concerning sexual difference. *Both* protagonists are exorbitantly spectacularized: Eddy's vocal exhibitionism makes him no less of an aural icon-fetish for her than she is for him. *Both* his and her voices are subjected, through visual and sound editing, to extreme synchronization and embodiment – epitomized by the extreme close-ups, centered on open mouths, that punctuate the climaxes of their solos and duets. Rather than imply inferiority and constraint, these operations promote extraordinary eruptions of freely circulating, virtually decorporealized libido. Compared with the Chevalier–MacDonald *oeuvre*, the unleashing of MacDonald's soprano and its coupling with Eddy's baritone work to deflate phallic authority and to impose a decidedly feminine imprint on their films.

Although a considerable body of psychoanalytic writing on music has been generated over the decades, little attention has been accorded to the singing voice, and, in particular, to the capacity of sopranos to provoke intense pleasure and displeasure.[12] I am proposing that a coherent line of inquiry can be built upon elements found in three major texts: *Project for a Scientific Psychology* (1895), in which Freud isolates the neonate's *scream* both as a motor discharge originating in instinctual requirements and as a communicative act signaling distress and helplessness to an environment obliged to respond; *The Ego and the*

[11] Silverman, *The Acoustic Mirror*, pp. 39, 56ff.

[12] Freud's admitted resistance to the pleasures of music notwithstanding (see *The Moses of Michelangelo* [1914] in *The Standard Edition of the Complete Psychological Works of Sigmund Freud*, ed. James Strachey [London: Hogarth Press, 1953–74], vol. XIII, p. 211), the founder of psychoanalysis was not so "*ganz unmusikalisch*" as he wanted people to believe. Limits of space and focus prevent me from developing this point here; see, for example, Martin Nass, "The Development of Creative Imagination in Composers," *International Review of Psycho-Analysis* 11 (1984), 481–91; and Guy Rosolato, "La haine de la musique," in A. de Mijolla, ed., *Psychanalyse et musique* (Paris: Les Belles Lettres, 1982), pp. 139–51.

Id (1923), in which Freud's diagram of the psychic apparatus includes a "cap of hearing" (*Hörkappe*, the auditory lobe, positioned sideways atop the ego), and where he insists that the superego, by maintaining intimate relations with the unconscious id, can in no way "disclaim its origin from things heard"; and *Inhibitions, Symptoms and Anxiety* (1926), in which adult anxiety is understood as the reactivation of primal states of danger triggering "fairly definite physical sensations," the most paradigmatic of which entail the "respiratory and vocal muscular apparatus" of the distressed infant as it alerts its mother to somatic needs.[13]

These insights, I believe, provide a conceptual framework for some intriguing hypotheses about song, sopranos, and cinema. If one posits vocal tone as a scream transformed by the organizing principles of musical acoustics (pitch, volume, timbre, duration), song can be construed as a heightening of the scream's erotic dimension (desire) and a reduction of its aggressive component (alarm). But if birth trauma is the prototype of anxiety activating the respiratory organs and the vocal apparatus, the singing voice, and especially the high-pitched female singing voice, has the capacity to invoke in listeners both the calming sensory orderliness of intrauterine existence (pleasure) and the invasive onslaught of uncontrollable auditory stimuli attendant upon separation from the mother (displeasure). The mother's voice may be associated with the lullaby, oral gratification, and regressive sleep. But it may also reactivate primitive fears of psychobiological destruction.

How does such speculation bear on moviegoers' responses to Jeanette MacDonald's voice? MacDonald was a light lyric soprano who, when paired with Eddy, had not yet performed opera on stage. But part of the MGM project to revive film operetta entailed establishing MacDonald – with the help of sound engineer Douglas Shearer – as an unquestionable match for Eddy's vocal prowess. In *Naughty Marietta*, where her spirited rendition of "The Italian Street Song" is a calculated response to Eddy's ostentatious display in "'Neath the Southern Moon," MacDonald puts to rest all suspicions that her natural endowment might prevent her from projecting exorbitant vocal strength on screen.

For the moviegoer who is well disposed to it, the intensity of sound MacDonald produces (especially at climaxes) and the progressive heightening of her vocal range throughout the 1930s (resulting in relative obfuscation of words to the advantage of musical line) reactivate the hallucinatory pleasures of acoustic omnipotence associated with prelinguistic, infantile narcissism. For moviegoers otherwise disposed, these same factors generate anxiety and embarrassment. At issue in both dispositions, I suggest, is the moviegoer's willingness to accept or to disavow the maternal voice as the agency of acoustic authority. MacDonald's

---

[13] Freud, vol. I, p. 318; vol. XIX, pp. 24–25 and 53; vol. XX, p. 137.

soprano is the manifest sign of that power, and her brand of singing requires audiences to acknowledge, by comparison, their insufficiency and subordination. MacDonald dares viewers to engage, along with Nelson Eddy, in a libidinal transaction that not only wholeheartedly embraces the feminine, but also takes male subjectivity to be dependent upon it and incomplete without it – gestures and postulates which patriarchal institutions, including Hollywood and psychoanalysis, tend to censor or repress. It is telling that Clark Gable, MGM's quintessential man's man, initially balked at co-starring with MacDonald in *San Francisco* (1936) on the grounds that "all he would have to do was stand there while Jeanette sang, not *his* idea of a good picture."[14]

From a psychoanalytic perspective, the disposition of male viewers and critics (and, as in the case of Gable, even actors) to respond defensively to the MacDonald–Eddy films may also relate to the fact that deepening of the voice during puberty is a gender-specific phenomenon: the degree of confidence in his masculinity which identification with Eddy's baritone inspires in a male viewer is inevitably at odds with that same viewer's identification with MacDonald's soprano – an identification generating memory traces of the strident infantile scream (signifying lack and helplessness), of that scream's projection onto the nurturing mother (granting her inordinate power and control), and of adolescent anxieties concerning gender identity. Jeanette MacDonald's physical appearance runs contrary to the Margaret Dumont stereotype of the fearsome, monstrous diva, but her vocal ejaculations make MacDonald no less subject to being perceived subconsciously as a phallic representation capable of engendering primal fears of bodily damage, castration, and even death.

III: An acoustic psychodrama

I Married an Angel (1942) makes explicit the destructive potential embedded in MacDonald's soprano. Numerous factors prevented the film from becoming a critical and box-office success. Having co-starred in seven previous pictures, the MacDonald–Eddy team was suffering from overexposure. The advent of World War II made moviegoers less responsive to musicals celebrating the splendid isolationism of romantic lovers. Films glorifying American nationalism, such as MGM's *For Me and My Gal* and *Yankee Doodle Dandy* or Paramount's *Star Spangled Rhythm* and *The Fleet's In* found more receptive audiences. The wartime climate also promoted public enthusiasm for screen singers who seemed to embody down-to-earth values, such as Judy Garland, Betty Hutton, and Gene Kelly. And fond memories of the 1938 Rodgers and Hart

[14] Eleanor Knowles, *The Films of Jeanette MacDonald and Nelson Eddy* (Cranbury, NJ: A. S. Barnes, 1975), p. 178.

Broadway success, in which the female lead was designed not for a singer but for the dancer Vera Zorina, predisposed New York reviewers to greet this expensive black-and-white adaptation with ample skepticism.

A less obvious cause of the comedy's financial failure lies in the self-conscious stance it adopts toward hitherto unexamined givens of the MacDonald–Eddy cycle, specifically its treatment of the psychodynamic binding Eddy to MacDonald's voice. In a switch from their prior movies, *I Married an Angel* begins by evoking the sophisticated and relatively decadent world of MacDonald's pre-Code films directed by Ernst Lubitsch and Rouben Mamoulian. An introductory title tells us that the action takes place in "Budapest in the gay days not so long ago." Taking on a role that would have gone to Chevalier in the earlier corpus, Eddy is the insouciant playboy Count William Palaffi, known as "Willie." Heir to a banking fortune, Willie's future is jeopardized by his chronic womanizing and his unwillingness to marry. He first appears arriving at his bank at 8 a.m., still sporting evening apparel and accompanied by two glamorous women. In an emphatic reinstatement of Chevalier's phallocratic regime, MacDonald first appears as Anna Zador, a bashful secretary who harbors a secret crush on the Count and who renders ritual homage to portraits of his ancestors – all male.

Except for four hummed and half-sung measures from Fritz Kreisler's "Caprice Viennois," intoned by Anna as she arrives at the bank on a bicycle, these opening scenes are devoid of song. But the following sequence, a costume party celebrating Willie's thirty-fifth birthday, overflows with witty rhymed dialogue set to music, elaborate ensemble singing, and a brief solo by Willie. (Although Anna is present, she does not sing.) The sequence's centerpiece is an extended number called "Tira Lira La," in which a parade of beauteous ladies costumed in lavish, exotic wedding gowns declare their mock qualifications for becoming Willie's spouse. While the sequence resurrects the buoyant hedonism of the Maxim's episodes in MacDonald's *The Merry Widow*, the number's musical style could not be further from the romantic waltzes and spirited marches of Franz Lehar – even as reinterpreted by Herbert Stothart, who served as musical arranger for both the 1934 MGM *Merry Widow* and *I Married an Angel*. Structured as a theme and variations, "Tira Lira La" begins with an expansive swing melody that is restated, first, in an upbeat, syncopated jazz version and, finally, in a jive rendition performed by a trio of dancing and singing black boys. This Middle European capital, at least when it parties, is steeped in the musical idioms of contemporary Manhattan.

A lyric sea change occurs with the onset of Willie's dream, which constitutes most of the remainder of *I Married an Angel*. Following "Tira Lira La," in which he rejects the glamour girls' coy proposals of marriage, Willie playfully announces that the woman he takes for a spouse will have to be "an angel" – and he points condescendingly to Anna, who is sporting a homemade angel costume and is decidedly out of place in this worldly, opulent milieu. In order to emphasize the ludicrousness of his choice, Willie callously asks Anna to dance, and the scoring – a Viennese-like waltz that segues into strains of "Spring is Here" – is nearly drowned out by the derisive laughter and verbal jibes of his female friends.

These raucous vocal ejaculations stand in stark contrast to the soothing acoustic gel that will bathe Willie at the start of his dream. To escape all expectations, both serious and mock, that a man of his age should be married, Willie – whose very name is British slang for penis – withdraws to his room, where he lies on a couch and falls asleep. His dream begins with eight bars of rubato soprano vocalization sung by the angel Brigitta (also played by MacDonald) as, in long shot, she descends from heaven to Willie's room. These measures are followed by a full and very slow-time refrain of the "I Married an Angel" melody, sung expressively by Brigitta in an extremely high register and filmed in a series of close shots of MacDonald.

The sonorous dimension of Willie's dream merits full attention. From a psychoanalytic perspective, Willie undergoes a symbolic regression to a state of prelinguistic narcissism that finds him blissfully submerged within a powerful, female-controlled auditory environment. His dream expunges the residue of American musical idioms as experienced at his party; it foregrounds the classical, European style which his lady friends sought to squelch when he was dancing with Anna; and it grants to Anna/Brigitta/MacDonald a central position in Willie's psyche, which the promiscuous women at the party were sure that they alone occupied. In other words, the dream effects a shift from a world dominated by patriarchal norms, which I have associated with the Chevalier-MacDonald comedies, to the symbolic realm of mother–child symbiosis characteristic of the MacDonald–Eddy pictures.

Indeed, the dream device allows for the symbolic expression both of Willie's ambivalence vis-à-vis the angel Brigitta and of the American public's vis-à-vis the later Jeanette MacDonald. More specifically, Willie's dream transcribes *male* subjectivity and its attitudes toward the deployment of MacDonald's soprano. Thus, despite Willie's acquiescence to Brigitta's control – in their initial encounter it is she who regulates Willie's ability to touch and kiss her, and it is she who protects and nurtures by feeding him a forkful of angel cake – Willie insists that she acknowledge his sexual needs, observing that marriage is an earthly as well as a spiritual institution. Brigitta's response, "Whatever you wish me to be I will be," harks back to the patriarchal ethos of the Chevalier movies. Moreover, the very next sequence – the couple's arrival in Paris for their honeymoon – offers a near quotation from Chevalier's "Song of Paree" in *Love Me Tonight* (also composed by Rodgers and Hart). However, where "Song of Paree" was initiated by Chevalier and remained his song, Willie's bouncy rendition of "I Married an Angel" is a reprise of Brigitta's statement of that melody at the dream's start. Willie here expands the song with the lengthy bridge interpolations "I'll Tell the Man in the Street" and "Hey, Butcher," but his vocal prowess is steadily subordinated to Brigitta's – as is confirmed by her seizing the melody at the song's conclusion, relegating Willie to the execution of a harmonious but subservient contrapuntal line. Similarly, Brigitta sings a half-chorus of the film's other principal song, "Spring is Here," before Willie joins her in duet. In point of fact, virtually *all* of Willie's singing in *I Married an Angel* derives from melodies first articulated by Brigitta. The reverse never occurs.

Willie's anxiety over his subordination to Brigitta becomes explicit when he reluctantly accedes to her request that they attend a harp concert at the Academy de Musique (*sic*). The new groom would prefer to indulge in stereotypic masculine activities – attending the *Folies Bergère* or the Longchamp races. But his bride chooses "to sing for you among the harps as I did back home." Staged within a *mise en scène* reminiscent of MacDonald's more genuinely spiritual moments in *San Francisco* ("The Holy City") and *Girl of the Golden West* (Bach–Gounod's "Ave Maria"), Brigitta's bravura display of coloratura at the Academy (she warbles the final strains from Eva dell Acqua's "Villanelle") prompts an invitation for her to sing daily with the harpists for the next two weeks. When she accepts, Willie swoons; notably, he is caught in his fall not by Brigitta-the-angelic-oral-nurturer, but by his male servant and confidant, Peter (Edward Everett Horton). In light of my hypotheses about sopranos and cinema, this instance of literal male bonding ("Willie" and "Peter") may be construed as a defensive maneuver against the primitive fears of psychobiological destruction which the high-pitched female singing voice is capable of reactivating. Playing against type, Nelson Eddy at this moment in the film disavows rather than embraces the maternal voice as an agency of acoustic authority and pleasure.

This momentary spoof on the dangers of overexposure to MacDonald's soprano takes on heightened significance as Willie's dream progresses. During the hilarious dinner party at which she is introduced to Budapest society, Brigitta alienates her guests by speaking the plain truth about their unwarranted pretensions and secret dalliances. When Willie finds her innocently kissing the bank's largest creditor, Baron Szigethy (Douglass Dumbrille), his jealous outrage jeopardizes the future of both his bank and his marriage. Willie's former girlfriend Peggy (Binnie Barnes) attempts to salvage this situation by remolding Brigitta's vision, demeanor – and voice. In the number "A Twinkle in Your Eye," Peggy instructs Brigitta in sophisticated traits of duplicity, complicitous winks, and seductive physicality. That is to say, Peggy/Barnes derides the angelic female persona of the MacDonald–Eddy pictures and literally *retrains* Jeanette MacDonald in the sex-kitten virtues prized by men in MacDonald's pre-Nelson Eddy musicals.

The next two sequences expose the degree to which toying with the MacDonald persona inevitably entails coming to terms with her voice. The first takes place in a nightclub that brings together Willie, his past girlfriends, and the guests Brigitta previously insulted. Arriving on the arm of Baron Szigethy and wearing a zebra coat and black sequined gown, Brigitta plays the consummate blasé sophisticate with heavy touches of the vamp as she slinks from table to table and offers mock apologies in half-spoken, half-sung couplets mouthed more or less to the tune of "A Twinkle in Your Eye" and accompanied alternately by accordion flourishes and a brassy orchestra. Most significant for our purposes, Brigitta flagrantly sings in chest rather than head voice, emphasizing a clear break with traditional codes of trained soprano vocalism. The result is arguably a parody more of, say, Mae West's attempt to crash society in *Going to Town* (1935) than of MacDonald in *Monte Carlo* (1930). But its effect on Willie is unambiguous. Shocked and angered at his angel's fall from propriety, he is reduced to a near-total state of emotional deprivation that corresponds, in our psychoanalytic framework, to a dislocation of the pleasurable fantasy of acoustic omnipotence enjoyed by the enthralled infant vis-à-vis its mother's voice.

As if to recover this lost sense of security, which Willie now sees as being tied to Brigitta's cultivated soprano, the next (and final) sequence of his dream showcases MacDonald's operatic talent. But it is precisely this onslaught of vocal excess and exorbitance that turns Willie's dream into a nightmare. The sequence contains five segments. The first, shot with Expressionistic decor, lighting, and angling, finds Willie running frantically after Brigitta and Szigethy as they escape by car. The next three segments present Willie on his bedroom balcony observing with horror three primal scenes: Brigitta seductively sings the "Chanson Bohème" from *Carmen* in a North African setting that evokes the nightclub where Dietrich performs in *Morocco* (1930); she then intones "Anges purs, anges radieux" from *Faust*, thereby evoking her own operatic performance in *San Francisco* but also adding a surreal touch by fondling a spaniel puppy held in the small of her right arm; and next, with her midriff bared and sporting a "grass" skirt made of black cellophane strips, Brigitta sings and dances "Aloha Oe" on the beach at Waikiki, cavorting with a group of scantily clad males who beat on drums and toss her about, ultimately making her fall into the Baron's lap – a probable reference to MacDonald's early anarchic comedy, *Let's Go Native*

117

(1930), directed by Leo McCarey. During each of these unrestrained vocal episodes, Willie, refusing to be a passive observer-auditor, sings contrapuntally in English and French, urging Brigitta to cease taunting him and to return. But Willie's prior state of vocal symbiosis is now utterly undone. The plaintive three-note motif repeated each time that Willie cries out for "Bri-*GI*-tta" – reminiscent of the cries of a distressed neonate as it alerts its mother to somatic needs – is consistently drowned out by MacDonald's more energetic, independent, and louder soprano line. With Brigitta occupying a physical and acoustic space from which Willie is emphatically severed (psychoanalytically put, Brigitta is now operating in a decidedly Oedipal sphere), it becomes impossible for her to hear and respond to Willie's (pre-Oedipal) needs, even if she so desired. Finally, Willie's dream screen portrays Brigitta and the Baron on water skis, with the boat that propels them racing straight for a collision with Willie – who thereupon screams, awakens, and rushes to find Anna Zador. In a brief coda that brings the film to its conclusion, Willie precipitously proposes marriage to Anna; she readily accepts; and together they sing a final chorus of "I Married an Angel," which, significantly, *he* initiates, and in which *he* carries the melody.

This hasty ending is deceptive in its apparent attempt to make *I Married an Angel* conform to the patriarchal ethos of romantic comedy: heterosexual courtship that culminates in socially sanctified marriage. In point of fact, the past tense of the movie's title refers to an illusion: Willie marries Brigitta in his dream, but the film ends with only the *expectation* that Willy and Anna will marry. In this regard, *I Married an Angel* maintains the fundamental MacDonald–Eddy principle of physical nonconsummation, providing us yet again with acoustic rather than physical climaxes.

The ending also seemingly reconciles thematic oppositions clustered around gender-based differences, in this case Willie's hedonism and Anna's decorum – a condition which Altman views as the *sine qua non* of American film musicals. But the ending's euphoric tone has little to do with the *couple's* being released from inordinate constraints: Willie and Anna do transcend class barriers, but *I Married an Angel* pays virtually no attention to this. The finale's euphoria derives instead from a swift disengagement from the acoustic psychodrama of Willie's dream-turned-nightmare, in which the antagonistic impulses may be defined as, on the one hand, regression to an imaginary, pre-Oedipal state of total identification with the mother's voice and, on the other hand, society's injunction that men must marry and indulge in full, "normal" physical relations with sexually mature women.

Epilogue

The present consideration of gender and voice in the MacDonald–Eddy movies suggests that by immersing the spectator-auditor into a world dominated more by melos than logos, film musicals hold great potential for stimulating unconscious responses. Moreover, when musicals require moviegoers to identify with the excessive quality of the trained soprano voice – a process that is virtually allegorized in *I Married an Angel* – there is an increased likelihood of reactivating, especially in men, unpleasurable primal affects such as oral anxiety, somatic dependence, and bodily insufficiency. In these instances, there is a heightened probability that defensive, aggressive derision will supplant feelings of euphoric seduction, although the latter are clearly plausible, appropriate, and proven alternative responses for male and female moviegoers alike. A challenge still remaining to film criticism and history is to comprehend the source and effects of such derision with sympathetic understanding. For this to occur, the special authority wielded by screen sopranos must be acknowledged. And the impact of this authority on gender representations and viewer-auditor reception must be explored further.

7

Adorno and the Sirens: tele-phono-graphic bodies

BARBARA ENGH

Employing a feminine figure, Theodor Adorno named an early essay on the phonograph "The Curves of the Needle," and published it in 1928 in *Musikblätter des Anbruch*, an avant-garde music journal founded in Vienna in 1919.[1] When Adorno joined the journal's editorial board in 1929, he recommended a number of changes, among them that the journal undertake the serious study of "light music" and kitsch, and that it do so with an attitude neither of arrogant dismissal nor of simplistic celebration.[2] He also called for a series of articles to appear under the rubric "mechanical music": "This grows out of the conviction that the mechanical presentation of music today is of contemporary relevance in a deeper sense than merely being currently available as a new technological means . . . The availability of means corresponds to an availability of consciousness."[3]

In "The Curves of the Needle," there appears a strange assertion concerning gender – strange in that it seems to stand apart from the argument of the essay as a symptom of an anxiety or a shock inexplicable within its own logic. Adorno claims that a woman's singing voice cannot be recorded well, because it demands the presence of her body. A man's voice is able to carry on in the absence of his body, because his self is identical to his voice; his body disappears. The prevailing paradigms of feminist interpretive practice – models indebted primarily to existentialist (problems of immanence versus transcendence) or to psychoanalytic theory (problems of the mother's body, voice, and labors) – seem fully prepared to interpret this passage. However, I will

---

[1] Theodor Adorno, "*Nadelkurven*," *Musikblätter des Anbruch* 10 (February 1928), 47–50; "The Curves of the Needle," trans. Thomas Y. Levin, *October* 55 (Winter 1990), 48–55.

[2] This is surprising in light of the prevailing dismissal of Adorno as an elitist and old-fashioned melancholic. Thomas Y. Levin makes this case, and discusses Adorno's essays on the gramophone in "For the Record: Adorno on Music in the Age of its Technological Reproducibility," *October* 55 (Winter 1990), 23–47.

[3] Levin, "For the Record," 28–29.

resist their efficacy, and instead attempt to interpret it through the Frankfurt School's analysis of subjectivity and the artwork in modernity. I begin with a story of the panic that ensued as humanity encountered its technologically disembodied voice. Then I turn to Adorno's discussion of the phonograph, and to the problem of the woman's voice. Finally I turn to the Siren, the singing woman as a problem, and to the cynosure in the epic development of bourgeois subjectivity, according to Adorno and Horkheimer, Odysseus. I supplement their reading with an episode in which he encounters song before the Sirens, before his body, tied to the mast, disappears.

I: Call girls

In *Discourse Networks, 1800/1900*, Friedrich Kittler analyzes the systems of inscription – the practice and pedagogy of reading and writing – that underpin the two historical moments of his title, assuming, after Foucault, that "such technologies are not mere instruments with which 'man' produces his meanings . . . Rather, they set the framework within which something like 'meaning,' indeed, something like 'man,' become possible at all."[4] In a wide-ranging series of analyses of texts from around 1800, Kittler demonstrates that "Romanticism is the discursive production of the Mother as the source of discursive production . . . Primary orality, the Mother, the self-presence of the origin: these are not merely sublimations or philosophical hallucinations, they are discursive facts, nodal points in a positive and empirical network."[5] The new technologies of inscription which take hold around 1900 – in the typewriter, the gramophone, film – institute a discourse network which is, Kittler argues, no longer organized around "the One Woman or Nature . . . If the phantasm of Woman arose in the distribution of form and matter, spirit and nature, writing and reading, production and consumption, to the two sexes, a new discourse network cancelled the polarity . . . Machines do away with polar sexual difference and its symbols."[6] In 1900, the relations between the sexes change. Instead of woman, there are women, everywhere, writing. They enter the universities, and the professions, particularly into positions of information transmission as secretary-typists and telephone operators.

The telephone was the first technology to disembody the voice. In the *Scientific American* of February 12, 1887, there appears an article that registers in an exemplary way the disturbance produced by that development. Its images of shipwreck and hysteria will recur. The anonymous

---

4 Friedrich A. Kittler, *Discourse Networks, 1800/1900*, trans. Michael Metteer with Chris Cullens, foreword by David E. Wellbery (Stanford University Press, 1990), p. xii.
5 Ibid., p. xxiii.
6 Ibid., pp. 347, 348, 351.

reporter confesses that he suffers from shock, from a "seasickness" due to the experience of the telephone. The shock is produced, he explains, by

> the mysteriousness, the sense of material non-existence, of that part of the machine and its belongings that lies beyond one's own instrument . . . My own material existence I am reasonably assured of. I can imagine my friend at the other end of the line. But between us two there is an airy nowhere, inhabited by voices and nothing else – Helloland, I should call it. The vocal inhabitants of this strange region have an amazing vanishing quality. Even while you are talking casually with one or another of them, you may become aware that you have been unaccountably "cut off;" and if you become impatient, and raise your voice in earnest demand or protest, the more you bellow, the more you become aware that you are idiotically shouting yourself black in the face against a mere inanimate box stuck against the wall. Nothing else than the supremest invention of the nineteenth-century could make man so supremely ridiculous as he is when shouting objurgations into a telephone transmitter that isn't "connected." The consciousness of such an experience produces in sensitive men, I am sure, a sensation of nervous shock, somewhat akin to seasickness. And sometimes . . . you hear the confused murmur of a hundred voices. You catch more expressions from private conversations than your nerves can transmit to the central office of your brain; and if you are imaginative, you may undergo, as I have, a feeling as if you had a hundred astral bodies that were guiltily listening at as many keyholes. The central office is not like any other business establishment whatsoever. The telephone seems to you to have no visible agency. If you have business with the company, you telephone it. Your applications and complaints go over the wire to that one impersonal, impalpable voice.[7]

If the human brain had at one time provided a "central office" which served to organize and process experience, it does so no longer. The reporter recommends a cure in the form of a visit to the central office of the telephone company.

There, that single, maddening, disembodied voice is nowhere in evidence – all is quiet. One's fear of the "ghostly"– and one's guilt – are alleviated by the sight of a score of eavesdroppers: "twenty comely young women sitting in a long row." The reporter suddenly feels strong enough to break into direct address: "'These seem to be young women of excellent physique,' I said to the superintendent. 'We insist on that,' said he." The excellent physiques are described, awkwardly and in some detail: a mass of steel bands, wires, receivers, transmitters, metal plugs, rows and rows of little holes – "an endless apparatus" born by each girl leaning back in an attitude "entirely cool and totally unconcerned."

Even so, five substitutes sit awaiting the call for their services, as the girls do "get rattled." The supervisor points to one – "that one with the slender figure and dark hair" – who the previous week "went into the

---

[7] "A Reporter's Visit to the Boston Telephone Exchange," *Scientific American* (February 12, 1887), 106.

girls' waiting room and had an attack of hysteria there . . . They generally go out into their room and have a good cry, and come back feeling better. They certainly seem to like the work, though the pay is only $7 a week." As the reporter and the supervisor speak, another succumbs. "Vexations" come in over the lines – from terrified, sick, and abusive customers if the reporter is any indication – and worse, from the boss himself, eavesdropping to ascertain that the girls not only listen politely, but also respond in the tones of that one disembodied voice that quietly goes out over the wire.[8] "Vexation makes the work harder for the operator, and she avoids it." She even cooperates with the suggestion that she go and throw her fit in private, out of sight.

As the boss engineers the hysteric's substitution, the reporter marvels at the quiet, and its paradox. Close enough to speak to the women directly, the superintendent calls them on the telephone, maintaining a hush over which "one clear voice in a good speaking tone might have been heard plainly across that whole room above all the business of making the connections for 2,000 people." That one voice is never heard. The hysteric and her replacement also manage quietly: "She could have spoken to him through the air by turning her head, but it would have made a little bit of noise and confusion in the room, and this modern tower of Babel, this vocal sensorium of a whole city, is as quiet as a public library reading room."

The reporter, who had dissolved into a hundred criminal astral bodies, goes away cured. The identity of the disembodied voice is revealed, in the paternal person of the supervisor, to be that of God, the Father, the phone company. The reporter has found, in the operators, the proper bearers of his hysteria, and the entire scene, far from the Babel of modernity, is a bastion of nineteenth-century culture after all, a public library reading room.

The phonograph proved to be even more disturbing. Its first auditors did not anticipate the pleasures of prerecorded music enjoyed in the privacy of their homes; rather the overriding initial concern was that now the dead would speak.

He will have no need of monuments or cenotraphs [sic] to sound his praises or record his benefactions; for, on the great highway of waters, to the utmost limits of America's rock-bound coast, and Albion's chalky cliffs, his Phonograph will speak to generations yet unborn, and tell of thousands rescued from shipwreck, and of nationalities made wealthy and powerful . . . and we shall be able *literally* to assert of Mr. Edison that, "He, being dead, yet *speaketh*."[9]

---

[8] See also Lana F. Rakow, "Women and the Telephone: the Gendering of a Communications Technology," in Cheris Kramarae, ed., *Technology and Women's Voices: Keeping in Touch* (New York and London, Routledge and Kegan Paul, 1988), pp. 207–28.

[9] Frederick Garbit, *The Phonograph and its Inventor, Thomas Alvah Edison* (Boston: Gunn, Bliss and Co., 1878), p. 7.

A year before this tribute, in 1877, Thomas Edison heard "his" voice emerge from the first phonograph. He later said, "I was never so taken aback in my life."[10] Initially, the "speaking machine" was a recording as well as a playback device. Edison brought it to the offices of the *Scientific American* where it introduced itself and inquired as to the health of its audience. "It is a little curious," the editors reported, "that the machine pronounces its own name with especial clearness." The machine presented "the illusion of a real presence," and one couldn't listen to it "without his experiencing the idea that his senses are deceiving him." They pronounced Edison the only man alive capable of raising the voices of the dead. Chief among the phonograph's functions, they imagined, would be the preservation of those "dead" voices, and not only famous ones: in the home, the phonograph would preside at the deathbed, recording final words, preserving the body's most distinctive feature, its voice, and providing an uncanny "Family Record" as a sort of living scrapbook.

Edison predicted that with the phonograph the blind would read and write. It would do more for the poor than the printing press. The "phonogram" would replace the newspaper. In the office, the phonograph would largely eliminate the position of secretary-typist, as it answered and recorded telephone calls, as businessmen exchanged wax cylinders inscribed by voices instead of letters inscribed by secretaries.[11] Interestingly, this possibility appears, and disappears, at more or less the same time that women enter the labor force *en masse* to fill these positions.

II: Tele-phono-graphic bodies

Among the proposed uses of the phonograph, but given no special emphasis by Edison and his cohorts, was the reproduction of music. Although its inventors had imagined that it would also record sound, the phonograph's commercial viability turned out to consist in its playback function, of mass-produced music. Capital prevailed in the form of the record industry, for as long as people produced their own recorded materials, the market for the phonograph was limited. Emile Berliner's gramophone was strictly a playback device using the more durable disc, and it came to define the form of the phonograph, whose other potentialities were largely abandoned for the time.[12]

By the time Adorno wrote "The Curves of the Needle," the uncanny qualities of the phonograph had been forgotten, and it had made itself comfortable in the bourgeois home as a modest cabinet. The brass

---

10 Roland Gelatt, *The Fabulous Phonograph 1877–1977* (New York: Macmillan, 1977), p. 21.

11 *Scientific American*, December 22, 1877; March 26, 1887; and November 19, 1887.

12 Jacques Attali, *Noise: The Political Economy of Music*, trans. Brian Massumi (Minneapolis: University of Minnesota Press, 1985), pp. 90–95.

horns of the early machines had presented the "mechanical being" of the phonograph, according to Adorno, and had thereby preserved a link outside the private home to loudspeakers, "fanfares of the street . . . disturbers of the peace." Inside the home, as respectable as the piano, the phonograph nevertheless retained a trace of its uncanniness in Adorno's mind, attesting to the passing of the bourgeois family: "Its cover provides a space for the artistic photograph of the divorced wife with the baby. Through discrete cracks comes the singing of the Revelers, all of whom have a soul; baby remains quiet."[13] The apparatus as such had receded from consciousness, becoming utterly submissive in its reproductive role – obedient, patient, and devout:

The mechanism of the gramophone effects only the reduced transmission, adapted to domestic needs, of preexisting works . . . The obedient machine – which in no way dictates any formal principles of its own – follows the interpreter in patient imitation of every nuance. This sort of practice simply assumes the unproblematic existence of the works themselves as well as the interpreter's right to that freedom, which the machine accompanies with devout whirring. Yet both of these are in decline . . . The archival quality of records is readily apparent: just in time, the shrinking sounds are provided with herbaria that endure for ends that are admittedly unknown. The relevance of the talking machines is debatable.[14]

In an essay published six years later, entitled "The Form of the Phonograph Record," Adorno would persist with the question of the unknown ends of records. Insisting that their aesthetic significance lies not in their transmission of music but in their "thingness," he wrote that, "if . . . notes were still the mere signs for music, then, through the curves of the needle on the phonograph record, music approaches decisively its true character as writing . . . Inseparably committed to the sound that inhabits this and no other acoustic groove," music writes itself indexically, and silently, as an inscription that is independent of human audition, and illegible to the human eye.[15] Records become a sort of nonsubjective knowledge and they preserve posthumously an archive of a subjectivity which Adorno – forced from his post at Frankfurt University into exile that year – believed to have been liquidated. "The dead art rescues the ephemeral and perishing art as the only one alive . . . This occurs at the price of its immediacy, yet with the hope that, once fixed in this way, it will some day become readable as the 'last remaining universal language since the construction of the tower.'"[16]

The earlier essay, "The Curves of the Needle," while no more hopeful about the future of music or of humanity, is less theological, and while

13   Adorno, "Curves," 52.
14   Ibid., 50–51.
15   Theodor Adorno, "The Form of the Phonograph Record," trans. Thomas Y. Levin, *October* 55 (Winter 1990), 59.
16   Ibid., 59. (Adorno is quoting Walter Benjamin's *The Origin of German Tragic Drama*.)

it, too, is concerned with the "thingness" of the phonograph, it pursues that question in the direction of the thing's role in the cultural reproduction of subjectivity. The essay begins by remarking on a paradox connected with the question of the fidelity of the sound. For Adorno, when the machine in its more primitive state had made its presence known, through its own noises and obtrusive machine-like presence, some presence, or proximity of the singer was likewise preserved. As the apparatus became more proficient and silent, "the subtlety of color and the authenticity of vocal sound declines as if the singer were being distanced more and more from the apparatus."[17] His concern is far from the humanistic plaint that decries the replacement of man by machine. What we would think of as the "failure" of the phonograph to imitate perfectly the human voice stands in other terms as the presentation of the inhuman, a crucial presence, for Adorno, in art. He states the paradox – wherein the more perfectly the machine is able to represent the human, the more thoroughly is the human removed – in another way: "The ambiguity of forward-moving technology . . . confirms the ambiguity of forward-moving rationality as such."[18] It would be some fifteen years before Adorno and Horkheimer would write *Dialectic of Enlightenment*, but already the argument of that work is being foreshadowed. That which in the discussion of the phonograph is presented as the encounter of the human and the machine, in *Dialectic of Enlightenment* is cast as the encounter of man and nature. What is crucial is the point that in the very distinction of the human and the inhuman lies a fatal misrecognition. The following passage encapsulates their argument:

As soon as man discards the awareness that he himself is nature, all the aims for which he keeps himself alive – social progress, the intensification of all his material and spiritual powers, even consciousness itself – are nullified, and the enthronement of the means as an end, which under late capitalism is tantamount to open insanity, is already perceptible in the prehistory of subjectivity.[19]

While now we tend to think of "the other" as having a human face, featuring racial or gendered difference, for Adorno, the oppression and exploitation of human beings is based on the prehistoric and ongoing distinction between the human and the inhuman. That necessary encounter results not only in the formation of human subjectivity, but also in domination, suffering, and the inhumane.

For Adorno and Horkheimer, the *Odyssey* "bears witness to the dialectic of enlightenment" in the hero's struggle to master the forces of

---

[17] Adorno, "Curves," 49.
[18] Ibid., 50.
[19] Theodor Adorno and Max Horkheimer, *Dialectic of Enlightenment*, trans. John Cumming (New York: Continuum, 1986), p. 54.

nature and magic through rational labor.[20] The encounter of Odysseus and the Sirens is crucial for its presentation of the master–slave dialectic which governs the enjoyment of art in Western civilization. Odysseus masters the elements and survives the crisis only at the cost of the renunciation of his body and whatever the participatory experience of the Sirens and their song would mean; the enslaved crew is entirely deprived of the pleasures and the knowledge of the song. Nevertheless, in song, in art, survive traces of a knowledge that would not be domination.[21] "Art keeps alive the memory of ends-oriented reason . . . Aesthetic behaviour is . . . a process set in motion by mimesis . . . The aesthetic mode of behaviour assimilates itself to [the] other rather than trying to subdue it."[22] Adorno insists that the concept of artistic expression has significance only as a non-subjective category. Things speak; there is meaning other than human meaning. While the technologization of art "is an extension of the subject's domination of nature," dialectically these processes enable a speech that "has nothing to do with the deliberate communication of a humane message or statement. What looks like reification is actually a groping for the latent language of things."[23]

Art is expressive when a subjectively mediated, objective quality raises its voice to speak . . . If expression were merely a duplicate of subjective feelings it would not amount to anything . . . A better model for understanding expression is to think of it not in terms of subjective feelings, but in terms of ordinary things and situations in which historical processes and functions have been sedimented, endowing them with the potential to speak.[24]

Skipping back to "The Curves of the Needle," we can understand the significance Adorno attaches to the silencing of the phonographic apparatus in the name of fidelity.[25] The more faithful the reproduction, the muter the language of things.

That silencing having been largely accomplished, to Adorno's ear, in the subjugation of the phonograph in the home, he turns to another, more immediate scene in "the prehistory of subjectivity," one more

---

20 Ibid., p. 43. Thanks to John Mowitt for observing that in the preface to the new edition of 1969, Adorno and Horkheimer recall the conjoining of their intellects in each sentence as together they dictated the manuscript to Gretel Adorno, their "precious helper."

21 See Calvin Thomas, "A Knowledge that would not be Power: Adorno, Nostalgia, and the Historicity of the Musical Subject," *New German Critique* 48 (Fall 1989), 155–75.

22 Theodor Adorno, *Aesthetic Theory*, trans. C. Lenhardt (London and Boston, Melbourne and Henley: Routledge and Kegan Paul, 1984), pp. 453, 455.

23 Ibid., p. 89.

24 Ibid., p. 163.

25 See the excellent analysis by John Mowitt, "The Sound of Music in the Era of its Electronic Reproducibility," in Richard Leppert and Susan McClary, eds., *Music and Society* (Cambridge University Press, 1987), pp. 173–97.

ontogenetical than phylogenetical. Despite the phonograph's reduced, domesticated circumstances, he accords it a profound power. He speculates on its psychosocial origins, and, in just a few lines, presents a proto-Lacanian schema of identity formation. It has a "mirror function" that stimulates in the listener a "primordial affect,"

which perhaps even gave rise to the gramophone in the first place. What the gramophone listener actually wants to hear is himself, and the artist merely offers him a substitute for the sounding image of his own person, which he would like to safeguard as a possession.[26]

What remains of the apparatus as it becomes transparent is an "acoustic mirror" which reflects an ever fuller, more authentic sound to and of the human subject, as a fantasy substitute for himself (and, for Adorno, as we will see, this figure is Caruso). Kaja Silverman, who has lent the term "acoustic mirror" its currency, borrows it from Guy Rosolato.[27] He grounds it ontologically, using it to refer to the phenomenon whereby one listens to oneself at the same time as one speaks. The reflective relation occurs in the gap of undecidability which the voice rends in the relations of inside/outside, subject/object. When Silverman maps her analysis onto Rosolato's analysis, arguing that gender gets mapped across those distinctions, gender too becomes grounded ontologically, and the question of the inhuman, and of the apparatus, drops from view, even as it silently "writes" itself on the bodies in question. Adorno emphasizes that "the mirror function of the gramophone arises out of its technology."[28] This distinction is important, because it grounds the social production of gender in social and historical processes, and because it acknowledges the inhuman as such, and therefore acknowledges relations of domination that are related to, but irreducible to, those of gender relations.

Again anticipating the psychoanalytic paradigm, Adorno proceeds to introduce the question of sexual difference. I quote the paragraph in full:

Male voices can be reproduced better than female voices. The female voice easily sounds shrill – but not because the gramophone is incapable of conveying high tones, as is demonstrated by its adequate reproduction of the flute. Rather, in order to become unfettered, the female voice requires the physical appearance of the body that carries it. But it is just this body that the gramophone eliminates, thereby giving every female voice a sound that is needy and incomplete. Only there where the body itself resonates, where the self to which the gramophone refers is identical with its sound, only there does the gramophone have its legitimate realm of validity: thus Caruso's uncontested dominance.

---

[26] Adorno, "Curves," 54.

[27] Kaja Silverman, *The Acoustic Mirror: The Female voice in Psychoanalysis and Cinema* (Bloomington: Indiana University Press, 1988), pp. 79–80.

[28] Adorno, "Curves," 54.

Wherever sound is separated from the body – as with instruments – or wherever it requires the body as complement – as is the case with the female voice – gramophonic reproduction becomes problematic.[29]

The tone is that of simple common sense: the female voice demands the presence of the female body, without which, paradoxically, it is fettered. There appears to be no male body at all, or if there is, it is identical to the body of the apparatus. Perhaps it is lashed to it, lashed to the mast of the stylus which traces the curves of the whirlpool that disappears into the center of the record. *Das grammophon,* a neuter noun, becomes a male body, a body which the gramophonic voice cannot require as a complement because the gramophone is already identical to it. As an instrument, separated from that body and singing like a woman, it becomes problematic.

This is really a very strange argument. At first glance it appears to be simply sexist. Adorno clearly privileges the male voice vis-à-vis the new technology, and to that extent there is nothing strange about it: many of the people who argued about these matters agreed that women's voices generally were unfit for reproduction. Amy Lawrence outlines the forms these assertions typically took: the woman's voice is "naturally" too small and soft; its higher frequencies translate poorly into electrical impulses; and there were reasons that amounted to what Lawrence calls a "'cultural distaste' for women's voices."[30] (None of this logic prevented the employment of female telephone operators.) However, it is important to notice that Adorno in no way invokes any of these arguments. His insistence that the woman's voice remain embodied does not rest upon an acoustical or an aesthetic claim. Women technically have access to the realm of artistic transcendence, "to unfetteredness," as long as they keep a human voice together with a human body as they sing.

This passage invites rebuke by two prevailing feminist critical paradigms. On the one hand, we can interpret it in the terms of de Beauvoir, as a presentation of the gendering of immanence and transcendence, the woman confined to the physical body and the man "free," his transcendence guaranteed by all the centuries of the disembodied phallic voice – of God, Reason, State, Corporation – and by her embodied immanence. The problem with this model, however, is that it presents itself as transcendent to history. What, in these terms, are we to do with the strange new body of the phonograph, which – as an object capable of singing like a man or a woman, or like something inhuman – threatens a pre- ndifferentiation of the sexes, a neutering, or a mix?

ho and Narcissus: Women's Voices in Classical Hollywood Cinema ngeles: University of California Press, 1991), pp. 29–32.

Further, if along these lines we charge Adorno with sexism, then what is the political demand associated with this charge? Equal phonographic reproducibility?

On the other hand, there is a psychoanalytic feminist model of the sort elaborated by Kaja Silverman in *The Acoustic Mirror*. Undeniably, Adorno's is a discourse of loss, which the psychoanalytic critic would term castration. Adorno, faced with the anxiety of castration through the disembodiment of the voice, anchors his thinking in an appeal to female corporeality, demanding that woman stand in as the bearer of his lack. But are we then to read the expression of the problem of the woman's voice in Adorno's text as Adorno's problem – do we psychoanalyze him, seizing the symptomatic thread which unravels the work? Again, to what end? Furthermore, feminist psychoanalytic criticism itself seems ill-equipped to encounter this other reproductive body – not of the mother but of the phonograph, productive of another uncanniness – without subsuming it into the binary paradigm of gender.

How, without Lacan, without the Mother, does Adorno arrive at his formulation of the acoustic mirror? Via the Radio Corporation of America (RCA) logo, "His Master's Voice," the image of Nipper the dog listening to the phonograph, which, Adorno points out, is the last legible image on the surface of the disc, and "the right emblem for the primordial affect the gramophone stimulated." Adorno says no more about Nipper, but the image is suggestive.[31] The listener sees an image of himself, but he has become a dog – another self-identical, albeit inhuman, body stands in for him. The beast, like the machine, is silent, the paragon of domestication. "Man's best friend" listens attentively for his master's voice, and comes when Caruso calls. Dr. Garbit, a doctor of medicine and philosophy whose tribute to Edison I quoted earlier, writing well before Nipper, warns of the indiscriminate mimetic capability of the phonograph: "It will whistle, sneeze, cough, sigh, echo or rather duplicate the agonized yelp of the unfortunate cur outside."[32]

Nipper represents the obedient watchdog protecting the disembodied voice of domination, as much as what threatens that: the work of Circe – "that divinity of reversion to the animal," who turns men into pigs and dogs, who told Odysseus how to survive the Sirens' songs.[33] In the analysis of Adorno and Horkheimer:

Circe's call-sign is ambiguity; she appears first as corrupter and then as helper. Ambiguity is already a mark of her lineage, for she is the daughter of Helios and the granddaughter of Oceanos. The elements of fire and water are undivided in her, and it is this nondifferentiation, as opposed to the primacy of a definite aspect of nature (whether matriarchal or patriarchal) which constitutes the

[31] Adorno, "Curves," 54.
[32] Garbit, *The Phonograph*, p. 9.
[33] Adorno and Horkheimer, *Dialectic of Enlightenment*, p. 33.

nature of promiscuity . . . The enchanted men behave like the wild animals who hear Orpheus playing.[34]

The problem seems to be not so much one of an originary encounter with woman as one of an originary confusion, ambiguity, undividedness. Adorno and Horkheimer understand that Circe is not a figure of the transcendental feminine: they position her, "made the prototype of the courtesan," amongst women, in a division of feminine labor that enables the hero to survive.

Adorno appeals to woman elsewhere. He might have written with Nietzsche: "Women and their action at a distance: Do I still have ears? Am I all ears and nothing else? Here I stand in the flaming surf whose white tongues are licking at my feet; from all sides I hear howling, threats, screaming, roaring coming at me . . . . It seems as if the noise here had led me into fantasies. All great noise leads us to move happiness into some quiet distance."[35] Woman, her silence ensured by her distance, floats by the hysterical man as a ghostly, beautiful sailboat. In a collection of aphorisms and fragments written during the Second World War, better accustomed to noise perhaps, and certainly to the disembodied voices of women, Adorno had this fantasy:

The sound of any woman's voice on the telephone tells us whether the speaker is attractive. It reflects back as self-confidence, natural ease and self-attention all the desirous and admiring glances she has ever received. It expresses the double meaning of graciousness: gratitude and grace. The ear perceives what is for the eye, because both live on in the experience of a single beauty. It is recognized on first hearing: a familiar quotation from a book never read.[36]

In any woman's disembodied voice one sees immediately a reflection of one's own self-desiring glance – or not. One bestows upon oneself a self-benediction, and guarantees self-presence from afar, even as, by authorizing that supervision, unwittingly one loses oneself. The redoubling provides an experience of the singular and the originary, a vision of one's unified body. But that body is gazed upon by a single Cyclopean eye: one that never reads the books, and through a single hearing makes all sorts of mistakes.

III: Sirens

Fredric Jameson writes that Adorno still worked on the "old-fashioned problem" of freedom, and points toward Adorno's discussion of the

---

[34] Ibid., pp. 69–70.

[35] Friedrich Nietzsche, *The Gay Science*, trans. Walter Kaufman (New York: Vintage Books, 1974), p. 123.

[36] Theodor Adorno, *Minima Moralia: Reflections from Damaged Life*, trans. E. F. N. Jephcott (London and New York: Verso, 1974), p. 111.

old-fashioned in a late fragment by Adorno entitled "Excavation."[37] I will quote from this fragment at some length, for several reasons: it gives us a sense of Adorno's thinking on "the woman question," and it offers a notion of hysteria which returns us to the question of artistic expression as the reified crying of things.

Where reasonable people are in agreement over the unreasonable behavior of others, we can always be sure to find something unresolved that has been deferred, painful scars. This is how things stand with the question of the condition of women. Through the distortion of the "masculine" liberal competitive economy, through the participation of women in salaried employment, where they have as much or as little independence as men, through the stripping away of the magic aura of the family and the relaxation of sexual taboos, the problem is indeed, on the surface, no longer "acute." Yet, equally the continued existence of traditional society has warped the emancipation of women. Few things are as symptomatic of the decay of the workers' movement as its failure to notice this. The admittance of women to every conceivable supervised activity conceals continuing dehumanization . . . We should think not only of their miserable working-day, and of their home-life senselessly clinging to self-contained conditions of domestic labor in the midst of an industrial world, but also of themselves . . . Most of the women who had gained some standing in bourgeois society were ready to turn and rend their hysterical sisters who undertook, in their stead, the hopeless attempt to break out of the social prison which so emphatically turned its four walls to them all. Their granddaughters, however, would smile indulgently over these hysterics, without even feeling implicated, and hand them over to the benevolent treatment of social welfare. The hysteric who wanted the miraculous has thus given way to the furiously efficient imbecile who cannot wait for the triumph of doom. – But perhaps this is the way of all outdatedness. It is not to be explained by mere temporal distance, but by the verdict of history. Its expression in things is the shame that overcomes the descendant in the face of an earlier possibility that he [sic] has neglected to bring to fruition.[38]

The hysterical protest, an example of which we saw at the telephone company, is a thing of the past. However, for Adorno, its expression remains in things as fossils to be excavated. In the documents which testify to what Jacques Attali has called "the emplacement of recording" – in the telephone operators, the reporter, the doctor, Adorno, and Nietzsche – there appear signs of hysteria. These symptoms may be read as indices, fossils, old things that give the lie to the "freedom" offered by the culture industry. These are the voices of the dead promised by the phonograph.

Odysseus, listening bodiless, lashed to the mast, provides us with a prototype of Adorno on the phonograph. It is instructive, therefore, to

---

37 Fredric Jameson, *Late Marxism: Adorno, or, The Persistence of the Dialectic* (London and New York: Verso, 1990), p. 77.
38 Adorno, *Minima Moralia*, pp. 92–93.

refer to an earlier episode in Book 8 of the *Odyssey*, in which the hero encounters song embodied. In this episode, Odysseus, nameless, and powerless to forget the past, himself embodies the hysterical protest, and relives the past in positions other than that of conquering hero, becoming a woman, and a slave. Alarmingly, this episode "returns" us to the scene of the telephone's central exchange, to the hysterical call girls. This time the hysteric is the shocked wanderer himself, who needs to "have a good cry, and come back feeling better." Odysseus is the anonymous shipwrecked guest of a king Alkínoös, who orders the preparation of ship and crew for an unknown hero's voyage home. He orders a feast, and summons a minstrel, whom Homer describes with a self-reflective gesture: "that man of song whom the Muse cherished; / by her gift he knew the good of life, and evil / for she who lent him sweetness made him blind."[39] At ease in a world of disembodied voices – or where the spectacle of the body does not constitute embodiment – the harper sings history.

The harper's song conveys the Trojan war; the past returns and "he of many wiles" breaks down, weeping into the privacy of his cloak. His host, observing him, orders an intermission, a break: a competitive sporting event at which the hero distinguishes himself from the others, reconstituting his unestablished and failing identity.

Dinner and the song resume – other histories, and, for a time, he enjoys himself. Then, with the song of the Trojan horse, and the fall of Troy, he succumbs to post-traumatic stress, to all-out hysteria:

> And Odysseus
> let the bright molten tears run down his cheeks,
> weeping the way a wife mourns for her lord
> on the lost field where he has gone down fighting
> the day of wrath that came upon his children.
> At the sight of the man panting and dying there,
> she slips down to enfold him, crying out;
> then feels the spears, prodding her back and shoulders,
> and goes bound into slavery and grief.
> Piteous weeping wears away her cheeks:
> But no more piteous than Odysseus' tears,
> Cloaked as they were now, from the company.
> Only Alkínoös, at his elbow, knew –
> hearing the low sob in the man's breathing –
> and when he knew, he spoke:
> ... "Break off the song!"   (8.521–37, pp. 140–41)

---

[39] Homer, *Odyssey* (8.62–65), trans. Robert Fitzgerald (New York: Anchor Books, 1963), p. 127. All quotations in the text are taken from this translation.

The king commands the guest to reveal his name, and pronounce what in performance sounds like both his name, Odysseus, and also Udeis, or "nobody." The musical indeterminacy of a pun, a slippage between signifier and signified, will provide him with the loophole he needs to survive.

Before he hears the Sirens' song again, Odysseus will employ the attentions of a call girl, Circe, and will learn to profit by deploying her knowledge. "The prophecies of the disempowered enchantress concerning the Sirens as well as Scylla and Charybdis indeed ultimately serve only masculine self-preservation."[40] He will learn how not to lose himself in hysterical remembrance. For Odysseus, the power of the Sirens' song lies not in its seductive beauty as such. The appellation "Siren," in its contemporary usage, designates the dangerous, beautiful, seductive *femme fatale* – the fearful and desiring projections of a disembodied aesthetics. What this sense of "Siren" has forgotten entirely is the historical power of the Sirens. Like the harper, they have an uncanny ability to raise the voices of the dead, to bring the past to life in the present. They sing to Odysseus of the Trojan war, threatening him with the subjective dissolution that he experienced in the presence of the harper's song. According to Adorno and Horkheimer:

Their allurement is that of losing oneself in the past . . . The compulsion to rescue what is gone as what is living instead of using it as the material of progress was appeased only in art, to which history itself appertains as a presentation of past life. So long as art declines to pass as cognition and is thus separated from practice, social practice tolerates it as it tolerates pleasure. But the Sirens' song has not yet been rendered powerless by reduction to the condition of art. They know "everything that ever happened on this so fruitful earth," including the events in which Odysseus himself took part.[41]

What is at issue in the Sirens' song is not immediately a question of gender. More significant is the extent to which the Sirens are not even human – depicted as half bird, half woman. The curves of the needle, which seemed to lead to the figure of woman, instead have led us to the question of music before gender. The voice, as posed in Adorno's texts, is not an inherently human problematic. Rather, the voice is the site at which, in the distinction between the cry and the song, the human and the inhuman are differentiated in a state of perennial irresolution.

In a discussion of the cognitive character of music, Adorno places the origins of music in tears – tears that are not properly subjective:

The beginning of music . . . extends beyond the realm of intention – the realm of meaning and subjectivity. The origin is gesticulative in nature and closely related to the origin of tears. It is the gesture of release . . . Music and tears

[40] Adorno and Horkheimer, *Dialectic of Enlightenment*, p. 73.
[41] Ibid., pp. 32–33.

134

open the lips and set the arrested human being free . . . The human being who surrenders himself to tears and to a music which no longer resembles him in any way permits that current of which he is not part and which lies behind the dam restraining the world of phenomena to flow back into itself. In weeping and in singing he enters into alienated reality.[42]

But boys – heroes – don't cry. As vulnerable to the Sirens' songs as he was to the harper's, Odysseus lashes his body to the apparatus, where ceasing to manifest its history it is lost, but preserved, fossilized. He listens, but cannot act: "The prisoner is present at a concert, an inactive eavesdropper like later concertgoers, and his spirited call for liberation fades like applause."[43]

[42] Theodor Adorno, *Philosophy of Modern Music*, trans. Anne Mitchell and Wesley Blomster (New York: Seabury Press, 1973), pp. 128–29.
[43] Adorno and Horkheimer, *Dialectic of Enlightenment*, p. 34.

PART III

Women artists: vocality and cultural authority

8

The diva doesn't die:
George Eliot's *Armgart*

REBECCA A. POPE

The strange thing about a singer's destiny is that you have to renounce everything for its sake, and then it's all over in a flash.

Soprano Lisa Della Casa[1]

Catherine Clément has suggested that nineteenth-century opera is a "spectacle thought up to adore, and also to kill, the feminine character."[2] If we see the woman who sings Carmen or Tosca, for example, as in some way participating in and collaborating with an art-form that rehearses and passes from one generation to another a masculinist gender code, then the large number of diva figures in nineteenth- and twentieth-century women's writing is at first glance surprising: the tradition stretches from, to name only a few, Eliot's Armgart and Sand's Consuelo to Cather's Thea Kronberg and the many divas in contemporary detective fiction by women.[3] Since so many operas depend on "the submission or death of the woman for the sake of narrative closure,"[4] and the women who play these roles, the prima donnas, are reputed to be rather deadly themselves – ruthlessly competitive, capriciously temperamental, extravagantly vain, and glamorously ornamental – the diva would seem a figure for the woman writer to avoid rather than privilege.

[1] Ethan Mordden, *Demented: The World of the Opera Diva* (New York: Franklin Watts, 1984), p. 90.

[2] Catherine Clément, *Opera, or the Undoing of Women*, trans. Betsy Wing (Minneapolis: University of Minnesota Press, 1988), p. 6.

[3] I have only named a few. For a survey of divas in texts by women and an examination of the issues and themes these characters call up, see Susan J. Leonardi, "To Have a Voice: The Politics of the Diva," *Perspectives* 13 (1987), 65–72. This essay is generated from research I am doing for a book on divas, real and fictional, which I am writing in collaboration with Susan Leonardi (working title the same as Leonardi's article, forthcoming Rutgers University Press).

[4] Susan McClary, "Foreword: The Undoing of Opera: Toward a Feminist Criticism of Music," in Clément, *Opera*, p. xvi.

The diva in women's texts, however, revises the representations of female singers we find in many texts by men and recoups for women themselves the woman who has, in every sense of the word, a "voice." Homer's Siren, figured as a monster – half bird and half woman – uses her voice to seduce and destroy men while, on the other hand, singing female muses like Wordsworth's solitary reaper are ultimately silenced. The reaper's inspiriting voice is lost in time and finally displaced by the male poet's text even as he memorializes it. More openly sinister is the fate of George Du Maurier's eponymous heroine Trilby, who becomes a great diva under the influence of the musician Svengali's mesmeric powers only to lose her voice after he dies. Even the stereotypical prima donna characterized above is, musicologist Susan McClary has argued, "a male-constructed fantasy image."[5] But most of the divas in women's texts are neither *femmes fatales* nor happy handmaidens to what is finally a male muse. They are more interested in music than marriage, and their voices are presented less as vehicles for seducing men than for empowering women – both themselves and other women.

The diva's "voice" in women's writing, then, is both a mode of and a metaphor for female empowerment in a culture that traditionally places women on the side of silence. Significantly, a recent study of women's intellectual development, *Women's Ways of Knowing*, observes that the metaphor women most often use to describe their epistemological growth and consequent coming to power is "gaining a voice."[6] It is in this context that women writers have placed their female singers and privileged the diva as the woman who has, preeminently and indisputably, gained a voice.[7] She garners the attention, admiration, and respect of the world with her singing voice, a voice which, importantly, men cannot reach, usurp, or displace. Moreover, thanks to this singing voice, she has a "voice" in the music she makes, in her own destiny, and in the larger world. A female success in a male realm, this privileged status gives her license to probe, revise, and even reject the traditional gender code.

George Eliot's Armgart is just such a figure and serves as an example of the tradition I have been sketching. This eponymous heroine of a verse drama written during a break in the composition of *Middlemarch* is renowned for her portrayal of Orpheus in Gluck's opera. At the height of her career she becomes ill, loses her singing voice, and thus gives up the stage and teaches singing to earn a living. The work has been neglected by critics, and most of the commentary that we do have reads it in the context of the novels, seeing Armgart as simply another of Eliot's egoists in need of chastening or as another of her angry and

---

5   McClary, "Foreword: The Undoing," p. ix.
6   Mary Belenky et al., *Women's Ways of Knowing* (New York: Basic Books, 1987).
7   Leonardi, "To Have a Voice," 66.

frustrated female artists.[8] While it is certainly necessary and revealing so to contextualize Armgart, to stop here leaves us with only part of the story and inhibits us from seeing the extent of her difference from other Eliot heroines and her revisionary force. Given Eliot's interest in and knowledge of music, our reading of the poem and the heroine remains incomplete until we take seriously Eliot's use of this specific opera, a very important one in the history of opera, which has, moreover, a specific and unusual performance history, a performance history especially important for tracing the progress of women's voices in opera.

Gluck is generally remembered as a reformer of eighteenth-century Italian opera, and his *Orpheus and Eurydice* is held up as a major step in the movement away from static conventionality and overelaborated virtuosity and toward a purer, simpler expression and greater fidelity to "dramatic truth." In its rejection of received conventions of form and its privileging of the archetypal poet/musician Orpheus, we begin to see the appropriateness of the references to *Orpheus* in a poem about a consummate vocal artist who refuses traditional social forms and conventional gender roles.

The performance history of *Orpheus* is revealing and relevant as well. Gluck set Calzabigi's libretto twice. The first version, in Italian, was written for the famous castrato Guadagni and premièred in Vienna in October 1762. Contemporary accounts of castrati voices describe them as brilliant, powerful, and ethereally superhuman, and thus, perhaps, the logic of Gluck's choice of a castrato Orpheus. Twelve years later the composer rearranged the work for the Paris Opera, this time using a French translation of the text and making numerous musical additions and changes, in particular rescoring Orpheus for tenor because the Paris Opera rarely used castrati. This change marked the turning point in the use of castrati to sing roles in the soprano and alto registers.[9] From the late eighteenth century on, the practice of castrating male singers steadily declined, and with this decline came the rise of the female singer, who

---

[8]   Among the critics who place Armgart in the context of female characters in the novels are: Sandra Gilbert and Susan Gubar, *The Madwoman in the Attic* (New Haven: Yale University Press, 1979); Kathleen Blake, "Armgart – George Eliot on the Woman Artist," *Victorian Poetry* 18 (1980), 75–80; and Marcia S. Midler, "George Eliot's Rebels: Portraits of the Artist as a Woman," *Women's Studies* 7 (1980), 97–108. K. M. Newton, in *George Eliot: Romantic Humanist* (Totowa, NJ: Barnes & Noble, 1981), places Armgart in the company of other Eliot egoists and pays little attention to gender issues in the poem. The only work I have found that attempts to read *Armgart* in the context of Gluck's opera is Mary Wilson Carpenter's *George Eliot and the Landscape of Time* (Chapel Hill: University of North Carolina Press, 1986), but Wilson's critical interests and investments are very different from my own. She, for example, does not push the intersections between the poem and the opera as far as I do, and she sees the gender issues in Eliot's text ultimately subsumed in more generally "humanist" ones.

[9]   Mordden, *Demented*, p. 19.

took over roles previously sung by men and ultimately made the upper registers her own.[10]

By the nineteenth century women were singing the castrato version of Orpheus, and George Eliot herself heard such a performance during a trip to the Continent in 1855. Johanna Wagner, niece of the composer, sang Orpheus, and Eliot described the production to Sara Hennel in a letter:

The scene in which Orpheus enters Tartarus, is met by the awful shades, and charms them into ecstatic admiration until they make way for him to pass on, is very fine. The voices – except in the choruses – are all women's voices, and there are only three characters – Orpheus, Amor [Cupid], and Euridice. One wonders that Pluto does not come as a Basso, and one would prefer Mercury as a tenor to Amor in the shape of an ugly German soprano – but Gluck willed it otherwise and the music is delightful . . . instead of letting it be a tragedy, Euridice is brought to life again and we end with another Ballet girl scene before Amor's temple.[11]

With this precedent of women singing the version originally written for castrato, in 1859, Berlioz, a great student and champion of Gluck's

10 Angus Heriot, in *The Castrati in Opera* (1956; reprinted London: Secker and Warburg, 1974), p. 9, asserts that the origins of the practice of castrating boy singers before their voices changed are "shrouded in mystery." Although castration was denounced by the Church, its ban on women singers in the Church and later, its ban, at least in parts of Italy, of women from the stage, indirectly encouraged the practice. From this vantage point, castration becomes the lengths to which patriarchy will go to sustain itself and to keep women out of public view. During the eighteenth century, Heriot maintains, castrati were the most popular and celebrated of all opera singers. They sang two sorts of roles, the "first man" roles – noble lovers, warriors, rulers – which exploited what contemporary accounts have described as the ethereal and "superhuman" quality of the castrato voice, and women's roles *en travesti*. Some castrati specialized in women's roles and even dressed as women off stage as well, and, conversely, some women passed themselves off as castrati and sang in public. The slippage and play between sex and gender (further complicated by the fact that these men were castrated and thus, in some eyes, not completely "men") which the cross-dressing castrati brings to the opera stage becomes an important feature of the art even after the decline of the castrati. Women, of course, took and still take some of these early "first man" parts, and operas written after women were allowed on stage, Strauss's *Der Rosenkavalier* for example, suggest with their trouser roles for women that the sexual ambiguity called up by the use of the castrati *en travesti* had a power and attraction that survived beyond the expedient of males playing female roles because women were banned from the stage. In *A Song of Love and Death: The Meaning of Opera* (New York: Poseidon Press, 1987), Peter Conrad argues that opera is an art devoted "to the definition and interchangeability of the sexes," and while the term "interchangeability" fails to capture all the complexities called up by these operatic gender-bendings and reversals, the cross-dressing motif in opera is certainly one of the vehicles through which opera displays, and perhaps critiques, cultural definitions of gender. For more on the history of castrati, see Heriot's *The Castrati in Opera*, and for cross-dressing in opera, see Will Crutchfield's "Giving Voice to Sexual Ambiguity," *New York Times* (March 31, 1985), 2.1.1.

11 George Eliot, *The George Eliot Letters*, ed. Gordon S. Haight (New Haven: Yale University Press, 1954), vol. II, p. 191.

music, took the French version for tenor and, with reference to the original version for castrato, reworked the opera and the role of Orpheus for the famous diva Pauline Viardot. The Berlioz–Viardot production of Gluck's *Orpheus* premièred in Paris to great acclaim and in 1860, ten years before the composition of *Armgart*, moved to Covent Garden. Dickens saw it in 1862 and Viardot's performance moved him to tears. The opera quickly became a Viardot vehicle, and she sang it across Europe. Although her repertoire of roles was wide – too wide for the health of her voice – she was, and remains, best known for her Orpheus.

Eliot and Viardot were friends, moving in many of the same artistic and intellectual circles. Indeed, Viardot occupied in the world of music a place parallel to Eliot's in the realm of letters. No mindless bird of song or stereotypical diva was Viardot.[12] Daughter of the famous tenor and voice teacher Manuel Garcia and younger sister of the renowned prima donna Maria Malibran, Viardot became a singer only after the tragic early death of her sister. She was an accomplished pianist – Liszt was one of her teachers – and composed as well. She arranged some of the piano music of her friend Chopin for voice, and after her retirement from the stage she had planned to write an opera, alas never completed, based on a libretto by George Sand.[13]

Accounts of Viardot and her performances repeatedly stress her intelligence, musicianship, discipline, and devotion to her art. Henry Chorley, the well known chronicler of the Victorian music scene, pronounced her a "consummate, devoted, and thoroughly-musical musician" and, after seeing her on stage, observed that her performance had "fire, courage, and accomplishment, without limit."[14] For Chorley, such artistry was all the more exceptional because her voice was uneven: "In spite of an art which has never (at so early an age) been exceeded in amount, it was to be felt, that Nature had given her a rebel to subdue, not a vassal to command, in her voice." Her remarkable voice was thus the product of a "despotic exercise of will" (vol. II, p. 49) in the service of thoughtful characterization. She was an acting singer who foreshadowed Callas, a performer with a limited instrument who used it

---

12 Most of the biographical information I present here can be found in the standard biography of Viardot by April Fitz-Lyon, *The Price of Genius* (New York: Appleton-Century, 1964). Generally, the material on Viardot's life in sources before Fitz-Lyon's book can be found there, and more recent, popular books on the diva, for example Rupert Christiansen's *Prima Donna* (London: Bodley Head, 1984), and Mordden's *Demented*, add little on Viardot that is new.

13 Or at least a manuscript for the proposed opera has never been found. Recently the manuscripts of Viardot's previously unknown voice transcriptions of twelve Chopin mazurkas with texts by poet Louis Pomey were unearthed in the British Library and Library of Congress by pianist Jerome Rose.

14 Henry Chorley, *Thirty Years' Musical Recollections* [1862], 2 vols. (New York: Da Capo Press, 1984), vol. II, pp. 46–47, 48. Subsequent quotations in the text are from this edition.

intelligently to achieve a stiking depth of characterization.[15] Moreover, she carried this devotion to playing her roles with accuracy and depth to degrees greater than any singer before her: she designed her own costumes and did research to insure their historical accuracy, for example, and she was one of the first divas to prepare a role by studying not just the music and libretto, but the opera's literary sources – in Shakespeare or Goethe, for instance – as well.

It is perhaps for her connections with the major writers of the age that Viardot is now best remembered in literary circles. She was George Sand's closest female friend, and Sand's novel *Consuelo* (1842), an account of a brilliant singer dedicated to her art with a missionary zeal, is a tribute to her. Viardot herself thought the novel so captured her ideals and temperament that she once told an acquaintance to read *Consuelo* if he wished to know her better.[16] Viardot was, in fact, so perfect an exemplar of Sand's notion of the great and committed artist that the novelist, hoping to protect her much younger friend from the wearying romantic entanglements to which she herself was prone, engineered her marriage to the stable and devotedly affectionate, but very much older, Louis Viardot.

The arrangement did not work out quite as Sand had planned. Turgenev fell in love with the married Viardot and remained so for the rest of his life. When not in Russia, he lived as near the Viardots as he could, and toward the end of his life actually moved in with them. She seems to have reciprocated his feelings, at least at times during her life, but also, according to the picture we see of her in April Fitz-Lyon's biography, seems generally to have kept this attachment, like all her attachments, second to her art. This willed refusal by a woman to subordinate art to love was, not surprisingly, misinterpreted in terms that cast her as a stereotypical prima donna who played men against each other and kept them on a string. Henry James, a regular at Viardot's musical gatherings while he lived in Paris, sums up the indictment against her:

I meant to add about poor Turngenieff that there [are] insuperable limits to seeing much of him, for the poor man is a slave – the slave of Mme. Viardot. She has made him her property, is excessively jealous, keeps him to herself etc. She, her husband, and her children (of one of whom T. is supposed to be the papa,) keep him as a sort of *vache à lait*, use him, spend his money etc. Such is the tale I am told[17]

James, ever astute, was quite correct to question the accuracy of these rumors.

15 Mordden, *Demented*, p. 59.
16 Fitz-Lyon, *The Price*, p. 281.
17 Henry James, *Letters*, ed. Leon Edel (Cambridge, MA: Harvard University Press, 1975), vol. II, p. 16.

It is, of course, Viardot's connection with Eliot – they were close enough for Viardot to visit the writer at home when Eliot was too depressed to leave the house – that most interests me here.[18] Rupert Christiansen writes that they socialized in Paris and London, which suggests that the two women had met before the Viardots, fleeing the Franco–Prussian war, took up residence in London in 1870, the year Eliot wrote *Armgart*.[19] If she did not personally know Viardot then, she would certainly have known her by reputation, and Lewes's letters provide evidence that they knew each other by 1871: he describes a lunch party hosted by Eliot and himself – the guests included Trollope, Turgenev and Viardot – at which Viardot "sang divinely and entranced everyone, some of them to positive tears."[20]

As I showed earlier, Eliot knew Gluck's *Orpheus* before it became a vehicle for Viardot, and she makes references to it in her fiction as early as 1857, in "Mr. Gilfil's Love Story." Her calling up of Gluck's opera again in *Armgart* requires us to take seriously the appearance of this particular opera with its particular performance history as we construct a reading of the poem. Moreover, as I suggested above, by 1870, when she wrote *Armgart*, Eliot could not have helped thinking of Viardot as she worked on this tale of a diva renowned for her Orpheus. Many of the divas in texts by women are inspired by historical singers – Consuelo by Viardot, Marcia Davenport's Lena Geyer by Alma Gluck, Willa Cather's Thea Kronberg by Olive Fremstad – and while I do not want to offer up Viardot as a transcendental signified here, I do want to begin the process of looking at the poem in its full operatic context.[21]

We first meet Armgart on her return from another triumphant performance of *Orpheus*. Like Viardot, Armgart is not a conventional beauty – "The women whispered, 'Not a pretty face,'" she says scornfully – thus her triumph is all the sweeter because it rests solely on the power and artistry of her singing and acting.[22] As the scenes with her suitor emphasize, marriage defines the lives and identities of most women in her culture, but Armgart finds her life in her voice. "What is my soul to me without the voice / That gave it freedom?" she asks, and after losing her voice she laments, "Oh, I had meaning once" (pp. 508, 495).

[18] Eliot, *Letters*, vol. IX, pp. 14–15.

[19] Rupert Christiansen, "George Eliot, *Armgart*, and the Victorian Prima Donna," *About the House* 7 (1986), 8–10. Also see note 21 below.

[20] Eliot, *Letters*, vol. V, pp. 143–44.

[21] Music writer Christiansen speculates that Armgart is modeled on Viardot in "George Eliot, *Armgart*, and the Victorian Prima Donna," a short article which has less to do with *Armgart* than its title might suggest. Christiansen is the only critic, musical or literary, I have found that so speculates. He finds the Viardot connection interesting, but not, as I do, necessary for a satisfying reading of *Armgart*.

[22] Page references to *Armgart* are from volume IX of *George Eliot's Works*, Warwick Edition (Edinburgh: William Blackwood and Sons, 1906). Later citations from *Daniel Deronda* are also from this edition of the *Works*.

Rebecca A. Pope

Awaiting her return are the nobleman Graf Dornberg and her cousin and companion Walpurga. In an exchange with Dornberg, whose repeated marriage proposals Armgart repeatedly rejects – they carry with them the expectation that she give up her career – the diva makes it clear that, for her, voice and gender are inseparable: "The great masters write / For *women's* voices, and great Music wants me!" she proclaims (p. 480, my italics), and she notes proudly,

> Men did not say, when I had sung last night,
> "'Twas good, nay, wonderful, considering
> She is a woman" – and then turn to add
> "Tenor or baritone had sung her songs
> Better of course; she's but a woman spoiled"
> (p. 478)

Armgart knows that she has a voice which, thanks to the waning of the castrati, men cannot duplicate or displace. To have such a voice, she implies, frees her from the strictures and demands of the traditional gender code. Further, the voice is a way of addressing and redressing patriarchal power, as Walpurga makes clear when she quotes her cousin to Dornberg:

> For herself
> She often wonders what her life had been
> Without that voice for channel to her soul.
> She says, it must have leaped through all her limbs –
> Made her a Maenad – made her snatch a brand
> And fire some forest, that her rage might mount
> In crashing roaring flames through half a land,
> Leaving her still and patient for a while.
> "Poor wretch!" she says of any murderess –
> "The world was cruel, and she could not sing:
> I carry my revenges in my throat;
> I love in singing and am loved again."
> (p. 457)

Armgart sees her voice as an empowering female difference in contention with patriarchy. From this vantage point, it is hardly surprising that when she loses it after an illness, she blames not the illness but the cure. The loss of her voice is a silencing of it by male medicine: "You have murdered it / Murdered my voice" she tells the doctor (p. 493). Later, she laments, "He cured me of my voice," as if having a voice is, from the masculinist perspective of her culture, a state of pathological defiance from which women must be saved (p. 498).

This use of voice as a mode of female redress can take the form of revising or supplementing the male-authored text.[23] Armgart repeatedly

---

[23] Leonardi, "To Have a Voice," 69.

figures her singing as a freewheeling flying and soaring, and one of the freedoms she appropriates for herself is the right to alter or supplement the text. In a moment which recalls Berlioz's complaints that in performance Viardot had altered words in the libretto and added roulades that he had not written into his rescoring of *Orpheus*, Armgart's singing teacher, Leo, complains that during a performance she had deliberately sung notes which "Gluck had not written, nor I taught" (p. 464). His insistence on fidelity to the score can be read as an attempt to keep the production – as opposed to the mere mimic performance – of art solely in male hands. His complaint, "I hate my phrases to be smothered o'er / With sauce of paraphrase, my sober tune / Made bass to rambling trebles" (p. 463) suggests as much. Armgart's response to his complaint is more a dismissal than denial; she will display her artistic vision and virtuosity. For Armgart, to have a voice is to have a say in production, to have the power to use the male text as, at least in part, a pretext for her own creative vision: "I gave that [the trill] up to you / To bite and growl at. Why, you said yourself, / Each time I sang it seemed new doors were oped" (pp. 466–67).[24]

All this should make the suitor Dornberg uneasy, but he persists in his suit. He is unsuccessful, first and foremost, because of Armgart's willed and single-minded dedication to her art: "I can live unmated, but not / Without the bliss of singing" (p. 488). In this refusal to divide herself and her energies – "I will live alone and pour my pain / With passion into music," she declares (p. 484) – Armgart recalls the dedication Sand so respected and admired in Viardot, who worked to extinguish all her passions save her passion for music because she believed that artistic achievement required that the artist become indifferent to all

---

[24] Mary Wilson Carpenter, in *Landscape of Time*, p. 169, argues that "by introducing a trill wholly for artistic embellishment, Armgart contravenes the artistic identity she claims to feel with [the reformer] Gluck and reveals both her ambition and her lack of artistic depth." Her line of argument echoes Leo's and neglects to account for the fact that Leo admits that her singing opens new doors, something mere "embellishment" generally doesn't do. Resonating in the background here is a movement away from florid operatic singing in the nineteenth and twentieth centuries. Mordden, in *Demented*, p. 44, argues that this fidelity to the written score is "counterfeit," that while composers banned "wholesale revision and rude improvisation . . . they were not composing for robots," and thus expected each singer to "inflect" the music according to her/his own "distinctions of voice and approach." Viardot herself was criticized for her florid singing in much the same terms Carpenter and Leo criticize Armgart, but she did have her defenders. In his discussion of the Viardot Orpheus, Chorley writes: "The torrents of *roulades*, the chains of notes, unmeaning in themselves, were flung out with such exactness, limitless volubility and majesty, so as to convert what is essentially a commonplace piece of parade, into one of those displays of passionate enthusiasm, to which nothing less florid could give scope. – As according relief and contrast, they are not merely pardonable – they are defensible; and thus, only to be despised by the indolence of the day, which, in obedience to false taste and narrow pedantry, has allowed one essential branch of art to fall into disuse' (Chorley, *Thirty Years'*, vol. II, p. 58).

save her/his art.[25] Thus Armgart declares, "I will not take for husband one who deems / The thing my soul acknowledges as good – / The thing I hold worth striving, suffering for, / To be a thing dispensed with easily" (pp. 484–85).

The overall effect of the exchanges with Dornberg is to suggest that Armgart has no intention of ever marrying. She never declares this outright, however, saying instead, "The man who marries me must wed my art – / Honour and cherish it, not tolerate" (p. 486). She knows full well that Dornberg, despite his sense of himself as liberal and progressive, is not such a man. For example, he too cavalierly and too patronizingly dismisses as "mere mood" Armgart's claim that she carries her revenges in her throat. He further declares that "too much ambition has unwomaned her," but even here he is smugly indulgent, confident that her "unwomanly" ambition is only a temporary state of defiance which marriage to him will cure (p. 458).

In a culture in which gender roles are rigid and ambition and "womanliness" are supposed to be mutually exclusive, Dornberg's charge is heavy with implications. Armgart knows what Eliot's later and better known diva, the Alcharisi in *Daniel Deronda*, openly articulates when she says, "Every woman is supposed to have the same set of motives [marriage and motherhood], or else to be a monster" (*Works*, vol. X, p. 345). But the Alcharisi goes further than Armgart does when she defends her abandonment of Deronda by saying, "you can never imagine what it is to have a man's force of genius in you, and yet to suffer slavery to being a girl" (vol. X, p. 349). Significantly, especially since the role that crowns her career is the trouser role of Orpheus, Armgart never figures herself, her voice, or her career in the masculine terms that the Alcharisi uses, terms which, no doubt, underlie Dornberg's charge of "unwomanliness." Armgart resists reifying the binary oppositions the traditional gender code depends upon and uses to keep women secondary.

For example, the singer repeatedly yokes together her voice and her gender, as if to forestall charges that by putting her art before the prescriptions of the gender code she will be seen as "monstrous" and "masculine."

> Yes I know
> The oft-taught Gospel: "Woman, thy desire
> Shall be that all superlatives on earth
> Belong to men, save the one highest kind –
> To be a mother. Thou shalt not desire
> To do aught best save pure subservience:
> Nature has willed it so!" O blessed Nature!
> Let her be arbitress; she gave me a voice

---

[25] Fitz-Lyon, *The Price*, pp. 321, 322.

> Such as she only gives a woman child,.
> Best of its kind, gave me ambition too.
>
> (pp. 477–78)

Armgart is quite deliberately picking up Dornberg's own terms here, for she later contends that male arguments to nature and biology are really ideology: "I am an artist by my birth – / by the same warrant that I am a woman: / . . . I need not crush myself within a mould / Of theory called Nature" (p. 480).

Within the context of these powerful assertions that to be woman and to be an artist are not mutually exclusive, how then are we to read the fact that Armgart gives voice to Orpheus, the figure who for Western culture allies the artistic with the male? What is the status of the Orpheus role in this work, given that years earlier Eliot had figured bad women's art as "an absurd exaggeration of the masculine style, like the swaggering gate of a bad actress in male attire"?[26] Eliot's choice of genre, an unusual one for her, and the operatic setting are critically helpful and suggestive here. The verse drama and theatrical setting both call up a thematics of "roles," and, following the arguments of Clément and Conrad, the operatic context suggests, in addition, issues of gender. Finally, the performance history of the specific opera embedded here, Gluck's *Orpheus and Eurydice*, calls up as well the issue of the relations between (gender) roles and biological sex. Thus we might be tempted to argue that because Armgart's identification with Orpheus is so complete – "Orpheus was Armgart, Armgart Orpheus," Leo marvels – she is, despite her rhetoric, masculinized (p. 464). Or, we might argue that by playing the manly part on stage, Armgart experiences not maleness (it is significant that we never see her in male attire), but the freedom, power, independence, and artistic creativity traditionally associated with the male role.

But the history of Gluck's *Orpheus*, as I suggested above, is one of gender reversal and slippage, and this, coupled with the poem's emphasis on the female voice, reminds us that Armgart consistently associates this very freedom, independence and power not with the masculine role, but with her female voice. A woman acting the manly part suggests the extent to which gender is a role, a "performance." Eliot's two divas know that this is especially true for women. Speaking of her years as a wife, Deronda's mother says, "I acted that part" (*Works*, vol. X, p. 362), and after losing her singing voice Armgart laments that she is "Prisoned now – / Prisoned in all the petty mimicries / Called women's knowledge, that will fit the world / As doll-clothes fit a man" (vol. IX, pp. 508–9). Gender roles are costumes for Armgart. Given the

---

[26] George Eliot, *The Essays of George Eliot*, ed. Thomas Pinney (New York: Columbia University Press, 1963), p. 53.

performance history of Gluck's opera we can push even further. The fact that the opera was a place where a female voice had replaced a male's and where a male's could never again displace a female's could not have been lost on Eliot. Moreover, thanks to Viardot and the other female Orpheuses before her, in Gluck's opera Eliot also found a tradition that allied women with the most powerful and moving art, art so powerful that it could "force hell to grant what love did seek." When we trace back the series of gender-bendings and reversals in the history of the operatic Orpheus, then, what may have appealed to Eliot is this: from the perspective of a nineteenth-century audience the figure of the first artist was always already in some sense female. (The image of Orpheus on the stage is, after all, a woman pretending to be a man who wears a tunic, a skirt.)[27]

Like Viardot, who sang roles out of her range and thereby prematurely ruined her voice, Armgart loses her voice in her prime and at the close of the drama is reduced to the prospect of being an unwed voice teacher in a provincial town. Given Armgart's long confrontation with Walpurga, in which Walpurga accuses the singer of blind egoism, we may be tempted to read Armgart's illness as a punishment for her aspirations to renown and for her refusal to renounce the rages in her throat. Such a reading has the appeal of providing a thread with which to seam the drama into the fabric of Eliot's fiction. It neglects, however, a subtle difference between Armgart's fate and that of so many other Eliot heroines: the Armgart we see at the close is chastened, but she is neither dead nor dependent nor, as the Alcharisi is, desiccated and bitter. Unlike Dinah Morris, she is not completely silenced. Unlike Deronda's mother, she is not driven to marriage by the prospect of artistic failure or decline: "I will not be / A pensioner in marriage," Armgart declares (p. 502). As a voice teacher, an occupation Viardot herself took up after she retired from the opera stage in the 1860s, Armgart still has a part, albeit a smaller and mediated one, in the production of art, and she still has the freedom and independence she has always associated with her female voice.

If I see this end as less punishing and/or tragic than other critics have, I appeal once again to Eliot's embedding of Gluck's *Orpheus and Eurydice*, especially its ending, for support. Monteverdi's operatic version of the Orpheus legend follows the traditional tale: the singer looks back and loses his Eurydice once again to the underworld. In Haydn's *Orfeo ed Euridice* (1791), Orpheus not only loses Eurydice, but is torn to

---

27 Although they differ in detail and motivation, cross-dressing motifs appear in a significant number of women's texts about female singers. For example, Sand's *Consuelo* dresses in boy's clothes to protect herself while travelling across Europe. Away from the stage and off in the country, both Cather's Thea (*The Song of the Lark*) and Sarton's Anna (*Anger*) adopt a style of dress described as masculine.

of the "straight geometric line," plays straight man to Louise Colet's womanly meanders, striving to contain lyricism's universal streaming by correcting Colet's bodily text and rewriting her verses.[1] As poor style comes to be embodied by Louise Colet's femaleness, and pure style by his own manhood, Flaubert tries singlehandedly to stop the overflow of Colet's feminine literary sensibilities by recommending alterations of her female physiology. The current of invectives reaches flood level when Flaubert reads *La Servante*: "Aren't you aware of how everything is being dissolved now, by a *letting go*, by all that is wet, by tears, by chattering, by milk. Contemporary literature is drowning in menstrual flow" (*Correspondance*, vol. II, p. 508). Through a metonymic collapse of writer and text, woman and writing, the writing itself becomes that ill-wrought urn, that leaking vessel to which women, particularly hysterics, are more ordinarily compared. Woman's writing (and by extension, womanlike writing), by implication the hysteric's text, becomes the hysterical text: an unshaped, spontaneous, gushing form of expression associated with a weeping, singing, babbling, corporeal voice.

There is no record of Colet's reponse to Flaubert's renovations of her body and text. All but a token few of her letters have disappeared. However, during the period Colet served as metaphor to Flaubert, she was writing, in *La Servante* – which can be read as an open letter to Flaubert – about women's ways of reading, writing, and negotiating reappropriation of their texts and reformulation of their voices.

As I read *La Servante*, following Colet's exploration of a woman's efforts to chart a passage through gendered conventions of plot, language, myth, and voice, to an open space outside – a blank page, as it were – I will come to focus on her confrontation with models of voice. In the course of my own text, again following Colet's, the figurative sense of voice as style, subjectivity, perspective, individuality – the textual voice, in the context of writing – slides into a more particular, literal sense of voice as corporeal: as the body's text. I insist on the textual element in reference to Colet's reconstruction of embodied voice, because her response to Flaubert's construction of feminine writing voice as uncontrolled corporeal force works to resituate this voice "between body and language," to cite Guy Rosolato's definition of human vocality.[2] Where Flaubert represents the writer's creativity in

---

[1] Gustave Flaubert, *Correspondance*, ed. Jean Bruneau, 3 vols. (Paris: Gallimard, 1973–91), vol. I, p. 40. All translations from the *Correspondance* are mine; subsequent references appear in my text. A longer version of this essay appears in Janet Beizer, *Ventriloquized Bodies: Narratives of Hysteria in Nineteenth-Century France*, copyright 1994 by Cornell University, and is used by permission of the publisher, Cornell University Press, Ithaca, New York.

[2] Guy Rosolato, "La Voix: entre corps et langage," *Revue française de psychanalyse* 38, 1 (1974), 75–94.

terms of bodily flow (controlled and measured, in the masculine form; unregulated and unrestrained in the feminine), Colet prefers metaphors of voice through which she challenges cultural models of feminine expression as unformed and freeflowing, linking creativity not only to the body but to the mind, and to the retelling of experience.

I: Reconstructing plot

The protagonist of *La Servante*, a young girl of humble birth, Mariette, one day finds a little red book – red like an apple of knowledge set temptingly in her path – in the garden of the château belonging to the Marquise for whom she works. The book that unbinds Mariette's desire (and to which the narrator attributes her fall) is not just any book, but the story of her life written before the fact. Captivated by this literary mirror, Mariette stops and reads her story, which entails loving a poet and dying in her prime.

A plot template is established in the first five pages of *La Servante*, in the form of the embedded novel *Mariette*. The remaining forty-odd pages of the text are devoted to testing the hegemony of this template: is Mariette condemned to repeat *Mariette*, to read and reread her story *en abyme*? To what extent can a woman whose life appears before her as a man's completed novel go on to change the plot?

Let us begin by flipping back to the garden of the opening pages of *La Servante*, to examine the forbidden fruit, the novel we have already paged through with Mariette. Given the length of the episode, the fetishistic detailing of the book as physical object lying "half open" – *entr'ouvert*, as if flashing its contents – and the narrative insistence on its seductive power, it is surprising to note how little we are told about the plot of *Mariette*, despite its centrality within the plot of *La Servante*. We know of only three actions that form the plot of *Mariette*: the heroine loves, is loved, and dies when she is twenty.

Mariette is framed as a citation of the limited plot functions available to women within the dominant narrative tradition – devotion to a man, and death – and, as such, is an Ur-text against which the framing text will be played out.[3] Through Mariette's reading and living of the novel she discovers, Colet anticipates Carolyn Heilbrun's perception that "We can only retell and live by the stories we have read or heard."[4] In

---

[3] On the limited narratives available to women, see Nancy K. Miller, *The Heroine's Text* (New York: Columbia University Press, 1980), p. 82; Carolyn Heilbrun, "What was Penelope Unweaving?" in *Hamlet's Mother and Other Women* (New York: Columbia University Press, 1990), pp. 103–11; Susan McClary, *Feminine Endings: Music, Gender, and Sexuality* (Minneapolis: University of Minnesota Press, 1991), p. 15; Catherine Clément, *Opera, or the Undoing of Women*, trans. Betsy Wing (Minneapolis: University of Minnesota Press, 1988), p. xi.

[4] Carolyn Heilbrun, *Writing a Woman's Life* (New York: Norton, 1984), p. 37.

the gap she introduces between *Mariette* and Mariette's dismal but critically divergent life story in *La Servante*, and in a second breach she opens between Mariette's voice and the narrator's voice, Colet strategically demonstrates both the difficulty of revising time-honored stories, and the urgency for doing so. The heroine of *La Servante* ostensibly complies with the pre-ordained love plot, and foils the death plot; however, in so doing, she complicates both.

After the fall comes greater temptation. Novel-reading opens loftier horizons: Mariette sets off for Paris as maid to the Marquise, whose brother Lionel, author of *Mariette* and object of her infatuation, is fortuitously ailing. Once Mariette has nursed him back to health, his professed love gives way to domination, and her status as lover and would-be writer is redefined as abused servant. When he abandons her, Mariette attempts suicide, but is rescued from a watery death in the Seine by her disdained suitor, the honest but oafish miller, Julien. After a brief (but interminably boring) rest cure in the country amidst his thriving family, she returns to Paris where by dint of two years of hard domestic labor, she purchases her independence, a *chambre de bonne*, and a bookshelf. A fatal encounter with Lionel leads to a renewed liaison and continued misery, until, victim of his own dissolute tendencies and a malady I take to be tuberculosis, he marries Mariette on his deathbed, and expires. Then there is a lacuna in the text. The next section is situated at the Salpêtrière Hospital in the midst of a city of madwomen, one of whom is Mariette. We are not told what precipitated her madness. The text ends with Mariette clinging to a tree that she would climb, we are told, were it not for her straitjacket.

There are several differences in the fate of the two Mariettes, the most obvious one being the iconoclastic survival of the diegetic Mariette at the narrative's end. Despite the apparent similarity of her love plot to the model plot represented by the metadiegetic Mariette (she loves, she marries), the tone and the structuring of this plot call for a different reading.

Colet frequently uses a strategy whereby sympathy is elicited for Mariette through narrative identification with her point of view, which is withdrawn whenever her character is too submissive, too complicitous with her ill treatment. This is one way of juggling irreconcilable subject positions: Colet wants to recount, from a feminine subject position, what it is like for a woman to live out the plots written for her by men, but if she carries through to the traditional endpoint without a twist, to show how well women have learned these plots, she ends up replicating them.

The death plot continues throughout the narrative to divide Mariette and the narrator; it creates an internal struggle for control that no doubt reflects unresolved narrative ambivalence. Although *La Servante* successfully resists Mariette's death, it is not for lack of a death wish on her part. We see her on three separate occasions leaning over parapets, lingering longingly at the river's edge, as if teasing, defying the narrator; on the second of these occasions, she leaps, only to be saved from drowning by a narrator determined not to give in to this plot, even if she is tempted to play with it.

By the time Mariette has been plucked out of the Seine and married to a corpse, she has been essentially disengaged from the conventions of female plot. Denied death, widowed without having known marriage, she has bypassed narrative convention; she has outlived her plot. She is left in a literal no man's land outside plot, outside language: it is the women's hospital called the Salpêtrière. There is a third alternative to female death and female submission: it is madness. But whereas death and marriage bring about narrative resolution, madness is a gaping space, a yawning question. The textual blank separating Mariette's marriage to Lionel and his death, from the Salpêtrière scenes, corresponds to the lacuna that is madness. The text does not name the cause of Mariette's folly; it simply moves into it.

Though female madness has been seen by some as woman's revolt against patriarchy, I do not want to champion Mariette's case as an overcoming of constraints or a celebration of the instinctual.[5] It is clear, in the terms of the present context, that madness is what is in excess of plot: it is the price exacted for living outside plot. It is less a sign of successful revolt than a symptom of the ills incurred for venturing into a region beyond or between cultural codes. Such a region is reached in *La Servante* by means of a mythic journey into language.

II: Reinventing language

What I have been calling the madness plot in *La Servante* is named for its endpoint; however, its evolution can be traced throughout the narrative as a mythological voyage into language and out again on the far side. The saga of Mariette is recounted in terms of a gendered passage from country to city, nature to culture, mother to father, concrete to abstract, unity to separation, imaginary to symbolic, voice to book. We will see dramatized here – but revised – a gendered myth of language acquisition that has changed little from the fiction of Colet's era to the theory of our own. Given that Colet writes from the paradoxical position of a woman writing about a woman striving to write in an order in which woman and writing are incompatible categories, revision is inevitable, but should not be construed as deconstruction. As Colet shuttles her character between a presymbolic language represented as natural,

---

5 See Hélène Cixous and Catherine Clément, *La Jeune Née* (Paris: Union Générale d'Edition, 1975) for a debate on the hysteric as heroine/victim.

material, fluid, embodied, and wordless, and a symbolic language represented as cultural, abstract, preinscribed, cerebral, and articulate, she reproduces conventional dualistic gender codes even as she valorizes them differently.

Mariette's trajectory in language bears the shape of a revisionary family romance. She moves from an initial mother-identified state of preverbal communion with nature to a liminal ground of literary aspirations that can begin to be realized only upon the death of her mother. At that point, reborn in an aristocratic milieu (ironically as servant), she enters the realm of symbolic language under the illusory patronage of the lover who is author of her identity if not her days. However, she can neither fully accede to the symbolic nor re-enter the repudiated presymbolic domain, and, caught between the two but belonging to neither, she falls out of language into madness. Let us review this itinerary.

For the child Mariette growing up in the provincial countryside, the world is split into realities of mother and fantasies of otherness, the other world associated with reading, education, and escape to Paris. With remarkable consistency, Mariette represents her mother as the obstacle to the larger world of Paris and books. She wistfully responds to her employer's invitation to serve in Paris: "Oh! as for me, that is my dearest wish / But my mother is ill, she would die without me."[6] Soon afterward, the mother's muffled moans and silent suffering yield to the printed word, when a letter coinciding with her death summons Mariette to serve the Marquise in Paris.

As I follow Mariette's passage to a Paris represented by books, writing, artful language and hypocrisy, I want to emphasize Colet's apposition of that sphere to the more dominant maternal voices of Mariette's childhood; I want also to suggest that these two apposed spheres anticipate the domains more recently theorized as "imaginary" and "symbolic" in Lacan's terms, and "semiotic" and "symbolic" in Kristeva's. I will use the terms "presymbolic" and "symbolic" to avoid specifically aligning Colet's myth with Lacan or Kristeva (that is, with a critical discourse it can only anticipate).

Mariette's "mother tongue" – the generally wordless, sometimes silent but always transparent voice of nature – described as song, is set against whispering breezes and singing birds; it is itself compared to the babbling of finches. This wordless communion with the voices of nature is interrupted explicitly by Mariette's sighting of *Mariette*. The written word effectively silences nature's voice for her, as it will quite literally suppress the mother tongue.

---

6 Louise Colet, *La Servante,* reprinted in Roger Bellet, *Femmes de lettres au XIXe siècle: Autour de Louise Colet* (Lyon: Presses Universitaires de Lyon, 1982; first edition 1854), p. 204. All translations from *La Servante* are mine; I have not attempted to reproduce Colet's verse. Subsequent references will appear in the text.

The parallels between Colet's story of a passage from preverbal communion to communication in language, and the Lacanian and Kristevan narratives of a child's insertion in the symbolic order, via paternal interruption of the mother–child dyad and suppression of the maternal sphere, are marked, and attest to the longevity of cultural myth.[7] Colet's version, however, presents critical variants that dislocate the customary structural elements, and denaturalize a too-familiar story.

First of all, there is no father in *La Servante*, no figure of the Law to sever mother and daughter, no *nom du père* to inscribe the daughter as a separate being within language. Mariette, "little Mary," which is to say, "little Mother," bears no patronym, and places herself under the sign of the Mother in a rhetorical move that feminizes the *pater* in the very act of naming him: "Mary is my patron [*patronne*]," she declares (p. 201). If Mariette's linguistic course runs parallel to contemporary theories of a passage from presymbolic plenitude to symbolic loss, it diverges from the theorized passage insofar as the move from presymbolic to symbolic for Mariette is gradual, nonviolent, and initiated by the mother (by nature as her surrogate). Not yet fully inscribed in the symbolic order, Mariette is still held in a symbiotic unity with a nature which converses wordlessly and intimately with her, but which incites her to pass into the symbolic order: "What did you say to her, voices of nature / . . . / To make this humble creature rise up / From her calm ignorance to burning dreams?" (p. 201). Mariette's aspirations toward the symbolic order are described as generated by the maternally associated preverbal sphere. This is an effective rewriting of the myth; it displaces the father's role as language-giver, attributing this function instead to the mother's sphere, thereby signaling that the entry into the symbolic order is situated on a continuum rather than precipitated by a rupture.[8]

Mariette never completes the transition from presymbolic to symbolic, matter to spirit, concrete to abstract. Her tenure in Paris, in writing, in the symbolic order, is marked by disillusion, incompleteness, and a sense of irretrievable loss. Whereas the voices of nature were transparent for her, meaning in Paris is mediated by an opaque language that disguises truth, superimposes a cosmetic cover upon it. Alienated within the order to which she aspired, she is haunted by the sense of a lost plenitude whose absence phantomatically intrudes upon her present, seizing

[7] Freud's version of this myth equates the progress of civilization with a move from the material to the spiritual sphere, which he respectively qualifies as maternal and paternal. *Moses and Monotheism, Standard Edition*, ed. James Strachey (London: Hogarth, 1964), vol. XXIII, pp. 112–15. On connections between culture and the mother's suppression, see Margaret Homans, *Bearing the Word* (University of Chicago Press, 1986), pp. 1–39.

[8] See Kaja Silverman's remarks on the mother's role as language-giver in *The Acoustic Mirror: The Female Voice in Psychoanalysis and Cinema* (Bloomington: Indiana University Press, 1988), p. 100.

upon the mother as figure of disappeared unity. But mother, nature, plenitude, unity become increasingly problematic concepts in *La Servante*. Images of fertility become sterility, flow turned to aridity, and mother's milk drying up are frequent. When, in desperation, Mariette throws herself into the Seine in an attempt to recuperate a primordial union, the nurturing fluid has disappeared; the river bed is a tomb: "Seine, that our ancestors called the nurturer / Your bed today is an immense ossuary!" (p. 232). What this *suicide manqué* makes clear is the utter estrangement of the maternal order Mariette reaches futilely to retrieve in dying.

Although Mariette's rescue from drowning and brief retreat into Julien's family is represented as a potential rebirth, reinsertion in the maternal order proves no more tenable than was inscription in the paternal. If the world inside the Lionel book is not equal to its cover, Julien's simple heart and beatific smile are not enough to make his confined life palatable. The narrative lack of clarity about what the right choice would be corresponds to the roots of Mariette's madness, which in turn responds to the imperative for an absolute choice. The daughter who would make her home fully in the symbolic must kill the mother. The daughter who would continue to reside in the maternal sphere finds all horizons closed.[9] Mariette is caught between two spheres, able to appropriate neither her memories nor her dreams, her voice or her pen.

After she leaves Julien's farm, we find her poised on a hill contemplating Paris. This pose is more accurately an equipoise, emblem of her suspension between feminine and masculine, country and city, nature and culture, wordless communication and linguistic opacity. Also a caricature of her social climbing, it prefigures the madness scene at the text's end, where only a straitjacket can keep her from clambering into the trees.

In the final scene, we find Mariette wandering barefoot and disheveled among the trees in the Salpêtrière courtyard, hair loose and flowing, wearing a crown of straw, weeping flower-like tears and song-like sobs. She has been saved from drowning, only to become Ophelia.

III: Refiguring voice

La Servante is framed by a five-page introduction, in the form of the *Mariette* novel, and a five-page epilogue, written in the shadow of the Ophelia story. Both stories constitute sanctified cultural models against which the body of *La Servante* must define itself. In fact the story of

---

9 See Jean Wyatt's analysis of the dichotomous choices awaiting daughters in *Reconstructing Desire: The Role of the Unconscious in Women's Reading and Writing* (Chapel Hill: University of North Carolina Press, 1990).

Ophelia, who, like Lionel's heroine, loves a poet and dies young, amplifies but does not diverge from the archetypal patterns of *Mariette*.

Colet spars with Ophelia as with *Mariette*, engaging with her plot but fracturing it, embracing but dislocating its central elements – its madness, song, silence, fluidity, fusion with nature, betrayed love, death – elements whose recasting would have been all the more unsettling to contemporary readers because of their familiarity with the Ophelia plot and character. For *Hamlet* had been rediscovered in France in 1827, in a production in which a young Irish actress, Harriet Smithson, stole the show as Ophelia.[10] Smithson's long black veil, straw-strewn hair and poetic delirium took Paris by storm; they were widely reproduced in prints and paintings, popular lithographs, and fashion design.[11] Trendsetters sported a "coiffure à la folle" – a black veil "with wisps of straw tastefully interwoven in the hair"[12] – which is faithfully reproduced in Mariette's mad scene: "Her hair, hanging like a veil of mourning, / Swept the ground, gathering wisps of grass and moss" (p. 245). The Ophelia figure continued to haunt the French imagination well after the 1827 ground-breaking performance. Delacroix executed a series of paintings and lithographs representing Ophelia in the 1830s to 1850s; George Sand represented her in *Indiana*, in 1832; Musset and Hugo alluded to her in the 1830s and 1840s; and in 1836 to 1839 Louise Colet was part of a team of translators who collaborated on an annotated edition of *Chefs-d'oeuvre de Shakespeare*. *Hamlet* was one of the works studied.[13]

When Colet becomes Ophelia's narrator she brings with her not only a stock familiarity with the popularized Smithson interpretation, but also an authoritative editorial knowledge of the play that lends to her plot revisions an element of calculation and consequence. Her portrait of Mariette at the Salpêtrière, hair hanging long and unbound, is particularly obedient to Elizabethan conventions of representation, which coded disheveled hair as a sign of immodesty and sensuality often indicative of female dementia.[14] Her allusions to Mariette's gentle madness ("Her derangement is so placid and docile" [p. 245]) also reflect the Shakespearean model, as does the Daphne-like potential indifferentiation

---

[10] The Smithson performance was the most dramatic moment in a more gradual romantic repatriation of Ophelia. See James M. Vest, *The French Face of Ophelia from Belleforest to Baudelaire* (Lanham, NY and London: University Press of America, 1989).

[11] Smithson's Ophelia dominated the character's iconography for generations. See Elaine Showalter, "Representing Ophelia: Women, Madness, and the Responsibilities of Feminist Criticism," in Patricia Parker and Geoffrey Hartman, eds., *Shakespeare and the Question of Theory* (New York and London: Methuen, 1985), p. 83.

[12] Showalter, "Representing Ophelia," p. 83.

[13] Vest, *The French Face of Ophelia*, p. 148.

[14] See Maurice and Hanna Charney, "The Language of Madwomen in Shakespeare and his Fellow Dramatists," *Signs: Journal of Women in Culture and Society* 3, 2 (Winter 1977), 451–60.

of woman and tree that emerges in the affinity of Mariette's own limbs for tree limbs.[15]

The iconographically correct detail of Colet's Ophelia renders her plot modifications even more conspicuous. Her most flagrant alterations, the transposition of the mad scene and the drowning scene and, correlatively, the transformation of drowning into drowning *manqué*, give pause for thought. The interrupted suicide must be viewed not only as a response to a narrative tradition of women sacrificed to men's plots, but also as a specific reflection on an abiding association – generally inscribed in the discourse of hysteria and particularly imprinted upon Flaubert's thoughts about Colet's feminine style – of women with water and all things flowing.

Colet's invocation of Ophelia in this text that I take as a response to Flaubert's denigration of her overflowing *style féminin*, fights water with water. If Ophelia's drowning represents "the [masculine] necessity of drowning both words and feelings," as David Leverenz has argued, then the homeopathic drowning of drowning that Colet writes into her Ophelia is a rescue operation: it combs not only the river, for the heroine's body, but her tears, for the feelings they contain, and her voice, for the drift of its words.[16] Mariette is an Ophelia who will not drown.

That *La Servante* has at its core a woman's unsuccessful attempt to return to a feminine source is especially poignant given Flaubert's reading of this text as emblem of a generalized cultural tendency toward effusiveness ("everything is being dissolved now . . . by all that is wet, by tears, by chattering, by milk" [*Correspondance*, vol. II, p. 508]). The text of *La Servante* moves like a thirsting Tantalus between wetness and dryness, flowing substances and desiccation. We have seen the life-giving, maternally figured Seine become a bed of bones when Mariette plunges into its waters. And Mariette's Parisian debacle is repeatedly figured as lakes drying out, or clear waters turning to mud.

The drowning of drowning or the recuperation of the feminine never effectively happens in *La Servante*, and Colet's narrative, like its Shakespearean intertext, speaks ultimately to the "dissociation of sensibility" that Leverenz locates in *Hamlet* as dichotomies of "role and self, reason and nature, mind and body, manly and womanly, or the language of power and the language of feeling."[17] It is in this space of limbo between womanly and manly codes that can never coincide, that Mariette's madness must be located.

---

[15] Woman as tree was a topos in nineteenth-century art and literature. See Bram Dijkstra, *Idols of Perversity* (New York and Oxford: Oxford University Press, 1986), pp. 93–101.

[16] David Leverenz, "The Woman in *Hamlet*: An Interpersonal View," *Signs: Journal of Women in Culture and Society* 4, 2 (Winter 1978), 303.

[17] Ibid., 308.

The originality of Colet's representation of madness is that it is not defined as that which speaks in woman's tongues, but rather that which lies *in between* feminine and masculine language. Feminine madness in Colet – that reader's disease, dreamer's mobility, flowing sensibility, and inevitable silence, forerunner of what would soon be popularized as hysteria – is that space of alienation that cannot be accommodated within either feminine or masculine spheres, plots, languages, and that therefore results in the gaping openness, excess, muteness of the unemplotted.

It is to achieve this sense of uncontainedness that Colet reorders Ophelia so that her madness is no longer that which leads to another action (her suicide) and is thereby recontained by it, but that which remains outside enclosing structures, that which resists closure. Colet's ironic strategy in the last pages of the text is to multiply discrete signs of enclosure (Mariette's straitjacket, Lionel's ring on her finger, the cell into which she is thrown in the last line of the text) that are, more globally, completely powerless to contain or to structure the formless space of Mariette's madness.

Mariette at the Salpêtrière has moved, in her course from mother to father to limbo, from the plenitude of preverbal voice, to the written word, and then to incoherence. I want to insist that the fall outside language into the Salpêtrière is not a return to the silent communion of natural/maternal voice, but a plunge into a communicatory void.

Colet presents the Salpêtrière as a city of silence (p. 244). In a single page of introduction to this scene, there are five references to the muted tongues and lives found there. When sound is to be heard, it is babble, or animal-like noise. The only other sound is song, as when we hear the idiots singing, or Mariette, whose own silence is broken by metaphorical song:

> Her beauty shines in her suffering today,
> Her tears are flowers crowning her brow.
> Her unheard sobs are magnificent songs
> Unequaled by those of her lover.
> (p. 245)

Here we must remember that music is traditionally associated with the irrational, and with the feminine. So when Mariette's weeping is exalted as song, I think we have to hear, beneath the trite romantic apotheosis of melancholy, the echo of Ophelia singing. Her echoing song serves not only as textual acknowledgment of Mariette's discursive breakdown (song understood as the pure sonority of voice deprived of signifying content), but also as reminder of the nexus, embodied by her story, of women, madness, fluidity, and song.[18] The link between fluidity

---

[18] On associations of music with women, materiality, and sexuality, see McClary, *Feminine Endings*; Silverman, *The Acoustic Mirror*; and Rosolato, "La Voix."

and voice is especially pronounced in these verses, for the passage from Mariette's suffering, *shining* beauty – which evokes tears without naming them – to her tears, now named, and then her sobs, and finally her song, first phrases female voice as inarticulate flow, and then rephrases female fluidity as vocalization, and even, as *song*, as incipient art.

Colet's penultimate articulation – and ultimate revision – of this connection between voice and flow furnishes the grounds for some concluding speculations on her recourse to a dominant metaphorization of creativity as voice (language and body) in response to Flaubert's recourse, in his own representations of creativity, to metaphors of flow.

Afterword

By means of a certain rhetorical alchemy, Flaubert consistently turns female voice into fluid, in this way not only liquefying but liquidating it, as if to dissolve the Medusa he embodied in Colet's voice when he wrote that it had "the power to make stones rise" (*Correspondance*, vol. I, p. 287). Colet reverses the metamorphosis by transforming flow into voice, albeit negativized voice. For, although the voice we hear at the end of *La Servante* is wordless, Colet's narrator makes madness speak by framing its speechlessness.

The transmutability of female vocality and fluidity speaks to an age-old mythic construction serving to naturalize a cultural representation of women's voices as corporeal, continuous, irrepressible, perilous – and implicitly powerful. It is best embodied by the figure of the Sirens luring men to a watery death with their song.

The identification of female voice with fluidity, and specifically, with female body fluids, effectively contains this voice, deprives it of its agency. Following Kaja Silverman's work on female voice in cinema, we can say that the process whereby female voice is embodied – interiorized or infused as body fluid potentially expressible through various organ holes – is more accurately repressive; each of the holes or points from which a woman's subjectivity is ostensibly to be expressed is more accurately "the site at which that subjectivity is introduced in her."[19] The embodiment of voice, most often culturally devalorized as feminine, is more generally one of the properties of human voice, which, again in Rosolato's words, is situated "between body and language." The feminization of embodied voice is then a gesture of projection (and rejection).

Our passage from Flaubert's representation of feminine voice as bodily effluvia to be contained, to Colet's version of feminine voice as framed discourse, reverses gender stereotypes as it moves from the materiality of his model to the abstraction of hers. For Flaubert's letters and Colet's reply in *La Servante* constitute a dialogue about containment

---

[19] Silverman, *The Acoustic Mirror*, p. 67.

within which he speaks in fluid metaphors of the need to channel a certain lyric, romantic style and furthermore *performs this channeling* by his rhetoric of female incorporation, while she replies by writing a text about the dispossession of female voice by male textuality, thereby reinterpreting his containing discourse in textual terms. In this way Colet's text is a distorted reflection of Flaubert's, and the resultant glare works both to highlight and displace his enclosing discourse.

There is a trenchant irony in my sense that the central interest of Colet's text is narratological (springing in part from its internal narrative structure but also from the internarrative structure constituted by its discourse with Flaubert's letters), because critical tradition has consistently read Colet's verse narrative with the accent on verse, and has insistently followed Flaubert in reading Colet's work with her person as quintessentially romantic to the point of sentimental drivel, effusively lyrical to the point of bathos, and most pointedly, hysterical.[20] Flaubert and the larger critical tradition tacitly echo cultural associations of verse with the feminine, music, materiality, the body, and voice as pure sonority unmediated by meaning. Although Flaubert (who reportedly could neither write a line of verse nor carry a tune) paid nominal homage to the quality of Colet's verses, he simultaneously dismissed them as insignificant products of her body: "I give you no credit for writing good verses. You lay them as a hen lays eggs, without consciousness of what you are doing" (*Correspondance*, vol. II, p. 480).[21]

My claim here is not that Colet deserves a place in the pantheon of aesthetic perfection; it is at once more modest and more complex. I want neither to be the apologist for her style nor the champion of her passions. I do, however, want to dissociate the two, and if I read *La Servante* as a text that could only have been written by a woman, it is because it displays a remarkable self-consciousness about women's position in patriarchal society, and not because it flows from Colet's lips in an oral/genital indistinction too often assigned by her culture as by ours to female discourse. Colet wrote her novel in verse. As such, she wrote a hybrid or even hermaphroditic text, according to gendered conventions of genre, once again manifesting a refusal to speak in a categorically feminine or masculine voice. It is this refusal to choose between two equally limiting alternatives that makes *La Servante* a protofeminist text in Nancy Miller's sense that feminist texts "protest against the available fiction of female becoming."[22]

---

[20] But see Julian Barnes, *Flaubert's Parrot* (New York: Knopf, 1989), and Marilyn Gaddis Rose, introduction to her translation of Louise Colet, *Lui: A View of Him* (Athens, GA: University of Georgia Press, 1986), for sympathetic presentations of Colet.

[21] I owe the information about Flaubert's nonmusicality to Herbert Lottman, *Flaubert* (Boston: Little, Brown, 1989), p. 66.

[22] Nancy Miller, *Subject to Change* (New York: Columbia University Press, 1988), p. 129.

The oppositional force of Colet's narrative can be gauged by Flaubert's scatological dismissal of it as "a sort of chamber pot in which the overflow of who knows what has dripped," and by his accompanying rejection of its anger: "That doesn't smell good. It reeks of hatred" (vol. II, p. 502). To read this text *à la* Flaubert as a purely personal expression is to infuse it within Colet's body as a sign of her leaking female physiology: to reduce a feminist text to a female vendetta, and in this way to defuse its more general ideological force.

It is the force of Colet's text as ideological commentary that prompts Flaubert's wrath, provokes the visceral outburst that he projects as scatological critique of her style. His reaction to her anger is a revealing measure of the threat of a woman's voice that escapes containment, a woman's discourse that, unlike Mariette's, resists circumscription, and a woman's pen that dares to express the extent of its repression. No wonder he reinscribed Louise Colet, stripped of her autonomy, deprived of her pen, as Emma Bovary. But that is another story.

10

Staring the camera down: direct address and women's voices

AMY LAWRENCE

Recent feminist film criticism has focused on how mainstream Holly-wood constructs women's voices in a way that denies them subjectivity.[1] Underlying the metaphoric uses of the term "woman's voice" is the physical reality of the voice as a manifestation of the body and of the will of a female speaker (through the physical aspects of pitch, into-nation, accent, and choices of tempo, volume, words, etc.). But access to that voice in film is not as simple as it appears. Because the image and the soundtrack are recorded separately, any material link between the woman speaking and the voice we hear is highly provisional. Our belief that the voice we hear belongs to the woman we see is mostly a matter of faith.

An occasional classic film, such as *Singin' in the Rain* (1952), has called attention to this regime under which a woman's control of her own voice is so precarious. But most often it is the goal of sound editing to make the technological separation of voice and image invisible through seamless synchronization.[2] Synchronization is always to some extent a fiction, with "invisible synch" testifying more to the sound editor's art, to how adeptly sound and image are joined, rather than to any authentic or natural link between body and voice.

The invisibility of synchronization does not make the process by which it is achieved neutral. One of its uses is to disguise the process by which a feminine ideal is constructed. A woman's relationship to her voice in film is necessarily a constructed one, situated by all of the discourses at work in cinema (the star system, narrative demands, con-

---

[1] See Kaja Silverman, *The Acoustic Mirror: The Female Voice in Psychoanalysis and Cinema* (Bloomington: Indiana University Press, 1988); and my *Echo and Narcissus: Women's Voices in Classical Hollywood Cinema* (Berkeley and Los Angeles: University of California Press, 1991).

[2] Mary Ann Doane, "Ideology and the Practice of Sound Editing and Mixing," in Elisabeth Weis and John Belton, eds., *Film Sound: Theory and Practice* (New York: Columbia University Press, 1985), pp. 54–62.

166

ventions of representation including lighting, close-ups, etc.). Whether synchronization restores an original unity or creates a fictional one, whether the process by which it is created is exaggerated (for comic effect) or invisible, it is clear that women in film cannot open their mouths to say a word unless it is allowed.

One of the cinematic conventions that is most dependent on synchronization's illusion of an unproblematic, unconstructed unity between image and voice is direct address. The term "direct address" refers to the effect created when a photographed subject looks directly into the camera and speaks. One of the primary injunctions for performers in classical film aesthetics is not to look at the camera. Doing so gives the uncanny impression that the actor can "see" the audience. The forcefulness of this break with the film's diegesis can be used to powerful effect when the director wants suddenly to confront the audience with its own presence/complicity (for example, the ending of *The 400 Blows*, 1959). This assumption of simultaneity between actor and audience threatens to expose the radical disjunction in space and time that underlies the cinematic viewing experience. Not only is the audience shocked out of its voyeuristic reverie, but by addressing the audience in an explicit "I/you" relationship, direct address demands some kind of response.

It is in documentary film that direct address is caught between an authenticating function and its disruptive potential. In the so-called "talking heads" documentary, the audience is encouraged to overlook any awareness of temporal and spatial disjunction because of the very urgency of the witness's testimony. Any awareness of cinematic construction (camera placement, synchronization, even the presence of an interviewer and camera crew) is suppressed in deference to the speaker.

The synchronization of image and voice in direct address stands as proof of the coherent and stable identity of the person we see speaking. The simulation of eye-contact also contributes a heightened sense of presence. Not surprisingly, feminist film production in the early 1970s favored documentary because it seems to challenge the camera's ability to objectify women, with direct address in particular enabling women to bypass the conventions of representation in favor of speaking directly to the camera that confronts them.

However, because of its dependence on two carefully constructed illusions – eye-contact and the synchronization of voice and image – direct address, like all conventions which present themselves as natural, simple, and unmediated, is actually a complex, ideologically loaded construction. In this essay I would like to examine two very different uses of direct address. In François Truffaut's *Les deux anglaises et le continent* (*Two English Girls*, 1971), direct address serves as a radical departure from traditional narrative style, calling attention to the film's status as an adaptation, and at the same time marking the moments of the most intense self-revelation when the characters burst out of the fiction and the text momentarily comes to full cinematic life. However, I will argue that the female characters who are presented in this way – and the literary genres their speech represents – are fully contained within a masculine authorial discourse. In Trinh T. Minh-ha's *Surname Viet, Given Name Nam* (1989), direct address is shown to be the site of the most multi-layered fiction where definitions of subjectivity, documentary, and adaptation are brought into crisis. Trinh's shared status with her characters (as outsider, woman, exile) underscores the problem of the speaking woman and raises crucial issues regarding the female voice in a medium dominated by the gaze. The fact that the *fiction* of direct address is centered on the speaking woman makes direct address *as used by women* each film's central paradox.

Truffaut's 1971 film *Two English Girls* is an adaptation of Henri-Pierre Roché's 1956 novel *Deux anglaises et le continent*. Truffaut had an international success adapting Roché's *Jules and Jim* (1961) roughly ten years earlier and his film of Roché's second novel was widely seen as a kind of self-referential gesture for Truffaut as the novel itself had been for Roché. Both men had a tendency to turn their lives into art. *Two English Girls* can be seen as a particularly personal form of adaptation where autobiography and biography, Truffaut's and Roché's lives, converge.[3] Where *Jules and Jim* was a fictional reworking of Roché's triangular relationship with his friend Franz Hessel and Hessel's wife Helen, Roché's second novel, written in his late seventies, fictionalizes an earlier relationship with two British sisters at the turn of the century.

The plot of novel and film recounts how Claude (Jean-Pierre Léaud) meets Anne Brown (Kika Markham), an art student in Paris and the daughter of one of his mother's school friends. During an idyllic visit to Anne's home in Wales, Claude is urged by Anne to court her sister Muriel (Stacy Tendeter). Claude proposes to Muriel but their mothers insist on a year-long separation. Within six months Claude decides he wants his freedom. Muriel is devastated and falls ill. Some time later, Anne comes to Paris to be a sculptress. She and Claude become lovers as she embraces a bohemian lifestyle. When Muriel finds out about his relationship with Anne, she renounces Claude. Shaken, Claude brings himself out of a deep depression by writing *Jérome et Julien*, the friends' story with the sexes reversed. After Anne dies of tuberculosis, Claude and Muriel consummate their relationship, but the next day Muriel leaves. The last scene takes place in a park years later. We are told

---

[3] Both were obsessive about women: Truffaut's *The Man Who Loved Women* (1977) deals with a modern-day Casanova who writes about his lifetime spent chasing women. Roché: "My desire [is] to write the story of my life one day . . . like Casanova, but in a different spirit." Carlton Lake and Linda Ashton, *Henri-Pierre Roché: An Introduction* (Austin: Harry Ransom Humanities Research Center, University of Texas, 1991), p. 217.

Muriel has married. Claude thinks he sees her daughter at the park and realizes that he has grown older.

What is notable about the film, as well as the novel, is not simply the plot but its presentation. In their catalogue for a 1991 exhibition on Roché at the University of Texas, Austin, Carlton Lake and Linda Ashton discuss the difficulties Truffaut had in conceptualizing the novel as a film. "The novel's unusual construction frustrated him and he concluded more than once that it was not adaptable to the screen." A nervous breakdown in 1971 and a consequent prolonged "sleep cure" with the novel his main source of consolation, decided Truffaut. Working with screenwriter Jean Gruault, he completed the film in 1972.[4]

One of Truffaut's more formally stringent works, *Two English Girls* aspires to an almost epistolary form, something rarely attempted in film. Nearly every scene is either prefaced by a letter, shows someone receiving a letter, illustrates the contents of a letter heard on the soundtrack, or shows the writing of a letter. There was widespread dissatisfaction with this technique which results in a marked distanciation effect unusual in Truffaut. Annette Innsdorf, for instance, gently suggests that "The proliferation of letters, diaries, books, and memoirs attests to the fundamentally literary sensibility and expectations of the characters which the director (perhaps too faithfully) mirrors."[5] But in fact both film and director are obsessed with the process of circumscribing a life with words. What I would call the film's hyperawareness of its status as an adaptation is clear from the opening credits where we see row after row of the novel, page proofs, title pages, and marginalia.[6]

When information is not presented through letters, it is presented by Truffaut himself as narrator telling us in voice-over what the characters are thinking or doing, a technique which makes the actors seem like puppets. This produces a hierarchy with the voice of the "author" coming between us and the characters. The only time the film seems to break through the mediation of the narrator/author, when words escape the page and the characters take on a life of their own, is when they speak directly to us.

Direct address stands out as a privileged signifier in *Two English Girls*, used when the pressure of the letter is too great to be contained. The first time it is used is when the puritanical sister Muriel has just learned about Claude's love affair with her sister Anne.[7] After a grueling

4   Ibid., p. 198.
5   Annette Innsdorf, *François Truffaut* (New York: William Morrow and Co., 1979), pp. 92–93.
6   Most of Truffaut's films are either adaptations or directly autobiographical. One could argue that his strongest works are based on historic journals whose writing is enacted in the film (*The Wild Child* [1969] and *The Story of Adèle H.* [1975]).
7   Earlier, Anne recites a letter she has sent Claude. She does not look directly at the camera. Significantly, she is pledging her devotion to Claude. The more commanding direct address is reserved for Muriel, the more intense sister.

scene where, seized with grief, she falls and hits her head, we cut to an extreme close-up of Muriel superimposed over a shot of a train rushing through the countryside. She recites a letter to Claude, repudiating any future relationship between them. Direct address usually gives the audience a sense of direct access to characters as they make eye-contact with us, their feelings expressed directly without the "fiction" of a scene. But clearly this isn't unmediated speech. The narrator tells us first, "Muriel wrote Claude a farewell letter." She prefaces her speech with the formal address of a letter – "Claude." Because of the use of direct address, this scene first calls attention to Muriel's speech as a *letter* and then, in a *coup de théâtre*, appropriates the letter, foundation of the epistolary novel, for cinema. Rather than breaking the diegesis, Muriel's address expands it to include the audience, situating them in an impossible fictional subject position (as Claude) that they can't wriggle out of.

Although presented in direct address, Muriel's speech is not presented as a "simple" outpouring of her feelings. In a film about art and representation (Claude collects paintings, Anne sculpts; they play "statues" and charades), it is important to remember that the women are artists. Muriel writes, but the genres she excels in are not those recognized in their period as "art" but as "merely" personal: diaries, journals, correspondence. Muriel's relationship to her work is also presented as different from Anne's to sculpture or even Claude's to writing. Muriel has ruined her eyes writing. When we first meet her she has bandages over her eyes; she sits down to dinner with a casual air as if a blindfolded woman was a common occurrence. Later, we see her writing late into the night, vowing to be the perfect daughter, sister, and a friend to Claude. The strain on her eyes is attributed interchangeably to her writing and to her feelings for Claude. She tells him later, "After you left I lost the normal use of my eyes . . . . I spent three months in total darkness." Women's relationships to their art are shown as more dangerously intense and obsessive than men's. The combination of passion, neurosis, and intensity focused by a woman on her written work makes Muriel an early model for Truffaut's Adèle H. (There is even a scene of her speaking out loud a letter she'll never send as she walks the streets of London, drawing the stare of a curious policeman.)

The final destination of Muriel's letters is not Claude but ultimately Claude's work. After the intense, dynamic close-up of Muriel rejecting Claude on behalf of her idealist vision of love, Claude is reduced to utter silence. He stays in bed for days until, the narrator tells us, "he healed himself by writing a book." Claude transforms the entire relationship into his autobiographical novel which we immediately see in press. Publication is what differentiates Claude's "real art" from Muriel's letters and diaries which never reach the public *as art* until they have been transformed by Claude into a published text. By writing a published work, Claude in effect has the last word.

It can be argued that *Two English Girls* is about the process of adaptation as the basis of art, yet the gendering of "who writes" versus "who is written" demands we look further. While the film actively illustrates the incorporation of Muriel's life and work into Claude's text, it is important to recognize that the entire project in all its manifestations is an appropriation of women's work – and not fictional women, as we might think. Women's work reconstituted as male autobiography grounds the fiction twice over, in both novel and film.

Roche's relationship with Margaret and Violet Hart (Muriel and Anne Brown in novel and film) began in 1900. "Margaret Hart's correspondence to Roche [was] written over thirteen years (1900–1913), even while she was nearly blind (she had taught herself to write in spite of the blindfold needed to protect her ailing eyes)."[8] As early as 1903 "Roché had asked Margaret [Muriel] . . . to turn over to him whatever documents she had pertaining to their forced separation. [H]e had anticipated that he would 'make a book from them one day . . . The story of our difficulties may prove helpful to others.'"[9]

It is clear from Roché's journals that he knew how valuable Margaret/Muriel's letters were even as he made them part of his own work. In 1950 "he remarked in his journal how 'extraordinary' they were . . . 'Some of them ought to be published.'"[10]

"[S]ome things [are written] in the first rush, with a 'Shakespearean' quality; other [passages] are more composed . . . It is almost a finished work in itself."[11]

At the same time, however, the film shows us what it will take to transform the letters from "*almost* a finished work" that "ought to be published" to one that is.

The process of co-optation/recuperation is made explicit in the scene where direct address has its greatest power: when Claude receives Muriel's diary. After he has broken with her, Claude receives a package from Muriel. He thinks she has returned his letters, but it is the diary she kept while they were separated. The narrator tells us this is "perhaps the most intimate confession that he would ever read." We cut to a close-up of Muriel speaking directly to the camera, shattering the realistic framing story. Not coincidentally, what Muriel tells Claude is meant to shatter his view of her as "pure" as it announces her (scandalous) ability to satisfy her own sexual needs. Everything she says

---

[8] Lake and Ashton, *Roché*, p. 183. "The correspondence ends in 1913, when, after three years of indecision, Margaret marries another man, Mr. Barratt, whom Roché had known in London in 1901" (p. 183).

[9] Ibid., p. 178.

[10] Ibid., pp. 178, 186. Roché's mother's letters were also important (see p. 178).

[11] Ibid.

threatens to displace Claude. She relates the passionate intensity of her physical desires, exemplified by her childhood habit of masturbating. We also see her first sexual interests being spurred not by Claude (who wants to be her "first") but by a cherubic female friend. When Muriel breaks through to direct address, she takes over the enunciation of the film itself, replacing the narrator and dictating the images, images that look like no others in the film. (It might also be more than coincidence that when the film was drastically edited during its initial run ["massacred, amputated and truncated," according to Truffaut], this crucial scene was cut and has only recently been restored.)[12]

When the scene ends, Truffaut the narrator tells us Claude's immediate reaction to Muriel's diary: "Claude thought it was marketable. He wanted to publish it in a limited edition." He adds, "Muriel refused, not saying how he hurt her." Nevertheless, the next shot shows Claude dictating Muriel's journal to a typist, turning her version of her experience into his product simply by respeaking it. "Now I know that I'm no longer a pure woman," Claude reads aloud, waiting for the female typist to get it down.

Claude's reaction mirrors Roché's use of Margaret and Violet Hart's work.

When Roché began to think in terms of incorporating original material into *Deux anglaises*, his first step was to copy out, on separate sheets of paper, each letter and journal entry that had potential use for the novel. In the process, he would *translate* into French the documents written in English and *tidy up* the ones already in French. His next step was to *revise* his copies, *modifying* the texts for precision and clarity *without changing the essential character* of the originals.[13]

Yet how free Roché felt to depart from the actual source material is made clear in the next sentence: "However, if a document was missing or nonexistent, Roché would either rely on his memory or resort to 'creative license' to supply it."[14]

In adapting *Deux anglaises*, Truffaut is, in effect, revising Rochés revisions. He begins by writing on the other's text (see the red-inked pages in the credits). Like Roché, Truffaut went beyond the text meant to be read (the Harts' letters, Roché's novel) to private diaries and journals

---

12 *François Truffaut: Correspondence 1945–1984*, Gilles Jacob and Claude de Givray, eds., trans. Gilbert Adair (New York: Farrar, Straus and Giroux), p. 565.

13 Lake and Ashton, *Roché*, p. 193, my emphasis. This echoes Truffaut: "I had been fascinated by the creative process of using real life events as the basis for a fiction story that would not distort the authenticity of the source material." *The Story of Adèle H.*, Helen C. Scott, ed. (New York: Grove Press, 1976), p. 7.

14 Lake and Ashton, *Roché*, p. 193. "Entries from Margaret's and Roché's journals for the year 1902 . . . are printed side by side" in the chapter of the novel entitled "The Separation" (p. 193). Placing the two works side by side to some extent preserves Margaret's voice as separate.

(Roché's journal was also "marked by Truffaut during the preparation of his film.")[15] But Truffaut's appropriation of Roché is fundamentally different from Roché's use of the writings of Margaret and Violet Hart. Truffaut adapts and pays homage at the same time, while Roché (and Truffaut compounds this) encompasses and absorbs the women's work.

The film buries the women's voices under layer after layer of male authorship. Here the "male author" exists as a triple threat: in the fictional character of Claude; in the film's author, Truffaut; and in the original novelist, Roché. Claude explicitly contains the passionate writing of Muriel through the institution of printing/publishing where he ascends to his identity as sole author. Roché is marked as progenitor of the seminal text in the title credits, the word from which the film has sprung. By positioning Roché as the textual and historical referent, the film works to suppress our awareness of the women's writing which pre-dated the publication of Roché's novel. The institution of cinema and the appropriation of Roché's language in the narration identify Truffaut as the ultimate in a line of male "auteurs," the one who envelopes the others (literally taking Roché's place as the narrator) as he pays filial homage to the texts that came before him.

As the women's voices are selected and shaped by this multiple male authorship, the women are in effect silenced as subjects. By the end of the film both Anne and Muriel have been removed from the text, romanticized and banalized, rendered dead or married. Anne has died for her freedom, and when we hear Muriel has married, instead of seeing an image of her we see a house. She has become literally a hausfrau (house/woman). The silence is deafening. All that is left with their passing are the (male) texts.

"A documentary aware of its own artifice is one that remains sensitive to the flow between fact and fiction."[16]

In Trinh Minh-ha's *Surname Viet, Given Name Nam*, the relationship between filmic text and literary source is more difficult to come at; it is actively obscured compared to the foregrounding of "literariness" essential to Truffaut's work. *Surname Viet*, like *Two English Girls*, is based on a book made up of the words of actual women.[17] While Truffaut and Roché subsume the women's work into their own by recontextualizing their words or making them muses to male authors, in a journalistic work like Mai Thu Van's *Viet Nam, un peuple, des voix*, which documents interviews with women describing their lives in post-war Vietnam, the lines between "author" and "subject" remain clearly marked.

---

15 Ibid., p. 220.
16 Trinh T. Minh-ha, "Documentary Is/Not a Name," *October* 52 (1990), 89.
17 Mai Thu Van, *Viet Nam, un peuple, des voix* (Paris: Pierre Horay, 1983).

However, unlike Truffaut, who casts Roché in the role of the father (to be idolized then superceded), Trinh actively resists constructing "a" source for her film. She argues that

meaning can ... be political only ... when it does not rely on any single source of authority, but, rather, empties or decentralizes it. Thus even when this source is referred to, it stands as one among many others, at once plural and utterly singular.[18]

We do not find out until the end credits that at least some of the film is based on a book.[19] At first it might seem as if Trinh is trying to suppress, even replace, the "original" author, but I will argue that this blurring of the connection between representation and reality is central to her radical deconstruction of the image of the speaking woman.

Displacing the "author" becomes a comparatively simple project compared to breaking the unexamined relationship between subject and speech that is at the heart of direct address. In order to undermine or reformulate the relationship between image/woman/speech, the film must systematically break the link not only between adaptation and source, but between the woman we see and the words she speaks – in other words, to expose the fiction of both documentary and direct address.

Trinh questions film's ability to represent reality by questioning documentary itself. In an article entitled "Documentary Is/Not a Name," Trinh blatantly avers that

There is no such thing as documentary – whether the term designates a category of material, a genre, an approach, or a set of techniques. This assertion – as old and as fundamental as the antagonism between names and reality – needs incessantly to be restated, despite the very visible existence of a documentary tradition.[20]

"Objectivity" is central to documentary's scientist pretensions which reach their height in ethnographic film. The very concept of "objectivity" is fraught with (and masks) ideological and hegemonic goals and processes. As in *Two English Girls*, Trinh's ethnographers are men who speak "for" others by taking and reshaping their words to create a text (recorded image and speech) that belongs to the new Creator – the male filmmaker.

But records are produced, not captured. All of Trinh's films, *Reassemblage* (1983), *Naked Spaces – Living is Round* (1985), and *Surname Viet*

---

[18] Ibid., p. 89.
[19] While the book was published in France in French, it is possible that some of the original interviews were done in Vietnamese and then translated into French. Trinh then translated them into English and adapted the interviews for the film. This removes us further from "direct" access to the women interviewed.
[20] Trinh, "Documentary," 77.

foreground the fact that what we see and hear, and the relationship between sound and image, are the result of post-production *creativity* by the filmmaker(s).[21]

Filmmaking is after all a question of "framing" reality in its course. However, it can also be the very place where the referential function of the film image/ sound is not simply negated, but reflected upon in its own principles and questioned in its authoritative identification with the phenomenal world.[22]

In Trinh's films, the locus of destabilization and the contestation of terms like "objective," "real," and "fiction," is the voice epitomized by the speech of women. The omniscient point of view in standard documentary is represented by so-called "voice of God" narration: a disembodied male voice reciting "facts" while speaking the dominant language without noticeable accent or use of the vernacular. Trinh uses her own voice and accented English for the poetically dense narration in *Reassemblage* and *Surname Viet*.[23] But beyond that most basic claim to authorship, Trinh's *construction* of women's voices and images challenges the ultimately hegemonic definitions of subjectivity reinforced in standard documentary/ethnographic film.

The first half of *Surname Viet* is made up of "interviews" with five women in Vietnam. Each scene becomes a staged monologue (some shot in single takes that last for several minutes). Posed on strikingly minimal sets, the women speak in heavily accented English.[24] Before each scene we see a written text appear over a black screen or over the image before the woman begins to speak. These are often transcriptions of what the women will say (though we soon find that the transcriptions are not complete and not always reliable).

While the interviews are unusually static, in one with a woman identified as Thu Van the camera is mobile, probing. The first time we see Thu Van, the camera moves up and down her body without a cut, stopping once to frame her expressive hands, and again on her feet in

---

[21] See Doane, "Ideology"; Rick Altman, "Moving Lips: Cinema as Ventriloquism," and Alan Williams, "Is Sound Recording Like a Language?" both in *Yale French Studies* 60, 1 (1980), 67–79 and 51–66; Thomas Levin, "The Acoustic Dimension," *Screen* 25, 3 (1984), 55–68.

[22] Trinh, "Documentary," 90.

[23] Trinh has been criticized for silencing women in *Naked Spaces* where the narration is fragmented into several voices/genders and in *Reassemblage* where the words of the Senegalese women are not translated. See Constance Penley and Andrew Ross, "Interview with Trinh T. Minh-ha," *Camera Obscura* 13–14 (1985), 87–103; Mary Kuryla, "Black Body: The Potential for a Non-Colonizing Cinema in Africa," *USC Spectator* 9, 1 (1988), 28–37.

[24] I have discussed the importance of accents and the cultural production of women's voices in the film in "Women's Voices in Third World Cinema: *Surname Viet, Given Name Nam*," in *Sound Theory/Sound Practice*, Rick Altman, ed. (New York: Routledge and AFI, 1992), pp. 178–90.

sandals. When we get to her face, she speaks directly to us but the camera bisects her, panning left, then right. Thu Van often speaks *through* a barrier of words. The written text fades in and out, superimposed over her as she leans toward the camera. The obstruction lends urgency to her effort to speak as it calls attention to the myriad obstacles (political, cultural, linguistic) threatening communication between her and the English-speaking audience she addresses.

Throughout, Trinh's *interested* camera (the opposite of disinterested objectivity) insists on an embodied discourse. When Thu Van begins to talk about her dreams as a girl, the camera tilts away from her face toward her hands: "When I was young, I wanted to become a writer. My parents told me, you have to write with your heart, but don't forget your heart belongs to the body." Throughout the shot, she discusses the specifically physical effects the post-war situation has had on women's lives.[25] "We don't want to admit – these women are tired." A woman only works "to deprive herself better, to eat less." Canonization is the official reward for the self-sacrifice expected of women. "The image of the woman is magnified like a saint and we are only human beings." According to state propaganda, women "are good mothers, good wives, heroic fighters. Ghost women with no humanity. They display us in shop windows for foreign visitors who come to look at our lives."

Yet the women in the film feel the loss of their youth, of husbands interned indefinitely, and worry about not being attractive any more. A middle-aged doctor tells of her sister's shock at seeing her after a long time; when the doctor looked in a mirror for the first time in years, she didn't recognize herself. Because direct address is rooted in the body, the synchronization of image and voice, it is necessary for the rest of the film to prove that body a lie.

The second half reveals that the women we thought were in Vietnam are actually émigrés living in California. Furthermore, they are not the women they "portrayed" in the first half, but five other women selected out of 150 Trinh interviewed. As "themselves," the women in California speak Vietnamese, subtitled in English. They are photographed outdoors in public spaces, frequently interacting with friends, as they explain how they chose to become "actresses" for this film.[26] There is also a dramatic stylistic shift from a "talking heads" documentary to *cinéma vérité* with its hand-held camera, imperfect framing, sound, and focus,

---

[25] I am indebted to Kaja Silverman for raising the issue of the film's presentation of the body in discussion at the Sound Symposium, Iowa, April 1990.

[26] According to Edward Branigan, Trinh asked the women in California to choose where and how they wanted to be filmed, inviting them to participate in their own construction, as it were – again problematizing the issue of authorship while trying to avoid the ethnographer's "desire to service the needs of the unexpressed" by "defin[ing] them and their needs." Trinh, "Documentary," 84.

location shooting, group scenes, and subjects caught "unawares," as if they didn't know they were being filmed – the opposite of direct address.

The second half of the film requires an act of rereading for the spectator as we see the women before us both as "themselves" and as the characters we have seen them play. In Trinh's film we have to relinquish a search for the "real" woman and adopt a more fluid conception of subjectivity. Both "Thu Vans" are representations of actual women; at the same time both are created by and for cinema. In an essay on *Surname Viet*, subtitled "Spreading Rumors and Ex/Changing Histories," Linda Peckham notes that

the artificial subject points to the absence of the "real" speaker, an absence that suggests internment, censorship and death, as well as the survival of a witness, a record – a history.[27]

The image of Thu Van is not that of a person "captured" on film but of a signifier with multiple referents.[28]

Direct address, which is predicated on the synchronization of image and voice, in Trinh's work points not to a singular cohesive female subject but to a more complicated conception of subjectivity as multiple, shifting, and communal, indicating not only the psychological but the social heterogeneity of a talking head.[29] Speaking, for exiles and the colonized, in effect "graft[s] several languages, cultures and realities onto a single body," the body becoming the site for multiple identities.[30] Each woman in the film restates the position/condition of the émigré, the exile, the "Third World Woman," and the colonized, as she simultaneously speaks for herself and embodies the words of others (presenting her body to the camera's gaze and giving her voice to their words). By exposing the mediation behind direct address, the "least mediated" technique of documentary, Trinh makes this complex subject readable in a film text.

Being simultaneously several people (who you were, who you are, who you played, who and where she is now and who she was) is a position shared not only by all of the women in the film but by Trinh and Mai Thu Van, the author of what might be called the *pre*-text for the first half of the film. Trinh's assertion that "Meaning" (like subjectivity?) "can only be political when it is destabilized and decentered"

27 Linda Peckham, "*Surname Viet, Given Name Nam*: Spreading Rumors and Ex/ Changing Histories," *Frame/work* 2, 3 (1989), 33.
28 The use of the name Thu Van may be in reference to the author, adding another layer or persona to this "character."
29 See Teresa de Lauretis, "Displacing Hegemonic Discourses: Reflections on Feminist Theory in the 1980s," *Inscriptions* 3/4 (1988), and Trinh Minh-ha, "Not You/Like You: Post-Colonial Women and the Interlocking Questions of Identity and Difference," *Inscriptions* 3/4 (1988), 76. In this article, Trinh discusses her refusal to play the West's authority on the Third World.
30 Peckham, "*Surname Viet*," 35.

applies to all of the women connected with the film, present and absent. Despite geographical distance, repression, barriers of words, the character of Thu Van insists that you listen to *her*, eye to eye and face to face, yet "her voice" comes from many sources and is addressed to a spectator who herself becomes a politicized, decentered series of listening positions.

In *Surname Viet*, Trinh belies the phenomenological impact of direct address, the "myth of an essential core, of spontaneity and depth as inner vision,"[31] and instead creates a multi-layered figure where an image and a voice occupy the position of an "other" without replacing, becoming, or defining that other. In earlier films, Trinh attempts not to "speak *for*" the other but "to speak *nearby*."[32] But in *Surname Viet* the women literally occupy the position of the women they play as they "give voice" to the testimony of their sisters in struggle. The women transform their bodies into the site from which the other can speak. The woman's voice is thus simultaneously embodied and displaced.

Both *Two English Girls* and *Surname Viet, Given Name Nam* challenge the boundaries of traditional film form, the first as a film about letters, an adaptation of a work that itself blurs boundaries as an autobiographical novel, and the second as a "fictional documentary." In each, direct address raises the stakes. In *Two English Girls*, Muriel's passionate outbursts shatter the surrounding diegesis. Its very power to disrupt shows why her voice must be contained, recuperated within a male authorial hierarchy. In *Surname Viet*, Trinh makes documentary's use of first person accounts told directly to the camera the crux of the film's deconstruction of female speech. Where Muriel's direct address has power and poignance as her bid for subjectivity, in *Surname Viet* subjectivity is redefined. *Surname Viet* exposes the way traditional direct address leans on our assumption of the singularity of the subject as it constitutes it.[33] For Truffaut, a woman's voice ultimately must be the construction of a male author. In Trinh Minh-ha's *Surname Viet, Given Name Nam*, a woman's voice becomes a *location* actively shared by a number of women joined in the political act of speech.

---

31 Trinh, "Not You/Like You," 77.
32 In *Reassemblage*.
33 See Doane, "The Voice in the Cinema," 54–62.

11

The voice of lament: female vocality and performative efficacy in the Finnish-Karelian *itkuvirsi*

ELIZABETH TOLBERT

Why the lament?

What better place to examine female vocality than in the ritual lament of Finnish-Karelia, a beautiful and moving genre associated almost exclusively with women? Given the overwhelming preponderance of women as lamenters in nearly all known cultures, and the fact that laments appear in similar forms and contexts throughout the world, vocality in the lament is an ideal case study, perhaps even a pivotal one, from which to understand the more general case of emotion, meaning, and gender in music.[1]

One of the most striking features of the lament throughout the world is its manner of performance, which has been characterized variously as "ritual wailing," "sung-texted-weeping," or "tuneful weeping."[2]

Material for this essay was drawn from fieldwork among Karelian refugees in Finland in 1984 and 1985, funded by a Fulbright Grant for Research and Study Abroad. Further support was provided by grants from the American Association of University Women, the University of California, Los Angeles, graduate school, and a Mellon postdoctoral fellowship at Cornell University. Earlier versions of some of the material in this paper were presented at the Thirtieth Conference of the International Conference on Traditional Music, Schladming, Austria, July 1989, and the Conference on Lament in Austin, Texas, April 1989. Special thanks to the Karelian lamenters who so graciously shared their knowledge with me, and to my colleagues Leslie Dunn, Nancy Jones, and Janet Chernela for fruitful discussion of the issues presented here.

[1] Reports of male lamenters exist in the interdisciplinary world-wide literature on lament; however, due to the lack of systematic attention to gender differences in lament performance, it is unclear whether male lamenting in any particular context is stylistically and functionally comparable to female forms.

[2] Graham and Urban both use "ritual wailing"; see Laura Graham, "Three Modes of Shavante Vocal Expression: Wailing, Collective Singing, and Political Oratory," in Joel Sherzer and Greg Urban, eds., *Native South American Discourse* (Berlin: Mouton de Gruyter, 1986), pp. 83–118, and Greg Urban, "Discourse, Affect, and Social Order:

Elizabeth Tolbert

Specifically, laments are performed with a texted melody infused with the "icons of crying,"[3] performative elaborations and stylizations of natural crying. However, in Karelia, as in many other areas of the world, it appears that the crying icons alone are not the essential formal criteria that distinguish the female lament from other genres; rather, it is the presence of *texted* and *melodic* stylized crying that characterizes the lament as intrinsically feminine. Women lamenters are said to "cry with words," as opposed to men, who merely "cry with the eyes," or ordinary crying. In the Karelian lament, iconic representations of emotion are embedded within the stylistic norms of language, music, and other expressive systems. This mixture of stylized weeping, singing, and ritual speech results in a powerful and moving manner of performance, one that is unique both to the lament and to women. The lamenter projects the experience of grief through her individual voice as a means to orchestrate the collective experience of sorrow. It is the very quality of the female crying voice, a voice that "cries with words," that is elaborated in performance to symbolize affect and to set this genre apart from others to accomplish cultural work grounded in the experience of grief.

The Karelian Lament

The primary source material for this essay comes from my fieldwork among Karelian lamenters in 1984 and 1985 in Finland. The Karelians are a small minority people closely related to the Finns in both language and culture, living along the border area between Finland and the former Soviet Union. For nearly 1,000 years they have been associated with Russia to the east and the Eastern Orthodox church, in contrast to the western Finns, who had ties to Sweden and Western Christianity. Up until World War II, the Karelian lament, or *itkuvirsi*, was an integral part of the non-Christian rituals of ancestor worship in the death and wedding ceremonies of peasant village life. It is probable that the lament survived in Karelia, and elsewhere in Eastern Europe, because the Orthodox church did not completely stamp out the indigenous religious tradition, as did the Roman and later Lutheran church in western Finland.[4] After World War II, when Karelia was ceded to the Soviets, the

(2 contd.) Ritual Wailing in Amerindian Brazil," *American Anthropologist* 90 (1988), 385–400. Feld uses "sung-texted-weeping" for the Kaluli of Papua New Guinea, while Tiwary uses "tuneful weeping" for tribal India; see Steven Feld, *Sound and Sentiment: Birds, Weeping, Poetics, and song in Kaluli Expression* (Philadelphia: University of Pennsylvania Press, 1982), and K. M. Tiwary, "Tuneful Weeping: a Mode of Communication," *Frontiers* 3 (1978), 24–27. In this essay, I use the term "lament" as the general cover term for genres that use the performance technique of stylized crying.
3 Urban, "Ritual Wailing," 389.
4 Lauri Honko, "Balto-Finnic Lament Poetry," *Studia Fennica* 17 (1974), 56.

ritual contexts for the lament were abandoned with the forced relocation of the Karelian refugees to Finland and the concomitant destruction
of their peasant culture. Today, a few older Karelian women still remember the traditions that were a part of their traditional village life. Among
them were the women that I worked with in 1985, women with remarkable memories, who with sensitivity and bravery faced the painful
memories of their refugee experience and their disappearing culture.

The *itkuvirsi* is performed only by women in an ecstatic manner
reminiscent of a shamanistic trance, showing influences from indigenous shamanism along with a thin veneer of Orthodox Christianity.
The prototypal context for laments is death, where the lamenter serves
as a conduit to *Tuonela*, the Finnish-Karelian land of the dead. The
lamenter is a magico-religious practitioner of considerable power; she
leads the souls of the dead to *Tuonela*, and brings messages back and
forth from one world to the next. She not only gives vent to her own
feelings, but through the projection of her individual experience of
grief, helps the society as a whole to mourn, and ultimately to preserve
the balance between this world and the next.

Lamenters emphasize that lament is a serious duty, not to be taken
lightly; each lament is a "work of sorrow," improvised anew for each
particular occasion. When the lamenter "cries with words," she uses a
special language appropriate for the dead, a ritual language full of metaphor, alliteration, parallelism, and nonreferential syllables, sung to a sigh-
like descending melodic line, and suffused with the icons of crying.

During a funeral ritual, as many as fifty obligatory laments are performed. At the moment of death, a lamenter is on the stairs before the
dogs of *Tuonela* start to bark.[5] She laments as a commentary on all
aspects of the funeral preparations such as washing and dressing the
corpse, making the coffin, and the burial. In addition to the funeral
preparations and the funeral itself, contexts for lamenting include
many remembrance feasts, both at home and at the grave. Lamenting
also takes place at home in front of the icon corner – a portal to the
other world and the center of the ancestor cult in the home – being,
according to lamenters, like a "speech to the dead, but in notes."

The primary role of the lamenter is that of a mediator between the
world of the living and the world of the dead. Her lament functions as
a "bridge between worlds," enacting the journey to the other world on
several levels of performance.[6] The lamenter guides the soul to *Tuonela*,
which is considered by the Karelians to be literally under the graveyard,

[5] Audio recording, Tampere University Folklore Archives, Erkki Ala-Könni, collector.

Accession Number	Date	Performer	Place of Origin
A–K 210	1957	Elmi Tsokkinen	Suojärvi

[6] Anna Caraveli-Chaves, "Bridge Between Worlds: The Greek Women's Lament as
Communicative Event," *Journal of American Folklore* 93 (1980), 129–57.

by "finding the words," *löytää sanoja*, words that gain power by being "cried" in performance. The special lament words mark the soul's departure from the intimate landscape of home and guide it across the unfamiliar white waters of the river of *Tuonela* in the north. The journey is visually represented by a path of towels stretched from the home to the graveyard, which is itself embroidered with tree-of-life symbolism, a representation of the shamanic world axis that links the land of the living with the worlds both above and below. The lamenter laments along the path of towels, accompanying the soul literally and figuratively to the land of the dead, performing the path both in form and function.[7]

The display of the icons of crying in the lamenter's voice is itself the means to travel to the other world; the crying manner of performance, along with other ritual actions such as covering the face and eyes, swaying, and holding the special lament cloth, the *itkuliina*, over the face, help to induce the trance-like state that enables the lamenter to "go to *Tuonela*." Furthermore, the crying voice signals the presence of spiritual power, reinforcing the validity of the performance, and thus facilitating the collective experience of catharsis.

Laments are also "cried" at weddings, where they mark the transition from girlhood to married woman. The lamenter, lamenting the part of the bride, protests that she is being sold to the "bears" or "wolves," as the groom's family is called in laments, for a few copper coins, and that the "white clothes," an allusion not only to her wedding dress but to her shroud, have been prepared before their time. She asks her relatives for her inheritance and for advice, and in reply is told to obey her mother-in-law, to "try to serve her and bow before her, water her feet with your tears."[8]

The contents of the wedding laments are characterized by the sharp contrast between the happy life of the girl and the misery of living among strangers. The wife was primarily thought of as a worker for the husband and his family, and if she did not survive well in her new surroundings, she had nowhere to go. As Martta Mikkilä reported to me, "before they lamented, now they divorce."

[7] For a more detailed exposition of these ideas, see Elizabeth Tolbert, "On Beyond Zebra: Some Theoretical Considerations of Emotion and Meaning in Music," *Pacific Review of Ethnomusicology* 4 (1987), 75–97; "The Musical Means of Sorrow: The Karelian Lament Tradition," unpublished Ph.D. dissertation, University of California, Los Angeles, 1988; "Magico-Religious Power and Gender in the Karelian Lament," in Marcia Herndon and Suzanne Ziegler, eds., *Music, Culture and Gender* (Berlin: Institute for Comparative Music Studies, 1990), pp. 41–56; "Women Cry with Words: Symbolization of Affect in the Karelian Lament," *Yearbook for Traditional Music* 22 (1990), 80–105.

[8] Audio recording, Tampere University Folklore Archives, Erkki Ala-Könni, collector.

Accession Number	Date	Performer	Place of Origin
A–K 128	1955	Elmi Tsokkinen	Suojärvi

As in death contexts, the ancestors figure prominently in wedding laments, where they are informed of the wedding plans and asked for their protection. Konkka compares the liminality of the engagement period to the mourning period for the deceased, as evidenced by external signs such as the loosening of the hair, and the special clothes that the bride wore that were analogous to mourning clothes.[9] She also proposes that the word for "wedding," *häät*, at one time referred to a festival for the dead.[10]

The many wars and eventual relocation of the Karelians to Finland, along with the inevitable influences of urbanization and modernization, have resulted in the disruption of the lament tradition. Today, the only traditional contexts still available for lament performance are private ones such as remembrance feasts for the dead, or informal ones such as communing with the ancestors at the icon corner or in the graveyard. New lament contexts are evolving, however; many Karelian lamenters now lament in Finland at artistic and tourist venues, for the media, or for Karelian cultural events. Along with other Karelian performance traditions, crafts, and even the practice of Orthodox Christianity, laments are performed not only as a reminder of the old ways, but as a means to re-create and affirm Karelian identity in the face of the dominant Finnish Lutheran majority.

Klaudia Rahikainen, while not a lamenter herself, heard lamenting in funeral contexts in her youth, and is quite sensitive to the increasing decontextualization and aestheticization of Karelian traditional practices. She criticizes today's lamenters who "lament for money" and not for a "real occasion," commenting that some have never heard lamenting at a wedding or funeral. She notes that

Prasniekka is a church holiday but it is also a general word for festival [and] a saint's name day. In Karelia it meant any holiday. Before there weren't laments at *prasniekkas*, but now there are. It's a performance . . . The *prasniekkas* now are *lammitetty* [meaning "warmed over"].

Further evidence of the "warmed over" nature of lamenting in Finland today is the way in which laments are learned.

You can't learn how to sing laments. You can teach yourself [*opitella*], but not learn [*oppia*]. It's not real if you learn it. In Karelia they didn't perform. It was natural, like drinking coffee. Now they perform and teach, but not then.

Knuuttila, a Finnish scholar who has worked extensively with present-day North Karelian performing traditions, explains that

in part keening and lamenting are a direct inheritance of the old culture but also keening and making up of laments has been expressly learnt because

---

[9] Unelma Konkka, *I kuinen Ikävä*, Suomalaisen Kirjallisuuden Seuran Toimituksia 428 (Helsinki: Suomalaisen Kirjallisuuden Seura, 1985), pp. 110–15.

[10] Konkka, *I kuinen*, p. 181.

demand for this type has, to some extent, increased in the last few years in the folklorism forum . . . [However,] I would like to claim that despite all the ballast today's [1985] North Karelian traditional performers are more genuine than their environment or their audiences; they are mediators of fragments of their own culture which is strange to most of us [Finns].[11]

I believe that Knuuttila has described the situation very well; the laments that were sung to me were fragments, yet were comparable musically and textually to archive examples recorded since 1905. Most importantly, although lamenting had acquired the tinge of aesthetic performance, to those who had actually learned lamenting in Karelia, it remained, at least conceptually, a sacred form of ritual expression.

A refugee lament

In Finland today, one of the most common topics for lamenters is the Karelian refugee experience. As the lament once helped to ease the transition from this world to the next, it now serves to mediate between the world of the past and the modern world. When Karelian lamenters mourn for their past, their lost culture, and their former homeland, they counteract their loss by lament performance, performance that not only helps to sustain the tradition, but that contributes to the ongoing re-creation of Karelian identity in new and evolving contexts.

In the following refugee lament, Alina Repo laments to her dead mother about the hard times during the war, and wistfully remembers her beautiful home in Karelia. Alina's lament contains elements of her own life intertwined with the collective experience of losing one's homeland, expressed in the linguistic and musical conventions of the lament form. Alina balances the personal and the traditional, the innovative and the formulaic, thus exhibiting an essential feature of lament performance – the "dynamic interplay of individual expression and collective forms and sentiments."[12]

Alina begins her lament with the traditional muffled sobbing, covering her face with the *itkuliina*, or "crying cloth," so that the evil spirits will not enter her mouth. Shielding her eyes with her hands, she sways gently in a circle and starts to lament, employing the icons of crying, the special lament words, and the sigh-like melody to contact her mother in *Tuonela*. As she begins to "find the words," the melody descends in an unadorned manner, interspersed with sporadic, forced crying. As the performance develops, the melody becomes more elaborated, more text is inserted into each sigh-like melodic phrase, and the crying icons intensify and gain momentum; each of these formal

---

11 Seppo Knuuttila, "The Last Rune Singer," *Musiikin Suunta* 7:1 (1985), 63.
12 Steven Feld, "Wept Thoughts: Voicing of Kaluli Memories," *Oral Tradition* 4, 2–3 (1990), 241.

intensifications in turn generates an increase in micro-modulations of pitch and rhythm, a sign not only of emotional intensity but of spiritual presence, an indication that the lamenter is entering a trance-like state to communicate with her mother in *Tuonela*.

Alina Repo, Juuka, Finland, August 1985
Refugee lament

1 *Kuule kuldaine kukad (i) päiväizeñi.*
   Listen my dear flower sunshine.
2 *Kallejen malittuizeñi majitciaizeñi.*
   My dear bearer, my mother.
3 *Emozeñi kallis kandajaizeñi.*
   My mother, my dear bearer.
4 *Kui jo liennet piässy igävie päiväizil (i) piälici.*
   I wonder how you passed the bad days.
5 *Oli ai katalaizel laizel kaiken (i) moized (i) igäväized da itkuized.*
   The times had all kinds of sadness and crying.
6 *O kallis kandajaizeñi.*
   Oh my dear bearer.
7 *Kui oli iliman suuruized igäväized.*
   It was such great unhappiness.
8 *Kui ai emmo voinnu ihastellakse izäizie laittuloiz (i) ikkunpiälyziz.*
   Because we couldn't enjoy the windowsill that father made.
9 *Emogo voinu veseldelläkse omis Karjalan vesirandaiziz*
     veseldelläkse.
   And we couldn't play in the waters off our own Karelian shores.
10 *Aa näin elee kaiken (i) moized (i) katalaizil laizil.*
   So, one lives in all kinds of unhappiness.
11 *Pidän ylästä (i) ylen suured (i) igäväized.*
   In very great unhappiness.
12 *Kui jo ollygö kotikujoized*
   Because the home lanes have
13 *kummalle kuksistuttu.*
   been given to strangers.
14 *Kai peltoizet kai pelloni piendaruized ylenä jäliközoiduttu,*
   and the fields and the sides of the fields have been neglected,
15 *Kui jo ei ole armahien askeluizeñi astujaizi,*
   and there are none of my dear steppers to walk,
16 *Eigö pienoizi pihamuahuizile pepettelemää.*
   and no small ones to putter in the yard.
17 *Oppikkoa vain ygö armahad andelaized elelä uuzil elin (i) tilaizil.*
   Try dear giver to live in the new circumstances.
18 *Ylen sulavis soguiziz suzien suzien da dien ker. (?)*
   In harmony with strangers.

19 *Oi kallis spoassaizeñi.*
Oh my dear saint.

20 *Anna suured (i) blauhostoveñiaized kaikil (i) rahvahaizil eliä yksisdummaizi.*
Bless all people that they live in harmony.

21 *Kui jo lien ollu ylen orboloin ozaized.*
If only I had been left to the orphan's fate.

22 *O katceldavannu.*
Oh protector.

23 *Suojelle (n) Siñjisokolan siibyizil pienoizi pezäize (i) peitelessää.*
Protect the small ones of Sinisokola, covered with wings in the nest.

24 *O kalledit kantomut. Kui olen (i)*
Oh dear ones who carried me. If only I had

25 *orboin ozaizil jäänny yksil elintilaizil.*
been left alone to the orphan's fate.

26 *Oi kallehet kandajaizeñi.*
Oh my dear bearer.

27 *Älgää yllägiä yksinäizi eläjäizi.*
Don't forsake me the lonely one.

28 *Kui jo ollygö armahavia talaviaigaized annettu omil (i) eländaigaizil.*
I have been given terrible winter time for my own life circumstances.

29 *Mindä lien ollu valgeat tzaugevoatteivo varusteltu ennen kaikki aigaizi?*
Why have the white clothes been prepared before their time?

30 *Eigö lie voinu stiästellä vieluveräjizipiälici.*
(?)

31 *On ajaa vied aigaized akkalaa lakkaized ollu.*
There would have still been time before I would have had to become an old woman.

The voice of lament

The lament, although expressed in traditional form, has its roots in personal experience; as Outi Repo remarks, "I learned them [laments] all my life long. The kind of life you have, so are your laments."[13] Within the formal constraints of the performance, the lament becomes personalized through improvisatory procedures such as specific reference to events, places, and persons, and through the manipulation of formal elements in the musical, textual, and emotive domains; these improvisatory

---

13 Audio recording, Tampere University Folklore Archives, Erkki Ala-Könni, collector.

Accession Number	Date	Performer	Place of Origin
A–K 1683	1970	Outi Repo	Suistamo

processes are crucial for the creation of the lamenter's own style, her own "voice," vocality steeped in and inextricably intertwined with symbolic values.

Alina sprinkles her lament with particulars, the particulars of her own life along with the particulars of the past, images that are personal yet which also communicate a lifestyle known to all Karelians. Alina evokes the common experience of the "bad days, the times [that] had all kinds of sadness and crying," the times when "the home lanes have been given to strangers," and links it with references to her own home and the Karelian landscape. She names the place Sinisokola, and situates especially poignant feelings in her own "home lanes," her own "Karelian shores," and her own "fields." She longingly remembers the "windowsill that father made," and playing "in the waters off our own Karelian shores."

Alina's personal experience of pain is highlighted when she cries to her mother "don't forsake me the lonely one," prefacing her pleas with traditional modes of address such as "my dear bearer," or "my dear flower sunshine." Crying "If only I had been left to the orphan's fate," and grieving that she has been "given terrible winter time for my own life circumstances," she uses traditional formulations for the deeply personal sentiment of unalloyed loss. When she prays to the Saints to "Protect the small ones of Sinisokola, covered with wings in the nest," and to "Bless all people that they live in harmony," Alina underscores the plight of the Karelian refugees while using traditional phrases from wedding and funeral laments. In this way, her individual experience of grief gains multiple voices in performance and is used to negotiate between individual meanings and the social goals of catharsis, the regulated expression of grief, anger, and sorrow, and in the case of the refugee lament, the ongoing creation of a Karelian past.

The structural elements of the text, such as stock metaphors, alliteration, and specialized grammatical forms, are a critical area of definition of the lamenter's "voice." Improvisation within these formulaic structures, into which the particulars of the situation are fitted, reflects the tension between the individual and the group by showing a balance between formula and innovation.

One of the most beautiful structural features of the lament is the virtuoso display of alliteration and end rhyme, along with a general sensitivity to the use of sound to create the special lament words, especially the metaphorical names. In the first three lines of the above refugee lament, Alina Repo laments to her mother with profuse alliteration of the "k" and "m" sounds, and, in so doing, places affective meaning in the sound of her words: *Kuule kuldaine kukad (i) päiväizeñi*, "Listen my dear flower sunshine," *Kallejen malittuizeñi majitciaizeñi*, "My dear bearer, my mother," *Emozeñi kallis kandajaizeñi*, "My mother, my dear bearer."

Sequences of similar suffixes also serve as a poetic device to unify long chains of words. For example, the verbal suffixes *ja, i, nen,* and *ni,* when strung together and subject to the requisite phonetic transformations of the Karelian language make for the recurrent verbal ending *jai-ze-ni,* meaning "my little one who does . . . " or the noun suffix *ze-ni,* "my little one." Again, in the first three lines of the above lament, there is a recurrent use of these endings: *Kuule kuldaine kukad (i) päiväizeñi,* "My dear flower sunshine," *Kallejen malittuizeñi,* "My dear bearer," *majitciaizeñi,* "my dear mother," *Emozeñi,* "My dear mother," *kallis kandajaizeñi,* "my dear bearer."

Parallelism, along with manipulation of phonetic features, is another locus of affective meaning in lament texts. Lamenting the desolation of her former Karelian homeland, again, replete with alliteration, Alina Repo cries: *Kui jo ei ole armahien askeluizeñi astujaizi, eigö pienoizi pihamuahuizile pepettelemää,* "There are none of my dear steppers to walk, and no small ones to putter in the yard." She also uses parallelism and alliteration to long for the joys of everyday life in Karelia: *Kui ai emmo voinnu ihastellakse izäizie laittuloiz (i) ikkunpiälyziz, emogo voinu veseldelläkse omis Karjalan vesirandaiziz veseldelläkse,* "We couldn't enjoy the windowsill that father made, and we couldn't play in the waters off our own Karelian shores."

Unfortunately, the English translation cannot do justice to the lament's beauty. Its meaning is not as straightforward as presented here, and although its metaphorical names and other conventions do have referential content, they are only a small part of its meaning. The sound of the words of the lament creates textual icons of emotion, equivalent to the icons of crying; the referential content of lament language is both enhanced and obfuscated by this "poetic function," and, as shown below, is even further transformed by the icons of crying and by singing.[14]

"Crying with words": music/text interaction

As can be seen in the musical transcription in example 11.1, the lament melody, improvised in its particulars in a manner analogous to improvisation in the lament texts, is largely defined by a sigh-like descending tetra- or pentachordal melody. The line is further delineated by breath demarcations consisting of an initial sharp, audible intake of breath, and a final sob. The melodic formula begins with an elongated highest note, represented in the transcription as a half-note "a," and descends in an undulating contour with step-wise motion to a repeated "d," the final note, also elongated. The musical elements of the lament are somewhat speech-like, and are not easily codified in the values of Western

14 For a discussion of "poetic function," see Roman Jakobson, "Closing Statement: Linguistics and Poetics," in Thomas Sebeok, ed., *Style and Language* (Cambridge, MA: MIT Press, 1960), pp. 350–77.

11.1 The relationship of music and text in Karelian lament, illustrating the technique of musical masking. Syllables other than the first are accented in the following ways:
  A melisma (more than one note per syllable)
  B elongated duration
  C fermata at end of musical phrase
  D raised pitch and stressed dynamic
  E wavering, trill-like voice
  F elongated duration and stressed dynamic

musical notation. Therefore, in the transcription, neither the rhythmic nor pitch values are represented literally; the rhythmic notation system denotes longer and shorter relative durations, while the pitch notation represents relative pitch between notes of the melodic line.[15] The voice

[15] A word about the transcription; all transcription represents analysis in that it renders a parsing of units of structure, which in turn represent an approach to a particular musical problem to be investigated. Therefore, there are no "correct" transcriptions, only transcriptions that are more or less useful for illustrating particular ideas. I have chosen to notate the skeletal formula of the lament, at the expense of a visual representation of micro rhythmic and micro tonal modulations, in order to best illustrate the relationship between musical and textual units in this genre.

of the lamenter is strongly suffused with the icons of crying throughout the performance. The pitches and rhythms are therefore not stable, and themselves index affect. The icons of crying intensify the musical representations of affect; by the end of the lament, or during particularly poignant passages, the pitch rises markedly, and the micro-variations in pitch and rhythm intensify. The text also becomes more dense with affective features, such as the vocative use of metaphorical names, non-referential syllables, parallelism, alliteration, and assonance.

The details of melodic contour are dictated by the demands of the prosodic features of the text. The text is for the most part set syllabically. When it is not, its melismatic setting serves to accentuate the text. Moreover, each word defines a melodic pitch contour that represents either a level contour, or a descent from its initial to its final note. This both serves to define words as units, and to fit the text into an overall descending pattern. The descending melodic word contours are roughly congruent with speech accent, in that the pitch contour of words in Karelian is falling.

However, there are additional musical features that are not congruent with speech accent, where musical means are used to mask the meaning of the text, a technique I have referred to elsewhere as "musical masking."[16] Specifically, within the sigh-like musical phrases, the meaning of the text is masked by musical procedures that transform its structural properties; among these are musical intonation contours that are not aligned with speech intonation contours, musical rhythms that deliberately obfuscate speech rhythm and word boundaries, and most importantly, "stress shift," a stylistic device wherein the normal syllabic stress of spoken language is shifted to unstressed syllables during singing.[17]

Example 11.1 illustrates stress shift in a Karelian lament.[18]

In this lament, stress shift occurs when musical accentuation of pitch or duration is displaced by occurring on syllables other than the first, due to the fact that in spoken Karelian, the first syllable is always stressed by both raised pitch and dynamic accent. This results in obfuscation of word boundaries and serves to disguise the referential meaning of the text. As shown in Example 11.1, syllables other than the first are accented in the following ways: at letter A, the last syllable of the word "kul-dai-*ne*" is accentuated by melisma and by an elongated duration

---

16 Tolbert, "Emotion and Meaning," 90.
17 For stress shift in Spanish song see Terrell Morgan and Richard Janda, "Musically-Conditioned Stress shift in Spanish Revisited: Empirical Verification and Nonlinear Analysis," in Carl Kirschner and Janet DeCesaris, eds., *Studies in Romance Linguistics: Selected Papers from the Seventeenth Linguistic Symposium on Romance Languages*, Amsterdam Studies in the Theory and History of Linguistic Science, Series IV – Current Issues in Linguistic Theory, vol. 60 (Amsterdam, PA: Benjamins, 1989), vol. LX pp. 273–88.
18 Adapted from Tolbert, "Emotion and Meaning," 90–91.

at the end of the melisma; at letter B, the second syllable of "päi-*väi*-ze-ni" is accented by a longer duration on the second syllable than on the first; at letter C, the melodic formula demands that the last note of the phrase is held, elongating the fourth syllable of the word "päi-väi-ze-*ni*"; at letter D, the second syllable of the word "mal-*it*-tui-ze-ni" is accented both by a rise in pitch and a dynamic accent; at letter E, the second syllable of the word "kal-*lis*" is accented by a trill-like wavering of the voice; at letter F, the second syllable of the word "li-*en*-et" is accented by both elongated duration and dynamic accent.

Performative efficacy

A good lamenter is one who can "find the words," and, as shown above, in "finding the words," the lamenter finds not only the text *per se*, but "words" infused with vocal expressions of affect, affect achieved through the manipulation of performative devices such as alliteration, musical stress shift, and stylized crying. The expressive qualities of the lamenter's vocality are a sign of both her individuality and her magico-religious power. Each lamenter laments with her own "voice," "like the birds who sing with their own voice," a voice that is ritually effective in leading the soul of the dead to *Tuonela*, or in sustaining marriage, as indicated by the testimony that the "master [lamenter] was really good. She gave away 44 girls in marriage and not one was divorced."[19] The power of the voice is also evident in some of the terms for lamenting. *Luvoitteleminen* or *loihtia*, literally means "to cast a spell";[20] likewise, the etymology of the word *laulaa*, "to sing," indicates that it originally meant "to exert a mysterious, magic influence."[21]

The emphasis on ritual efficacy through vocal expressivity highlights one of the most important characteristics of lament performance; it is not merely a display of grief, but an interactive performance that demands a response. A skillful lamenter carries the group along with her, and in Karelia is known to "make even a stone weep." While the lamenter "cries with the voice," those around her respond by "crying with the eyes." The use of the crying voice in the lament serves as an attention-getting mechanism to promote intersubjectivity, allowing for individual experience to be experienced as social and vice versa.[22]

The powerful nature of the crying voice is further highlighted by the fact that it is not necessarily an index of the internal state of the lamenter,

[19] Konkka, *I kuinen*, p. 107.
[20] Ibid., p. 10.
[21] Martti Haavio, *Vainamoinen, Eternal Sage*, Folklore Fellows Communications 144 (Helsinki: Suomalainen Tiedeakatemia, 1952), p. 73.
[22] For a discussion of the role of intersubjectivity in processes of meaning formation, see Bradd Shore, "Twice-Born, Once Conceived: Meaning Construction and Cultural Cognition," *American Anthropologist* 93, 1 (1991), 20.

but a metasymbol of emotion; nevertheless, the fact that the lament is being cried by an individual woman gives prominence to the fact that it is the individual experience of grief that is being generalized. The quality of the lamenter's crying voice points to the somatization of grief, a process that is only possible through the experiences of the individual body. Thus the quality of the voice itself is crucial to the negotiation between the personal and the collective; every woman cries her own grief with her own voice, yet her voice is also a collective sign of grief.

Although the stylized melodic crying of the female lamenter's voice is unquestionably allied with performative efficacy, paradoxically, at least from the standpoint of a Western ethnopsychological bias, it is also allied with powerlessness and lack of emotional control, and the implication that women "cry" in laments because they are "emotion-expressing surrogates" of low status.[23] Recent work has countered this claim by focusing on how lament performance allows for the creation of women's "affective enclaves," gender defined spaces of protest, solidarity, and affirmation that maintain separateness yet also allow for influence and access to social power outside of strictly delineated female realms.[24] By framing crying as a stylized form within the context of lament performance, women reverse the power imbalance inherent in their purported "surrogate" status. As Gal, among others, points out, the persistence of devalued forms of expression betrays resistance to the dominant order and the existence of an alternative world view.[25] However, in the lament, it is not merely the *presence* of stylized crying, but specifically the *form* that it takes, that allows the lament to be both a powerful instrument of ritual efficacy and an instrument of empowerment for those who perform it. It is the very quality of the female lamenting voice, vocality that embodies musical, textual, and iconic expressions of affect, that transforms the powerless crying of an individual woman into the collectively powerful form of "crying with words," an expression of courage and beauty that defies helplessness in the face of death.

[23] An example of the depiction of the female lamenter as one who lacks emotional control can be found in Bade Ajuwon, "Lament for the Dead as a Universal Folk Tradition," *Fabula* 22 (1981), 274. For discussion of "emotion-expressing surrogates," see Paul Rosenblatt, Patricia Walsh, and Douglas Jackson, *Grief and Mourning in Cross-Cultural Perspective* (New Haven: Human Relations Area files, 1976), p. 26.

[24] Constantina-Nadia Seremetakis, *The Last Word: Women, Death, and Divination in Inner Mani* (University of Chicago Press, 1991), p. 5. Also see Tolbert, "Magico-Religious Power," 41–56.

[25] For a recent discussion of the relationship between discourse, power, and gender, see Susan Gal, "Between Speech and Silence: The Problematics of Research on Language and Gender," in Micaela di Leonardo, ed., *Gender at the Crossroads of Knowledge: Feminist Anthropology in the Postmodern Era* (Berkeley: University of California Press, 1991), pp. 175–203.

Conclusion

As shown above, the lamenter's voice gains its power through the interplay of "words," music, and crying, each mediating the other in a complex and multi-layered manner of performance. Both text and crying in the lament are themselves mediated; lament text is mediated speech, a special form of communication appropriate for the lamenter's "work of sorrow," and, likewise, the lamenter's crying is a mediation between the natural cry and the culturally specific and stylized icons of crying. Through hierarchical levels of formal constraints, these interacting textual, musical, and emotive systems draw attention to themselves, and by means of this self-reference, or "poetic function," index their ritual function.[26] Laderman notes a similar phenomenon for Malay ritual performance, proposing that "the extent to which language is transformed by music [or in the case of the Karelian lament, by music *and* crying] constitutes the ritual reframing of reality through sound."[27] When the Karelian lamenters interweave text, words, and music to "cry with words," they create "wept thoughts," mediations between thought and feeling that have the power to mediate between the worlds, between the individual and the collective, and between the past and the present.[28]

This complicated manner of performance, one which requires extensive transformation and inversions of the norms of both speech and music, is actually an inverse mode of performance that is appropriate for communication with *Tuonela*, conceived by the Karelians to be an inverted mirror of this world. The formal procedures in the lament therefore suggest that religious principles and cosmological associations are encoded into the musical improvisational process, and are the essential means by which the lament is imbued with ritual efficacy, efficacy manifest as magico-religious power in the musically transformed and mutated performance of the word.

It is significant that Alina Repo uses the powerful performative style of "crying with words" in the non-ritual context of the refugee lament. The memory becomes "truth" in part because of a ritual performance technique that draws on the power of the crying female voice as a way of witnessing and creating a consensual reality.[29] She thus uses the power of her voice, her "crying with words," as a means to reposition

[26] For discussion of poetic function in reference to laments, see Urban, "Ritual Wailing," 385–400. Also see note 14.

[27] Carol Laderman, *Taming the Wind of Desire: Psychology, Medicine, and Aesthetics in Malay Shamanistic Performance*, Comparative Studies of Health Systems and Medical Care (Berkeley, Los Angeles, Oxford: University of California Press, 1991), p. 107.

[28] See Feld, "Wept Thoughts," especially 256–58.

[29] For discussion of this idea in reference to Greek laments see Seremetakis, *Last Word*, pp. 120–23.

the relationship of the Karelians vis-à-vis their history, and to create a performative link with the past. When Alina grieves to her mother about the hardships of the refugee experience, she is calling upon her to authenticate a memory of Karelia that has become irrevocably lost; by forming her appeal as a lament, she widens her audience to include all of the Karelian people.

Alina and other present-day lamenters perform laments to commemorate the plight of the Karelian refugees, to comment on the errors of the younger generation, to mourn the loss of Karelian traditions, as well as to reaffirm Karelian identity and to enhance individual status. These new contexts only reinforce the fact that the voice of lament is truly a powerful one; the lamenter carries the bodily experience of crying in her singing voice, using it to transform and empower her words. Her voice thus creates a bridge between the world of the living and the world of the dead, the past and the present, weaving individual lives into collective remembrances.

PART IV

Maternal voices

12

The lyrical dimensions of spirituality: music, voice, and language in the novels of Toni Morrison

KARLA F. C. HOLLOWAY

In the final pages of Toni Morrison's *Song of Solomon*, an aged, weary, and dying Pilate grants her nephew Milkman her supreme gift – she gives him her voice and urges him to sing. His song, "Oh Sugargirl don't leave me here" that "he could not stop . . . from coming," is a passioned embrace of his lineage. Through voicing the "worn old words" of the text that links him to his past, Milkman acknowledges his ancestry.[1]

Passages like this indicate the ways in which Morrison's literary voice is linked to ancestral and modern voices of the black diaspora. As I read this novel, a distant memory of my mother's singing crystallized. Mother's voice, a constant hymn throughout my childhood, is connected to the voices of my grandmothers, churchwomen, and my black teachers. I remember all of their tones with great specificity, and their words constantly invade my present with their wisdom.

In the novels of black women writers, women's voices claim ownership to a creative word – a force not unlike the West African concept of *nommo*, in which the creative artistry of voice connects generations.[2]

This essay is a version of three of my chapters from Karla Holloway and Stephanie Demetrakopoulos, *New Dimensions of Spirituality: A BiRacial and BiCultural Reading of the Novels of Toni Morrison* (Westport, CT: Greenwood Press, 1987). I extend my appreciation to the publishers for permission to reprint this text.

[1] Toni Morrison, *Song of Solomon* (New York: Alfred A. Knopf, 1977), p. 340. Parenthetical references in the text are to this edition.

[2] Among the Dogon of the Upper Volta, the spirits of Nummo were represented by the divine number of eight – the symbol of speech. In *Conversations with Ogotemmeli: An Introduction to Dogon Religious Ideas* (Oxford University Press, 1965), Marcel Griaule interviewed an elder of that clan, Ogotemmeli, who explained that "when Nummo speaks, what comes [forth] is a warm vapour which conveys, and itself constitutes speech . . . the first word had been pronounced before the genitalia of a woman . . . and came from a woman's genitalia" (pp. 18, 20). In the 1970s, some African American

Women's voices in these novels are like my mother's; they control and advise through their soft or strident, careful and caring language. These voices make certain that the loss that women of the West African diaspora experienced through the systems of slavery, colonialism, and racism would not be the final measure of their experiences. Instead, an insistent and gendered voice that extended the idea of generation to embody spiritual generation and linguistic creativity salvaged and revised the potential of their womanhood. As a result, the distant and persistent echoes of song maintain a memory, despite the ravages of diaspora fracture, of a West African legacy.

In this essay, I explore the dimensions of voice in two of Toni Morrison's most lyrical novels – *Song of Solomon* and *The Bluest Eye*. A scene from Morrison's *Sula* introduces this author's vision of the (re)creative potential of voice.[3] I focus on the ways that Morrison's novels reveal the complex and necessary presence of women's voices and song. These voices echo through generations of African and African American women and enact the memories that assure the continuity of their cultural traditions.

Because these voices resonate as well to my own cultural and gendered memories – the rituals, ceremonies, and language of my own experience as an African American woman – I have allowed an italicized voice to emerge in this essay as a means of acknowledging the force and flow of my own memories that persistently invade my reading and scholarly interpretations of Toni Morrison's stories. Instead of insisting that these readings – the scholarly and the personal – distance themselves from each other, Stephanie Demetrakopoulos and I chose to model a "passionate scholarship" that acknowledges feelings as well as ideas as our critical methodology.[4] I intend for this essay to indicate the necessity of both voices as they speak to the community of voices who are the universe within and without these stories.

The idea of community may be the most visible cultural context within the stories by black women writers. Whether as text or subtext,

(2 contd.) literary essays and anthologies used the concept of nommo (Nummo) to associate that sense of creative generation with their work. See, for example, Paul Harrison, *The Drama of Nommo* (New York: Grove Press, 1972) and William H. Robinson, ed., *Nommo: An Anthology of Modern Black African and Black American Literature* (New York: Macmillan, 1972). The attention to Afrocentric critique in the 1970s and 1980s, and the enthusiastic, but often superficial embrace of the term in critical essays and reviews, led literary theorist Henry Louis Gates, Jr., in a speech before the African Literature Association, to call for "no mo' nommo."

3 Toni Morrison, *Sula* (New York: Alfred A. Knopf, 1973); *The Bluest Eye* (New York: Washington Square Press, 1970). All references cited in the text are to these editions.

4 See *New Dimensions*, p 1. The term is Barbara Du Bois's from her essay, "Passionate Scholarship: Notes on Values, Knowing, and Method in Feminist Social Science," in *Theories of Women's Studies*, eds. Gloria Bowles and Renate Duelli Klein (London: Routledge and Kegan Paul, 1983), p. 112.

the interpretive significance of the community's cultural identity and African genesis plays a critical role in articulating the gendered sphere of its enactment.[5]

Toni Morrison's novels reveal this community dramatically and sustain its imagery through the cultured and gendered dimensions of language. For example, in *Sula* there is an immediate reference to voice and song. The novel's opening scene fleetingly reflects the harmonious vision of an African village that its community has lost. Morrison indicates that this town where (by the novel's end) "there will be nothing left of" has "quiet days, when people in valley houses could hear singing sometimes, banjos sometimes . . . [and see] a dark brown woman in a flowered dress doing a bit of cakewalk . . . her bare feet . . . raise the saffron dust" (pp. 4, 5). Morrison quickly brings the disruptive and abusive present into this image. The harmonious, vital village vanishes and the story sustains instead imagery that draws us towards the novel's conclusion where Suicide Day, a noisy celebration of death, is its final image. In *Sula*'s final pages, Shadrack, a man whom the violence of Western civilizations has rendered mute and mad, leads a cacophonous and clamorous clan that has lost its connection to the harmony of the African village that the novel's opening scene briefly glimpses. It is left to Morrison's character, Nel, to recognize and name the nature of this loss in the book's final pages. The stylized presentation of Nel's weeping over the death of her friend Sula recalls a ritual lament.[6] In "circles and circles of sorrow," a lyrical metaphor that evokes both the circumlocutions of her generational legacy as well as the emotive potential of song, Nel's voice folds her grief and loss into one long, lonely cry, "we was girls together," and signals the spiritual epiphany of this novel.

the loss pressed down on her chest and came up into her throat."We was girls together," she said as though explaining something."Oh Lord, Sula," she cried, "girl, girl, girlgirlgirl." It was a fine cry – loud and long – it had no bottom and . . . no top, just circles and circles of sorrow. (p. 149)

Her voice reconstructs the physical loss of place and potential that are thematic foci in this story, and forces the remnants of her own memories and the community's lost spirit into a dimension that can contain her grief. The generational voice recalled in the embracing, concentric ripples of Nel's soulful cry, resonate for me in three critical ways as I read Morrison's novels.

First, Morrison's own narrative emphases consistently engage a lyrical strategy and foreground a musical motif. Especially in *Song of Solomon*

---

[5] See Melvin Dixon, *Ride Out the Wilderness* (Urbana: University of Illinois Press, 1987), for a discussion of the relationship between place and cultural identity in African American literature.

[6] See Elizabeth Tolbert, "The Voice of Lament" in this volume, especially with respect to the ritual aspect of the lamenter's voice and its identity with the feminine.

and *The Bluest Eye*, as well as in her most recent novel, *Jazz* (1992), the narrative voice regenerates the poetic expressivity of song.

Second, the fictive maternal singers within her stories themselves layer her authorial narrative strategy, repeating its emphasis on the lyrical dimensions of voice and encouraging our attention toward the musical timbre of the words within her worlds.

Finally, Morrison's novels become a catalyst for my personal memories of the lyrical voices of my own mothers – the black women of my family and community whose words follow, instruct and encourage my connection to their traditions.

Nel's echoing cry ululates as a plaintive lament, re-membering the voices of West African women whose songs inscribed the loss of Goree island, and echoing the voices within the ships of the middle passage, the auction block, and the fields of southern plantations. It powerfully evokes the spiritual generational community. Both the idea and the visual presentation of "girls together" and "girlgirlgirl" communicate the interconnectedness of a womanist re-membrance. They illustrate what Demetrakopoulos notes as the "life stages of [Morrison's] women" (*New Dimensions*, p. 63), and they are for me intimate reminders of maternal singers and storytellers – the linguistic necromancers of my community.

I : The lyrics of salvation – Song of Solomon

Morrison's novels recall a West African version of reality that allows the coexistence of the spiritual and physical worlds within the same narrative spaces. In these spaces, mythic voices reconstruct an African American universe.[7]

Consider Milkman's acknowledgment of the power he has gained from Pilate's voice in *Song of Solomon*. Here, Morrison articulates and merges the creative and mythic traditions of black women who have celebrated the mystical and powerful potential of voice.

Milkman is the focus of this far-ranging and complex story; his birth is foretold in the novel's opening scene. On the day that marks the novel's opening, his mother Ruth, who sells velvet rose petals to local shopkeepers, watches a man threatening to leap from the roof of the city hospital. His Aunt Pilate, a "singing woman," accompanies this dramatic moment with song. Her melody and its confusing lyrics haunt the story and eventually follow the grown Milkman's flight south to reclaim what he thinks will be material wealth. Instead, he finds the

---

[7] For an extended discussion of voice in twentieth-century African and African American writers, and a theoretical exploration of the idea of multiple narrative designs, see Karla F. C. Holloway, *Moorings and Metaphors: Figures of Culture and Gender in Black Women's Literature* (New Jersey: Rutgers University Press, 1992).

spiritual wealth of his legacy through the intervention of Circe, a highly symbolic sibyl-like figure and Susan (Sing) Byrd. Both women reconnect him to the song and memory of his family. Pilate's song about Solomon (Sugarman), sung at the opening and closing frames of the story, is revealed as the remnants of an ancestral praise-song that celebrates Milkman's great-grandfather who literally lifted his body into the air and flew back to Africa to escape the abuses of slavery. Knowing the legacy of the song allows Milkman to claim dominion over his physical life and ownership of his spirit.

In the summer of their fifth and sixth years, my children devoted themselves to flight. My daughter's attack was methodical. She planned the mechanics of her flight first on paper, with Da Vinci-like designs. Then, scissors, scraps, and collected pigeon-feathers in tow, she lugged her imagination to the backyard and attempted to implement her plan. My son was more direct. He scaled the nearest tree and, wings of plastic garbage bags extended, he magnificently thrust himself into the air. After he and his recyclable wings crumpled to the ground, he'd extract himself from the pile of grass clippings he had chosen as his landing site and return to the tree.

I watched their adventures from the kitchen window. I was, at that time, involved in reviewing African American spirituals for references to flight. "Review" meant singing them, humming them, accompanying my children's flight with them. I was easily distracted from my task, probably because my once-viewed-as-magnificent idea that the source of the symbolic networks in Song of Solomon *was somewhere hidden within those early black songs was not developing as I had planned. However, as I watched my children play at what I was researching, I gradually realized that the source of the network was more extensive and more resonant than only those spirituals.*

For some time, I had been disturbed with the elusiveness of Song of Solomon. *I had struggled to grasp some single solid sense of this novel and had been uncomfortable with what I felt as its shifting presence. As I watched my children at play, I recalled the scene that initiated my review of the spirituals and that clarified for me the novel's context. The extensive and complex network of flight and song is the theme of this story – and its multifaceted and shifting presence is its identity.*

Early that spring, before the summer of my children's obsession, my uncle had died. It was an especially difficult occasion for my family. My aunt had died of breast cancer only a few years before that; they had been a young and wonderful family, and two sons were left parentless.

At the funeral service, the minister prayed an extemporaneous prayer to help guide us through those wretched days. The cadence of his voice slowly rose and fell, a contrapuntal accompaniment to the few audible sobs in the gathering. The upper room of the funeral home was heavy with our collected sorrow. As if to relieve some of this pressure, someone in the back of the room began to hum. We all knew the song, so another voice sang the lyrics until all of us softly relinquished our tears or our sighs into this music. The minister's resonant voice became the rhythmic punctuation to our melody. Soon, instead of his prayers, it was the song's lyrics that he called out to us: "Soon one morning when this life is over . . . "; and we responded "I'll fly away . . . " And at that moment our spirits were literally lifted up and out of that sorrowful place and sent to rest in some more nurturing, more forgiving dimension. It was an overwhelmingly emotional

201

event and later, as I remembered that day, I remembered most of all the sensation of being elevated from my sorrow and pain. Either that song or that collocation of music and event and emotion sustained and rescued all of us.

That summer Saturday, as I watched my children's developing design on flight, I realized that the background of their play was the background of this novel as well. Pilate's song accompanied incidents of liberation, flight, birth and remembrance. "Soon One Morning" elevated our spirits with the same objective result in those upper rooms of the Detroit funeral parlour.

The haunting poem by Robert Hayden, "O Daedalus, Fly Away Home," echoes the myth of this novel and repeats the rhythm and substance of African American spirituals.[8] The "two wings" reference in Hayden's poem

> Night is an African juju man
> Weaving a wish and a weariness together to make two wings.
> *O fly away home fly away*

recalls the spiritual's lyrics: "Lord I want two wings to veil my face, Lord I want two wings to fly away" and another's as well: "I'm gonna fly from mansion to mansion – when I'm gone."

Flight is a recurrent image in these African American songs, and Morrison's story foregrounds cultural metaphors of flight and dominion. This symbolic opportunity for oppressed slaves to free themselves spiritually from the shackles of slavery is the mythic source of this novel. One of the ancestors in this story is Solomon, a member of an ancient tribe of flying Africans, a West African clan whose ability to fly appears even today in legends about this community. Captured and brought to America, these enslaved Africans escaped their bondage by flying back to their African home. The legends of their escape from this continent have been mythologized into the spoken legacy and song of West African and African American history. The rich and complex spirituality of these West Africans paired a miraculous liberation with a similarly miraculous event – the power of flight as transformation and transcendence. Christianity may have offered a religious frame for the displaced African to contextualize this spirituality within the Americas, but the texture of that picture was distinctly black and African. In *Souls of Black Folk*, DuBois's description of a southern revival is dominated by imagery that suggests this collusion between flight and the musical cadence and timbre of a spiritual voice:

---

[8] Demetrakopoulos's essay in *New Dimensions* discusses this poem. See especially pp. 86–87 where Demetrakopoulos draws an essential parallel between the literature in this tradition and Morrison's own "eloquent" reflection on this theme of flying and song. Demetrakopoulos quotes Morrison as saying: "That is one of the points of *Song*: all the men have left someone, and it is the children who remember it, sing about it, mythologize it, make it a part of their family history" (p. 87).

The black and massive form of the preacher swayed and quivered as the words crowded to his lips and flew at us in singular eloquence.The people moaned and fluttered and then the gaunt-cheeked brown woman beside me suddenly leaped straight into the air and shrieked like a lost soul.[9]

Flight and song are woven together at every crucial juncture in this novel. Milkman Dead's birth is accompanied by the song of his ancestor Solomon. His cousins Hagar and Reba, and his Aunt Pilate sing it to him when he visits their home. At the end of the novel, the song appears again in an older, revised version. Here, children's voices remind Milkman of his own childhood and he comes to understand how physically close, yet spiritually deaf he had been to the heritage that echoed in the community's music.

In Countee Cullen's poem, "Heritage," a rhythmic and pulsating verse taunts the poet with an insistent memory of Africa and destroys his equilibrium. *Song of Solomon* is similarly unrelenting. Until the reader acknowledges the resonance of its voice, and until Milkman makes the necessary journey back and reclaims his past and his community, the myth is discomfiting and the song repeats endlessly and without resolution. From its first gripping funereal imagery of red velvet rose petals scattered across the frozen snow, we know that something will be buried in this book, and something born.

The singing woman . . . walked through the crowd to the rose-petal lady . . . she whispered . . . "A little bird'll be here with the morning." . . . The women were looking deep into each other's eyes when a loud roar went up from the crowd . . . Immediately the singing woman began again:

> O Sugarman done fly
> Sugarman done gone . . .

Mr. Smith had seen the rose petals, heard the music, and leaped on into the air.

(p. 9)

Women's voices and maternal songs preach cultural wisdom in Morrison's novel. They dictate cultural identity and bring order to the African American community. The universe of this novel is negotiated through linguistic metaphors that make both family and event vulnerable to myth-making and spiritualism. The language and the music of *Song of Solomon* imaginatively reconstruct cultural memory and are clearly a part of the "spoken library" of African American culture. Morrison has acknowledged her intent to value this collaboration between oracy and literacy in African American communities and to convey to her reader the images and cosmology of black language.

---

[9] W. E. B. DuBois, *Souls of Black Folk* (Chicago, 1903; reprinted New York: Fawcett, 1961), pp. 140–41.

The spoken library . . . [the] children's stories my family told, spirituals, the ghost stories, the blues, and folk tales and myths, and the everyday . . . instruction and advice of my own people . . . I wanted to write out of the matrix of memory,of recollection, and to approximate the sensual and visceral responses I had to the world I lived in . . . to recreate the civilization of black people . . . the manners, judgments, values, morals.[10]

Music is the umbilicus between the children and the men and women they become. In the earliest pages, Milkman's father, Macon, finds himself "surrendering to the sound" of his sister Pilate, who had been "his first caring for" (p. 29). Like his son, Macon feels the absence of Pilate's nurturing presence. His need of her lifeline symbolically engages the creative potential of song and draws him to his sister's window. Macon is vulnerable to her "memory and music" and succumbs, albeit briefly, to his link to the familial unit just inside the window where Pilate frames a generational picture of three singing women – her daughter, Reba, her granddaughter, Hagar, and herself – the elder – the grandmother who sways "like a willow," tall, strong, gentle, and serene over this scene (pp. 29–30).

Unfortunately, Milkman disrespects the bonds of family and enters into a selfish and abusive relationship with his cousin Hagar that eventually leads to her death. Because his actions fracture Pilate's generational unit, he is left with a debt that extends not only to Hagar's mother and grandmother, but to his own spirit. Milkman disrupts the force and power of their lyrical memories and consequently endangers their generational continuity. The scene of Hagar's funeral, heavy with the musical metaphors of Morrison's methodology make clear this lost lyricism.

Pilate burst in, shouting "Mercy!" . . . a command . . . "Mercy?". . . a question. It was not enough. The word needed a bottom, a frame. She straightened up, held her head high, and transformed the plea into a note. In a clear bluebell voice she sang it out – the one word held so long it became a sentence – and before the last syllable had died in the corners of the room, she was answered in a sweet soprano: "I hear you." (p. 320)

Here, Morrison's narration recalls the West African cultural artistry of call and response.

The people turned around. Reba had entered and was singing too. Pilate neither acknowledged her entrance nor missed a beat. She simply repeated the word "Mercy," and Reba replied.The daughter standing at the back of the chapel, the mother up front, they sang.

---

10 Toni Morrison, "On the 'Spoken Library.'" Excerpts quoted in the *English Journal* (Urbana: National Council of Teachers of English), February 1978. Morrison further commented that this library must be "interpreted, used" as a source of truth, and that the images, cosmology, and humanity of truth lie within spoken language.

In the nighttime.
Mercy.
In the darkness.
Mercy.
In the morning.
Mercy.
At my bedside.
Mercy.
On my knees now.
Mercy. Mercy. Mercy. Mercy.

They stopped at the same time in a high silence. Pilate . . . addressed her words to the woman bordered in gray satin who lay before her. Softly, privately, she sang to Hagar . . .

Who's been botherin my sweet sugar lumpkin?
Who's been botherin my baby?
Who's been botherin my sweet sugar lumpkin?
Who's been botherin my baby girl?

. . . "My baby girl." The three words were still pumping in her throat as she turned away from the coffin.   (pp. 320–322)

At the novel's end, Milkman's surrender to Pilate's song earns him back his spiritual and ancestral place. The echoing strains of the ancient song of Sugarman/Solomon appear again, but this time Milkman is the singer and he is able to regain the power of woman's song. Morrison makes it apparent in this final scene that voice – spoken or sung – contains this potential.

"Sing," she said. "Sing a little something for me."Milkman knew no songs, and had no singing voice . . . but he couldn't ignore the urgency in her voice. *Speaking* the words without the least bit of a tune, he *sang* for the lady. "Sugargirl don't leave me here . . ." [I]t took a while for him to realize she was dead. And when he did, he could not stop the worn old words from coming, louder and louder as though sheer volume would wake her. He woke only the birds, who shuddered off into the air.   (p. 340, my emphasis)

At the moment of Pilate's death, two birds swoop down to the dead Pilate and the reborn Milkman enacting the metaphor of the spiritual "Lord I want two wings." In his final generous moment, Milkman literalizes the potential of Pilate's song, re-members his grandfather's flight and assures his own salvation. His liberation into the embodied voice of the female enables the reclamation of his birthright.

In *Song of Solomon*, childhood, ideally a time of intimacy with things spiritual, is threatened by the loss of cultural identity. This novel demands our attention to the possibility that we may reclaim the strength of the spirit if we recall our ancestral songs. When Pilate sings, her face is "all mask; all emotion and passion . . . left her features and entered her voice" (p. 30). When that African American spiritual calls for "two wings to veil my face," it is both an affirmation and a promise of the strength of an African spirituality that assures endurance and spiritual dominion.

That summer, when my son pulled himself back into that tree and when my daughter furiously erased her design and modified her drawings, they were assuring themselves a future where flight was always in potentia. It did not need to have been actualized during that season. The next spring, Bem rediscovered that tree and Ayana whirled in March winds as if she had wings. I hummed their imaginations along, firm in my belief that childhood is a spiritual pause – a moment of memory and an assurance of the creative potential held within our cultural legacies.

II: The legacy of voice – *The Bluest Eye*

The Bluest Eye, Morrison's first novel, illustrates the promise of childhood but, with strategies similar to Morrison's later works, challenges her reader to explore with her an alternative text – the bleak remnants of creativity that has no dimension for its expression.

This novel chronicles the destruction of the sensitive, reflective young Pecola Breedlove who is pushed into insanity after her father rapes her. The MacTeer family – mother and father, sisters Claudia and Frieda – is the background image for the more central and symbolic Breedloves, a family of social outcasts internally disintegrating under the weight of various horrors. Pecola's parents are Pauline and Cholly.

The world of the children in this novel is uncompromisingly grim and, accordingly, the haunting strains of the blues accompany its often desolate images.

I thought of Shirley after I read this story. Shirley was a childhood playmate. I remember her linty braids, her snotty, self-assured play, and how the piece of sugar bread and her recitation of real or imagined slights to her leadership of our games kept her lips constantly moving.

The Bluest Eye is a journey into the spaces of cultural and gendered memory, and as I remember Shirley I do not know whether she is the sisters Frieda and Claudia, or whether she is Pecola – whether or not she is a child of hope or of despair. Somehow, though, it does not matter, because this is a novel in which I can recall the scope and feel of my own childhood.

Morrison does not allow me to linger long over the comfort that these early memories bring with them. Instead, she arrests my reverie with an episodic narrative that eventually forces me to understand the rape of the child Pecola. The memories stop here. As strongly as I have known and felt this story of black girlhood, as clearly as I had remembered the slick nauseating feeling of Vaseline or a sugar-coated spoon of Vicks sliding reluctantly down my throat during some distant illness; as longingly as I have recalled those precious and abbreviated hugs and remembered, shuddering, the quick angry switches – it all stops with the rape of the child Pecola.

Morrison both encourages reminiscence and disrupts it with the force of voice in this story. Story-telling and stories told access the narrative structures of this text and compel close and anguished attention.

Claudia's opening reflection tells about planting marigold seeds in the fall of 1941. She and her sister, Frieda, felt that planting the marigolds and then saying "the right words over them" would cause them to blossom, and would alleviate the smothering disarray of their friend's life. They hoped their words would work some magic to erase Pecola's ugliness, ensure the life of the child she carried, obliterate the gossip about her, as well as inform their own ignorance. They must indeed be potent words. The sisters were to learn that year about extremes – innocence, lust, faith, and despair – all equally nonproductive. Claudia's reflection leads her to understand that "there is nothing more to say" because her words cannot contain the overwhelming sorrow of this story. Herein lies its tragedy. When a community's language is disabled by its trauma and when its expressive potential is erased, spiritual desolation is the result. As Claudia, Cholly and Mrs. Breedlove, and finally Pecola lose their verbal expressivity, they fall more deeply into a chasm of despair. But Claudia, who distances herself from the tragedy, ultimately regains the promise of her voice – "I *talk* about how I did not plant the seeds too deeply" (p. 160, my emphasis) – and survives that year.

Claudia's reflections affirm the value Morrison places in artistic expressivity. She describes a conversation between her mother and one of her friends as a "gently wicked dance" (p. 16), an artistic metaphor that will be recalled to *Sula* as the "dark brown woman in a flowered dress doing a bit of cakewalk." Visual and aural artistry exchange their strategies and intimately interact in Morrison's fiction. Whether as dance or song, visual scenery or verbal artistry, all collaborate in *The Bluest Eye* to indicate how this creative potential is lost in the fractured communities of diaspora peoples.[11] Artistic allusions animate the verbal symbol and, in Morrison's work, the animated word is musical. Indeed, the children in this novel listen to their mother's conversation for "truth in timbre" (p. 16).

However, it is the mothers in this novel, studied contrasts, who guide our vision and our hearing. Mrs. MacTeer allows us to understand the impetus toward desolation, and also how to resist it. Claudia and Frieda listen to her voice for signs of her temperament; but it is not only the spoken voice that signals their mother's demeanor.

[11] In *The Fractured Psyche* (unpublished manuscript), Joyce Pettis explains the notion of fracture with critical insight relevant to the traditions of African American women's literature. Pettis suggests "linking the ability to talk in certain culturally specific ways . . . maintain[s] a fragile mental equilibrium" in Paule Marshall's work, and implicates the work of other black women writers as well in "Talk as Defensive Artifice," *African American Review* 26, 1 (Spring 1992), 109–117.

If my mother was in a singing mood, it wasn't so bad. She would sing about hard times, bad times, and somebody-done-gone-and-left-me times. Misery colored by the greens and blues in my mother's voice took all of the grief out of the words and left me with a conviction that pain was not only endurable, it was sweet. (p. 24)

The musical voice, their mother's singing, becomes a means of spiritual catharsis and, following slavery's field days rituals, the mask of song signals surreptitious actions.

My soul look back and wonder / How I got over . . . In Black America, the oral tradition has served as a fundamental vehicle for "gittin ovuh." That tradition preserves the Afro-American heritage and reflects the collective spirit of the race. Through song, story, folk sayings, and rich verbal interplay among every-day people, lessons and precepts about life and survival are handed down from generation to generation.[12]

Language in our communities is a historically powerful medium. In this novel, Claudia reflects that "my mother's fussing soliloquies always irritated and depressed us" (p. 23) and "if Mama was fussing . . . it was like somebody throwing stones" (p. 24). The actual dialogues between mother and daughters are not particularly eloquent or mellifluous – they contain mostly ordinary sentiments and necessary directives. But it is not only these dialogues that teach the girls how to reflect on their lives. Instead, the melodious fussing soliloquies and the "songs my mother sang" offer them their instruction.

In contrast to the creative expression that Mrs. MacTeer salvages, Mrs. Breedlove (Pecola's mother) has lost her voice. A distant narrator takes over the telling of her story because she has lost contact with sound. Silence characterizes her tragedy. We meet her slipping "noise-lessly out of bed" and attempting to regain her control as she berates her husband Cholly to get her some wood. But her tirade may as well be noiseless. It is met by Cholly's silence and the narrator comments that "to deprive her of these [verbal] fights was to deprive her of all the zest and unreasonableness of life" (p. 36). Unlike the sisters' mother, she was unable to claim the refuge of soliloquy or song. Separated from this tradition, all her energy is spent trying to engage in verbal battle one who refuses her fuel for the fire. Although Cholly pours out his "inarticulate fury" on his wife, during their battles they did not "talk or groan or curse" (p. 37). Although Mrs. Breedlove's prayerful conver-sations with Jesus do attempt some engaged language, her environment is too dark and brutal to allow her this spiritual escape. In conse-quence, Pauline Breedlove loses any creative, expressive potential and Claudia and Frieda's mother endures.

---

[12] Geneva Smitherman, *Talkin and Testifyin* (Boston: Houghton Mifflin, 1977), p. 73.

These women's strength lies in real speech – the creative and generative power of voice. The background of the Breedloves' anger is their inarticulateness, as well as the functional inarticulateness of the words they do exchange. The only time we learn of the potential force and violence of Mrs. Breedlove's words is when they are directed toward Pecola. And we shudder at the intensity of the mother's bitter confrontation of her daughter who has spilled blueberry pie on the floor of the white folks' kitchen.

"The blacker the berry the sweeter the juice" – a folk refrain that is a familiar lyric in the African American community – may come to some readers' minds as Morrison sculpts this scene.[13] It is a referent that makes obvious the cruel twist within this episode. The mother's words, "hotter and darker than the smoking berries," cause the girls to "back away in dread" (p. 87). Even more bitter is the final narrative in this section. Here, the little white girl that Polly Breedlove cares for gets the benefit of the warm and soothing language that Pecola desperately needs. With the connotation in mind that the folk line evokes – the positive value of darkness and the pleasure it holds – this scene is pathetically inversive. Instead of her own dark Pecola, Mrs. Breedlove salves the quizzical uneasiness of the white child saying: "Hush. Don't worry none," in a whisper where "the honey in her words complemented the sundown spilling on the lake" (p. 87).

Pecola is the pathetic victim of her mother's verbal and her father's physical abuse. Both diminish and destroy their daughter. Cholly's violent inarticulateness is easily traced. He is an abandoned child. Everything we learn about his background, every hurting and abusive gesture and every humiliation pushes him toward the extremes he eventually expresses. Guileless, and primed with ready sympathy for the tragically abused Cholly, the reader is easily led to the scene where we are forced to confront Cholly's rape of his daughter. And, as we look back at the life that Morrison has unrelentingly traced as abusive and painful, we *almost* understand this climactic event.

However, if we don't understand it, Morrison explains that it is only because we lack the musical metaphor.

The pieces of Cholly's life could become coherent only in the head of a musician. Only those who talk their talk through the gold of curved metal, or in the touch of black-and-white rectangles and taut skins and strings echoing from wooden corridors could give true form to his life. (p. 125)

---

[13] The epigraph in Wallace Thurman's novel, *The Blacker the Berry* (Macauley, 1929; reprinted New York: Macmillan, 1970), cites these lines. Within the African American community, this well-known aphorism reflects on the sweet sensuality and value of a dark-skinned woman. Although sensuality is not relevant to this scene, skin color certainly is.

Because we are denied music's cohesive power in the deafening scene of his child's rape, our understanding of Cholly's fracture is piecemeal and reluctant. The blues that saves Mrs. MacTeer is no solace for Cholly, Pecola, or even the reader who has come to depend on its mediative power. Cholly's creativity is frustrated and fractured, and the balm of spirituals, blues, or jazz (even though they are near – attached to the stories of others in this novel), is unavailable to him. Cholly never speaks again in this novel after a childhood encounter with his father who refuses to acknowledge his paternity. From that moment forward, a narrator presents a third-person perspective of Cholly's thoughts and mediates the music that Cholly cannot claim. Only the narrative's creative mesh enables the reader to bear the story of the rape of his child.

The "floodlight of drink" illumines this dark incident and the sequence of Cholly's emotional releases – "revulsion, guilt, pity, then love" – flow toward his daughter and drag us along with him. We know he was voiceless. Physical expression – his crawl across the kitchen floor toward his wife-like child, his nibble at her ankle, his confusion of tenderness and lust – was all that was left for him. Because he has been rendered inarticulate and silent, the force toward expressive action – an incoherent and blasphemous behavior – explosively speaks for him. Unlike the control Mrs. MacTeer maintains because of her spiritually enabled and creatively engaged song, what is left to Cholly is absolutely uncontrollable. Pecola's only left legacy is her mother's dim hatred and her father's desperate rage. In this moment of violent abuse, Pecola's own voice is ripped away. She is left silent and insane.

If language and speech do offer retribution and salvation, then Pecola's silence indicates the hopelessness of this child. At the novel's end, Claudia and Frieda sign and say "magic" words and offer Pecola their linguistic enchantment. But Pecola is mute and their incantations – their call to her spirit – have no potential response.

The only insight we have left of Pecola is her own – through the dialogue of her unconscious with itself. For Mrs. MacTeer and her daughters, magic words, song, and soliloquy brought grace. But there was no grace, no mediative musical magic for Pecola. We learn through her internal dialogue that Mrs. Breedlove does not speak to her daughter, that no one at school speaks to her, and that the rape on the kitchen floor was not the only time Cholly violently molested his daughter. We learn that even this internal voice does not bring Pecola solace because it taunts her with the possibility that the blue eyes she dreamed of having are not quite blue enough.

At the novel's end, the pathetic Pecola – who was "so sad to see" sifts through the garbage. Her sky-blue eyes and the sunflowers that grow wild around her metaphorically mix light and air into the earthy refuse of a garbage dump. Sadly, the image of waste remains the most powerful metaphor in the story. There are no words left to explore her loss, and no song can embrace or contain her spiritual desolation. This pitiful vision – clear, uncompromised, and silent – is all that remains.

I've grown past my childhood memory of Shirley and her sugar bread sandwiches and her brother June-bug. Shirley's memories of me may be similar – if they exist at all. And perhaps Morrison is saying that the extremes of our childhood memories etch them-selves against the present only if we have the voices, or call upon the music, or re-member the refrains clearly enough to recall them into our lives at the critical moments of conflict and crisis. Today, my mother's hymnal sits on my piano. I've placed it inside a worn lacy leather bookcover that once covered a bible in my grandmother's home. Mother's inscription on the inside cover says "For my children – so that they might remember." This is Toni Morrison's legacy as well. If we remember our mothers' singing, we embrace the hymn of generation.

In the literature of black women writers, interpretive spaces gain cultural dimensionality through metaphoric and linguistic manipulations of ancestral patterns of oracy. Mythic recursion, a *recherche du temps perdu*, is the linguistic vehicle that embodies the creative vision in Toni Morrison's novels. Her recovery of the language of creative generation encourages the memories of music in our own lives. They enable the clear and powerful reach of a lyrical voice that emerges inversively from the tragedy of the child Pecola, whose lost soul is symbolically imaged through her silence. It swells with the magical, powerful older women of *Song of Solomon*, whose voices and songs insist on a return to our state of natural grace; and it sweeps through the Bottom land of *Sula* until Nel, full of the memory of her friend Sula cries "circles and circles" of sorrow around that memory. Morrison's novels celebrate a woman-centered spirituality, the reclamation of legacy, and the right-eous and lyrical acknowledgment of a memory of things past.

13

Red hot mamas: Bessie Smith, Sophie Tucker, and the ethnic maternal voice in American popular song

PETER ANTELYES

I'm a red hot woman
Just full of flamin' youth.
I'm a red hot woman
Just full of flamin' youth.
You can't cold me daddy,
You're no good, that's the truth.

Bessie Smith, "Worn Out Papa Blues "(1929)

I could make a music master
Drop his fiddle,
Make a bald-headed man
Part his hair in the middle.

'Cause I'm a red hot mama, red hot mama,
But I'll have to turn my damper down.

Sophie Tucker, "Red Hot Mama" (1924)[1]

It is not surprising that little has been written about the red hot mama performers of the 1920s. Their prominence in popular entertainment was relatively brief. Prototypes began to appear at the turn of the century with such figures as blues singer Gertrude "Ma" Rainey and vaudevillian Eva Tanguay, but it wasn't until the early 1920s that entertainers such as Bessie Smith and Sophie Tucker took advantage of improvements

I would like to make special thanks to my editors, Nancy Jones and Leslie Dunn, for their keen advice and kind patience, and to David Goldenberg for his generosity of time and effort in supplying me with many currently unavailable Sophie Tucker recordings.

[1] Because of my interest in the performative elements of the embodied voice, I have preferred transcriptions to sheet music lyrics. Unless otherwise noted, then, all song quotations in this essay are from my transcriptions of recordings made in the year indicated.

in touring, recording, and distribution facilities to flesh out the mama to a broader audience. The figure was directly named in 1924 with the publication of the song "Red Hot Mama," but only two years later the mystique of the mama had reached a peak with the production of an all-black musical entitled "Red Hot Mama." And by 1929 the figure had come to take its last bow, as Sophie Tucker sang its swan song, "The Last of the Red Hot Mamas."

Yet the mama's existence would have been remarkable no matter what her life span. Her defining features, taken individually, were conventional enough. As spelled out in her name, the mama was "red hot" in her sexual appetite, and maternal in her authority, her allure, and her dangerously enveloping possessiveness. What was extraordinary was her embodiment of these traditionally opposed patriarchal fantasies of female power. More extraordinary still was her use of that embodiment to critique those fantasies, and demonstrate her own presence and authority. That artistry of embodiment is the subject of this essay.

A discussion of that artistry must begin at the intersection of ethnicity, gender, and voice. The figure of the mama was developed first out of the traditions of black women's blues; gradually, along with other elements of African-American musical culture, the figure entered into the entertainment arenas of minstrel shows, "coon" songs, and songs of ethnic nostalgia, arenas which had themselves been cultivating traditions of mother figures. Within a short time, this modified figure reentered the blues through the forms of black female vaudeville, and a general process of cross-cultural musical influence evolved. In an effort to capture some of the shadings of this multi-ethnic musical history, I have chosen to focus my essay around the careers of Bessie Smith and Sophie Tucker. In the discussion that follows I explore how notions of race, ethnicity, gender, and sexuality positioned these red hot mamas in the entertainment industry, and how their art, as exemplified in two characteristic performances, responded to, and made use of, that positioning.[2]

The first signs of the red hot mama can be traced to the entrance of the denomination itself into the vernacular of the blues in the late 1890s. One of the most prominent features of this vernacular was its eroticization of familial relations. Unlike the secure genteel home depicted in the white Victorian popular music of the time, these early blues evoked an eroticized arena of loss and contention: the union of

---

[2] I should note that restrictions in length limit the elements that I can examine here. A fuller study would include discussion of such factors as advances in recording technology and distribution. The decade of the red hot mama's popularity, for instance, precisely coincided with the emergence of recordings as the primary form of reproduction and distribution of popular music. The mama's art, including its dimensions of ethnicity and gender, was thus integrally related to these new developments and the mass audience constituted by them.

white mother and father became the disunion of black forlorn lovers, the familiar "mama" and "papa" of the blues.

One can only speculate on the sources of this new vernacular and the African-American perspectives it represented. One obvious factor was the instability of the family under economic discrimination. During the early twentieth century, the black family was particularly hard hit by the great migrations north and west. Black men were forced to travel to find work, while black women were largely confined to domestic work, which kept them fixed geographically, economically and socially. This phenomenon was the source for one common pattern found in blues songs of the period: the men sang of the sadness, anger, and relief of being on the move, the women of watching them go.

The language of family became a key medium for the expression of these feelings, partly because that language was also a medium for the oppression of blacks. In the rhetoric of racism, references such as "boy", "girl," "mammy," "pappy," and "auntie," were used to promote a prejudicial paternalism. By reinvesting familial terms with sexual overtones, black blues singers were practicing a characteristically African-American satiric inversion of racist language, revealing the destructive effects of its racism while reclaiming the individual autonomy and communal affiliation associated with the expression of adult sexuality.

Not surprisingly, women, in their roles as both lovers and mothers, were focal points of this language, signifying the various, often contradictory, responses to "home" that resulted from these conditions of economic and social discrimination. According to the point of view expressed in many of the male downhome blues songs of the time, a mama might be a vessel of warmth and stability, a seductress calling one back into the past, or an admonisher of one's infidelity. Leroy Carr's "Papa Wants a Cookie" (1930) offers an example of this particular tradition of mama figures:

> Mama's baking cookies: out in the kitchen
> Papa smells the cookies: and his nose starts to itching
> Papa tried to steal one: like he did before
> But mama's got the lock: on the kitchen door
>
> Papa says to mama: come a little closer
> Mama looks at papa: says oh oh no sir
> Papa turns around: starts to go away
> Comes right back: when she hear him say
>
> Papa says to mama: you a real nice-looker
> You turn on the heat: like a fireless cooker
> Come a little closer: in your papa's arms
> Another little kiss: wouldn't do us any harm

Papa comes home: when his work is over
Mama says to papa: you sure ain't clover
Guess what I cooked: for you today
Mama just smiles: when she hear papa say[3]

But if economic conditions kept many black women in the kitchen, so to speak, they also provided the impetus for some women to seek the economic mobility assigned to men. The black vaudeville circuit offered black women one of the few means of escaping from, or at least resisting, that life of fixity. These women became a different kind of mama, a figure of resistance, resilience, and authority, who was capable of expressing her own desires. Unlike the mama of Carr's song, this mama had the last word: she had the "lock" on the kitchen door in more ways than one.

As the blues queen, the mamá inspired both adulation and anxiety. Musician Danny Barker expressed both in his description of the great singer Ma Rainey's presence:

When you say Ma, that means mother; Ma, that means the tops, that's the boss, the shag bully of the house. Ma Rainey, she take charge; Ma, Ma Rainey's comin' to town, the boss blues singer. And you respect Ma, Grandma, my Ma and Ma-Ma, that's Ma. That's something you respect. When you say mother, that's the boss of the house, the shack, y'hear?, and not Pa. Ma-ma.[4]

By virtue of her maternal attributes, the blues queen gained respect. Yet, as Barker's repetition of "Ma" suggests, that maternal authority could also be seen as excessive. As "Ma-ma" she could negate the papa's power, even the papa himself ("not Pa").

This ambivalence often took the form of a struggle between desire and fear. Generally depicted as sexual aggressor, the blues queen was thus both mother and lover, both alluring and unsettling. One sign of the power accorded this interweaving of maternalism and sexuality was the commercial circumscription of the mama's art. On the level of race, for instance, the black vaudeville circuit and "race" record industries limited the reach, and profitability, of the mama's artistry. The advertisements appeared mainly in black newspapers, and the shows and records generally appeared within black neighborhoods. On the level of gender, the mama's music was advertised through a variety of female stereotypes, including the weeping mama, the vengeful Hottentot, and the red hot mama. Their personae were represented as racially other and their records as "racy," that is, as expressions of black female sexuality.

---

[3] The text, which is a transcription of a recording, comes from Michael Taft, *Blues Lyric Poetry: An Anthology* (New York and London: Garland, 1983), p. 46. The colons are Taft's mode of representing caesuras that he sees as implicit in the structure of the text; they do not necessarily correspond to actual caesuras in the performance.

[4] Barker interviewed in "Wild Women Don't Have the Blues," Calliope Films, 1989; prod. Carol Doyle Van Valkenburgh and Christine Dall, dir. Christine Dall.

While one mustn't underestimate the negative effects of these restraints, one must also recognize the extent to which the mamas' art constituted a response to, and even circumventing of, those restraints. Bessie Smith's career demonstrates all these facets of that art, particularly in her use of the attributes of the red hot mama.

In both her recording and stage performances, Smith typified the red hot mama. Her performances were built around her ability to ground her voice in her body. Few visual records exist of her work on stage; she only made one film during her lifetime, the 1929 short "St. Louis Blues." But that film, in which she both sings and dances, is enough to confirm the written descriptions of many of her contemporaries. It offers a brief glimpse of her domination of space through vocal control and projection, slow physical movement, and mannerisms drawn from mime and acting.[5] While the specific meanings conveyed by these actions differed according to song, performance, venue, and audience, they were generally associated with the characteristics of the red hot mama. Through her embodied voice, Smith represented herself as a person of great appetites, her blues inflections and movement on the stage a call for gratification – in food, in love, in sex. At the same time, those inflections and movements revealed the pain of her constraints, her rage at the attempts to objectify and disempower her.

The power of these features was represented by the one indisputable dimension common to all mamas: size. Many people wrote about Smith's ability to fill an auditorium with her voice alone, unaided by a microphone. Pianist Art Hodes wrote that "she don't need a mike; she don't use one . . . Everybody can hear her . . . She never lets me get away from her once"; and Danny Barker noted that "she could fill up Carnegie Hall, Madison Square Garden, or a cabaret. She could fill it up from her muscle and she could last all night. There was none of this whispering jive."[6] Jazz musician Mezz Mezzrow extended this perception to encompass Bessie Smith herself as a person:

Bessie was a real woman, all woman, all the femaleness the world ever saw in one sweet package. She was tall and brown-skinned, with great big dimples creasing her cheeks, dripping good looks – just this side of voluptuous, buxom and massive but stately too, shapely as an hour-glass, with a high-voltage magnet for a personality.[7]

[5] For a more detailed description of Smith's performing style on stage, see Chris Albertson, *Bessie* (New York: Stein and Day, 1972), especially pp. 50 and 135.

[6] Art Hodes in Hodes and Chadwick Hansen, eds., *Selections from the Gutter: Jazz Portraits from "The Jazz Record"* (Berkeley: University of California Press, 1977), p. 63; Barker in Nat Shapiro and Nat Hentoff, *Hear Me Talkin' To Ya: The Story of Jazz As Told by the Men Who Make It* (New York: Dover, 1955), p. 245.

[7] Mezz Mezzrow and Bernard Wolfe, *Really the Blues* (New York: New American Library, 1964), pp. 102–103.

Note how the trope of largeness is associated with her gender, as a woman, and her race, as black. Note, too, the anxiety implicit in the reference to the phallic dimensions assumed by the singer's voice and body. Bessie didn't need a microphone because she *was* a microphone, or rather, she had swallowed it; and she would fill you up with her own "muscle."

But if size represented the mama's embodiment, it also represented the capacity of the mama, through her embodiment, to escape reduction to, and containment within, her body. On the one hand, then, the mama's size, including the volume not only of her physical girth but deepness and loudness of tone, and broadness of style, signified particular racial, ethnic, and gendered identities; on the other hand, by containing the uncontainable – the maternal and the sexual – and exposing the contradictions of the oedipal fantasy, the mama's size signified her ability to transgress those boundaries. The mama was too big to be herself contained.

This paradox of embodiment and indeterminacy was the central complexity of the mama's art. As Steven G. Smith has written of the blues, "What is lived through [such music] is a struggle for liveable embodiment on what are acknowledged to be decisively disadvantaged terms."[8] In their articulation of desire and joy, vengeance and contempt, in their explorations of poverty, adultery, and prejudice, the red hot mama's songs acknowledged that the singers lived in their bodies and in the world that surrounded them, a world of racism and sexism. Their bodies were, for them, the site of history. At the same time, they reclaimed the female body from the patriarchal reductionism that objectified women as bodies alone. By investing those bodies with a fluidity of viewpoints, they transformed them into the very foundation of subjectivity.

By this artistry of embodiment, performers such as Smith created what might be called an "ethnic maternal voice." In adopting and embodying the persona of the mama, and in using their performances to comment on that act of embodiment, these singers brought the power associated with music, with non-representational sound, into direct dialectic with the power associated with language; and they brought the power associated with body into direct dialectic with the conditions and struggles attendant upon living in a patriarchal and racist culture. The maternal voice developed by the red hot mama performers was thus racial or ethnic as well, a mode of self-expression which allowed them to have many voices, constituting both music and language, body and mind, both a subjectivity freed from the constructed boundaries of

[8] Steven G. Smith, "Blues and Our Mind-Body Problem," *Popular Music* 11, 1 (January 1992), 41.

gender, race, ethnicity, and class, and an identity embodied in those constructions.

Smith's recording of "I Used To Be Your Sweet Mama" (1928; words by Leslie Miller; music by L. Miller and Fred Longshaw) offers a useful example of some of these features of the ethnic maternal voice:

> Yes I'm mad, and have a right to be,
> After what my daddy did to me.
> I lavished all my love on him,
> But I swear I'll never love again.
>
> All you women understand what it is
> To be in love with a two-time man.
> The next time he calls me "sweet mama" in his lovin' way,
> This is what I'm going to say:
>
> I used to be your sweet mama, sweet papa,
> But now I'm just as sour as can be.
> So don't come stallin' around my way
> Expectin' any love from me.
>
> You've had your chance and proved unfaithful
> So now I'm gonna be real mean and hateful.
> I used to be your sweet mama, sweet papa,
> But now I'm just as sour as can be.
>
> I ain't gonna let no man worry me sick,
> Or turn this hair of mine gray.
> Soon as I catch him at his two-time tricks
> I'm gonna tell him to be on his way.
>
> To the world I'll scream, no man can treat me mean
> And expect my love all the time.
> When he roams away, he'd better stay.
> If he comes back, he'll find:
>
> You've had your chance and proved unfaithful
> So now I'm gonna be real mean and hateful.
> I used to be your sweet mama, sweet papa,
> But now I'm just as sour as can be.

The song is structured around the conventional reversal, the two-timer two-timed, found in many classic blues songs: the man has left the woman, so the woman will leave the man. This reversal, though, as worked out through both the lyrics and the voice, reveals a red hot mama's rejection of her objectification and insistence on her own embodiment and unfixable subjectivity.[9] Beginning on the level of

9 In the reading that follows, I have chosen not to include considerations of authorship. While Smith wrote many of the songs she recorded, she also sang many written by

These figures had their counterparts in various contemporary traditions of mother songs, particularly the black and ethnic mamas of popular nostalgic laments, and the red hot Hottentot of coon songs. Expressing the anxieties and excitements of the new immigrants, and evoking as well the broader culture of nostalgia, recordings such as Irish tenor John McCormack's "Mother Machree" (1910) became enormously popular among both ethnic and non-ethnic audiences. Al Jolson became famous for his recording and stage renditions of "My Mammy" (1921), and Sophie Tucker for her "My Yiddishe Momme," which she sang in both English and Yiddish.

At the same time, Jewish composers were making use of the Hottentot tradition, as demonstrated in the appearance of such song figures as "Sadie Salome" and "Lena from Palesteena."[12] In fact, the source of the phrase "red hot," which Tucker claimed as referring to her own Jewish version of the mama, first appeared as a modifier of the mama in coon and ragtime traditions. "Hot," in particular, was a word specifically associated with blacks, as one finds in such songs as "The Hottest Coon in Dixie" (1898), "A Red Hot Coon" (1899), and "Hottentot Love Song" (1906). As evident in the last example, the word was most often used to describe black women, particularly the sexualized dancing which had come to represent their "nature"; "Hotfoot Sue" (1896) was a prime example. This sexual dimension was further underscored by the coon song commonplace associating sexual desire with body temperature: the dance of the Hottentot was sex, and that sex was "red hot."[13]

The Jewish vamp figure was similar to other ethnic vamps of the time. "Sheik" and "sheba" had become common terms for lovers in popular songs, drawing on the same cultural currents that were to produce Rudolph Valentino. In Tucker's recording of "There's Something Spanish in My Eyes" (1928), the singer takes to comic extremes the process by which all ethnicities were brought under one umbrella in the assignment of female stereotypes: "There's something Spanish in my eyes / My mother is Jewish, my father is Irish / Which proves that I'm Spanish, and I love you." While Tucker sings the lines to a sexy minstrel-Spanish beat, she allows the final phrase to hang awkwardly out of sync, as if the peculiar joint-identity were finally impossible to realize in the one voice.

The prominence of these ethnic vamps in the 1920s was a consequence, in part, of the forces of urbanization. By placing into proximity different classes, races, and ethnicities, and mixing them in an atmosphere of great social fluidity, these forces had led to a period of remarkable

---

[12] "Sadie Salome (Go Home)" (1909), words by Edgar Leslie, music by Irving Berlin; "Lena from Palesteena" (1920), words by Con Conrad, music by J. Russel Robinson.

[13] For a description of the treatment of the Hottentot figure in early popular song, see Sam Dennison, *Scandalize My Name: Black Imagery in American Popular Music* (New York: Garland, 1982), pp. 398–416.

---

lyrics, one finds an undermining of certain racist and patriarchal distinctions. The shift from sweet to sour plays on a term more common to white songs than black, "sweetheart," and undercuts the conventional gender roles found in these songs by turning the expected feminine sweetheart into the very image of anti-femininity: mother's soured milk. This image is later reinforced by the rhyme which identifies the man as unfaithful and the woman as correspondingly hateful (the word "faithful" was more commonly applied to women, and "hateful" to men). This tactic both acknowledges and, through inversion, undermines the underlying oedipal narrative, central to the traditions of both white popular song and black downhome blues.

This act of repossession is echoed in the way that the singer claims for herself the act of naming, a common strategy of black culture. She sings first of being *called* "sweet mama" but then announces that *she* has some naming to do – "This is what I'm going to say" – and that the man is the object of that naming: "sweet mama, sweet papa." At the same time she acknowledges the ties that remain between herself and her lover by keeping the same word, "sweet," and by placing a pause in the phrase not after "mama" but after the first "sweet," thus uniting mama and papa around the second use of the word: "mama sweet papa." The phrase is both ironic and sadly earnest, a complex interweaving of perspectives that might be realized in different ways in different performances. She may no longer be sweet mama, but she is still the mama. The intensity of those mixed feelings reveals itself later in the song when the singer moves from naming to screaming: she finds her own voice, but the gesture is as painful as it is liberating.

This shifting of position – from victim to victimizer, from object to subject, from sung about to singing, and singing to screaming – places the singer beyond easy definition. The song thus also displaces the listener's position as arbiter of the song's "meaning." The singer begins by addressing an unspecified audience, then shifts to women in particular, and then to a particular man. Significantly, this last addressee is framed in quotation: the address to the women is markedly more intimate than the more public setting to the man. By resisting a fixed position in relation to both her audience and her lover, the singer does not keep herself free of entanglements, but does keep herself free to comment upon them.

others; "I Used To Be Your Sweet Mama" fits into this latter category. That most of these composers were male adds another dimension, another double-voicing, to both lyrics and music that should not be overlooked. My interpretation, though, is designed to enunciate the elements of Smith's own artistry. In this context I read even those parts of the song not strictly authored by Smith, such as lyrics and music, as finally inseparable from their realization in her performance. As Ma Rainey sang in her "Last Minute Blues" (1923), "If anybody asks you: who wrote this lonesome song / Tell them you don't know the writer: but Ma Rainey put it on" (Taft, *Blues Lyric Poetry*, p. 219).

The uncertainty of this positioning, which conveys the poignancy of both embodiment and indeterminacy, is evident in the song's tense as well. The singer's rage consumes her present; yet her gesture of vengeance, played out in the song's refrain, takes place in an uncertain future ("If he comes back, he'll find"). She has to wait for, even long for, his return to gain the satisfaction of leaving him. What she can do now – and throughout the song, she places special vocal emphasis on the word "now" – is to sing.

The lyrics, then, provide a moving and thought-provoking combination of rage and longing, an awareness of the dangers of patriarchal popular song narrative with the recognition that any bid for independence is a difficult one at best. But this perspective only becomes fully realized in the movement and tonal quality of the voice. Three elements stand out: the restriction and sudden expansion of the range of notes, the movement from singing to speaking and back again, and the precise placement and weight of blues melismas.

For most of the song, Smith confines the vocal range of her repetitions of the two central lines – "I used to be your sweet mama, sweet papa, / But now I'm just as sour as can be." Only at the final iteration, in the song's last lines, does she allow her voice to soar upward on the word "now," and she keeps it high until "sour." The effect is a momentary operatic sense of liberation, though one that is quickly contained by the voice's adjustment to the melody in the final words. This back and forth movement is evident in other vocal effects as well. For the fifth and sixth stanzas Smith unexpectedly shifts into spoken patter, a convention more common in white than black vaudeville. The oddness of the shift within the frame of a classic blues delivery broadens the claims to self-possession she has made throughout the song: she is not to be mastered, and can say so in masculine- and white-identified speech as well as black and female song. The mention of a scream to come ("To the world I'll scream") adds, in this context, a potent promise of an even more uncontainable response. Smith further underscores the power that resides in her vocal resources, and her rage, by moving into stop-time in the delivery of two lines: "You've had your chance and proved unfaithful / So now I'm gonna be real mean and hateful."

Finally, Smith uses blues notes throughout the song to keep the motion between love and anger vividly present in the voice. Smith was especially effective in her use of the blues melisma, a microtonal movement of voice that involves both precision and indeterminacy of expression.[10] The effect is especially marked in the song's two main

---

[10] The most characteristic blue note, in Western musical terms, is the note that slides between the major and minor third of a chord in a blues progression. Historically, it was most likely created out of interactions between African and American musical cultures. The African contributed a finer range of microtonal movement and more

---

lines: "I used to be your sweet mama, sweet papa, / But now I'm just as sour as can be." The blues melismas are strongest on "no[w]" suggesting, in musical terms, the sense of bitterness acco[mpanying] transformation. By the end of the song, such technique [gives] body to the voice, and identity to the singer. She is a moth[er], a woman in her own right, a black woman and a singer. H[er] of the red hot mama.

Not all mamas were the same, of course. Where Smit[h] exemplified certain aspects of the black experience, Sophie [Tucker] did the same for the Jewish experience. Tucker's career reve[aled] striking differences within familiar contours. Many of the sam[e areas] of contention appear, including perceptions of the role played by [mama] in the family, attitudes toward female sexuality, conditions surro[unding] the economic opportunities for women, and women's role in the [enter]tainment industry.

As with the black family, the Jewish immigrant family faced a [great] deal of stress as a result of migration, and that stress was often ass[oci]ated with new roles assigned to women. As the second genera[tion] daughters entered the work force, images of the Jewess as worker a[nd] temptress appeared. At the same time, as the first generation mothe[r] retired to the home, the archetypal "Jewish mother" began to emerg[e], selfless but also demanding, drawing the children back into the pas[t] even while providing for their movement out into America. In this sense, the Jewish mother can also be said to contain elements of the worker and the temptress. The Jewish red hot mama was a variation of these types, a combination of sexy transgressor and "Yiddishe mama" who represented the tensions and ambivalences of not only oedipal but assimilationist impulses.[11] Tucker's recording of "You're Got To See Mama Ev'ry Night," as we will see, illustrates and comments upon this combination of personae in its movement from one kind of mama to another, from the homebound mother to the "mama" on the move.

---

fluid movement between tones than existed in the fixed whole- and half-tone divisions of Western culture; and the American contributed a distinction between major and minor modalities as representing various positive and negative polarities, from happiness and sadness to triumph and tragedy. By slipping between major and minor, the blue note challenges the conventional meanings of those polarities, signifying not positive or negative, not happiness or sadness, longing or contempt, but both at once and neither. The note thus not only implicitly undermines the rigidities of American musical language, but also allows for a broader, and less fixable, range of expression.

[11] The oedipal conflict, particularly as a representation of generational differences, was a common feature of assimilation narratives during these early decades of immigration. Henry Roth's Call It Sleep (1934) may be the most popular example. For a text more focused on the woman's point of view, see Anzia Yezierska's Bread Givers (1925), in which the heroine, Sara Smolinsky, comes to realize that for her to assimilate, she must bear the burden of her own, and her father's, unresolved longings and fears. At the end of the novel, she manages to become both her father's mother and her husband's daughter.

experimentation in the forms of self-imagining: Jews in blackface, blacks in "blue vein" societies, people of wealth in "slumming" guise, women in men's clothing and vice versa. This experimentation was especially visible in the flexibility and hybridity of the early forms and arenas of mass culture, from vaudeville to cabaret to cinema, from coon songs to Tin Pan Alley to red hot mama songs.[14] That much of this "cultural cross-dressing" took the form of oedipal self-fashioning should come as no surprise, since the oedipal drama had often been the stabilizing narrative resorted to during such periods of social mobility.

Tucker's career as a red hot mama embodied these tensions, and provides a fascinating example of how differences between racial and ethnic identities affected the artistry of the mama. Tucker stands out, in part, because, in Mark Slobin's characterization, she essentially had a man's career: "she so closely followed the path of male Jewish colleagues and has so few female counterparts that one is constantly surprised."[15] In fact, Tucker challenged many of the conventional roles assigned to Jewish women precisely by placing her career first. She was also never less than direct in declaring this independence. "I'm not to be had," she sings in the characteristically titled "I Ain't Takin' Orders from No One" (1927). She will be neither possessed by men nor distracted from her own self-possession: "I've got no weeds in my patch, no eggs to hatch, / My heart's unattached, my door is unlatched, / But I'm not taking orders from no one."

In keeping with her claim to a place in the male realm, she aggressively challenged even her male contemporaries in the entertainment field. In the song "I Don't Want to Get Thin" (1929), she translates her physical size into a statement of vocal authority by singing of how "many a sonny boy has tried to climb up on my knee." The sonny boy reference, of course, is to her competitor Al Jolson, here reduced to just another married man over whom she has the power of seduction.[16]

[14] For a full discussion of the relations between urbanization and the development of mass culture during this period, see Lewis A. Erenberg, *Steppin' Out: New York Nightlife and the Transformation of American Culture, 1890–1930* (Connecticut: Greenwood, 1981).

[15] Mark Slobin, *Tenement Songs: The Popular Music of the Jewish Immigrants* (Urbana: University of Illinois Press, 1982), p. 202.

[16] In a newspaper article about this time, Tucker carries her criticism further by suggesting that Jolson is imitating her style by singing songs upon request: "Al is a dear, and I like him, but I wish he had not thought it necessary to follow in my footsteps in this respect." Note how casually she claims the traditionally male role, relegating Jolson to following in her footsteps. This competition between the two performers also found expression, albeit indirectly, in the stage version of *The Jazz Singer* (1925). The play's main character, Jakie, modeled on Jolson, introduces himself as a vaudeville singer by offering his own version of what had, the year before, been one of Tucker's popular recordings: he sings "Red Hot Mama." The newspaper article can be found in Envelope 2391, p. 1, of the Tucker scrapbooks, now housed in the Locke Collection of the New York Public Library, Lincoln Center.

Her assertiveness was based, in part, on her shrewd use of the minstrel traditions she learned from her early years on the burlesque and vaudeville circuits. Not only was she able to claim a male performance arena, but she was also able to use the cover of black culture to represent her own subjectivity as a Jew. Her first forays as a performer were, in fact, in blackface. "Coon shouting" had emerged in the 1890s, popularized by such performers as May Irwin and Marie Cahill, and was becoming a means by which ethnic performers sought to locate themselves in American culture, specifically by identifying themselves with, and distinguishing themselves from, blacks. Tucker's approach to coon shouting was somewhat unusual in that she presented herself at the beginning of the performance as truly black; only at the end of the set would she peel off a glove to reveal, to the astonishment of the crowd, the white skin underneath. Yet despite her success, she hated the disguise; she wanted to bring herself into the spotlight. And so within only a few years she dropped the act. The influences remained central to her art, however.

Out of these influences she developed her own version of the red hot mama. The critic June Sochen has described that version as "a brilliant merging of maternal Jewish and sexy black themes."[17] I agree with Sochen in her focus on the combination of Jewish and black elements, but I think she misses the point in the way she distinguishes them. By identifying the maternal with Jewishness and sexuality with blackness, she accepts the conventional oppositions between the groups as well as between types of women. Tucker's red hot mama rejected these oppositions; she was also a sexy Jewish woman and a maternal black woman. She was, that is, both sexy and maternal as a Jew and a black. While she did structure her stage act around alternations of maternal and sexy songs, moving, say, from "My Yiddishe Momme" to "Papa Better Watch Your Step," the figures were, in fact, fused in the figure of Tucker herself. The red hot mama was not a different figure from the maternal mama, but a larger figure, enfolding the properties of the maternal into the sexual, the Jewish into the black, the mama into the Hottentot. In Yiddish terms, she was *zaftig*, large and sensual, specifically "full-bosomed" (*American Heritage Dictionary*).

This complex process of empowerment through the endorsement and undermining of ethnic female stereotypes is evident in Tucker's recordings and performing style. Early on in her career, Tucker became well known for recording minstrel-style vaudeville songs, such as "That Lovin' Rag" (1910) and "That Lovin' Soul Kiss" (1911). The lyrics were predictably minstrel-oriented, emphasizing profligacy and sexual

---

17 June Sochen, "Fanny Brice and Sophie Tucker: Blending the Particular with the Universal," in Sarah Blacker Cohen, ed., *From Hester Street to Hollywood: The Jewish-American Stage and Screen* (Bloomington: Indiana University Press, 1983), p. 48.

appetite, and she sang in a minstrel-ragtime style. According to contemporary reviewers of her stage performances: she "chopped off her words" in a voice of "Ethiopian volume."[18] By the 1920s, though, she had modulated these inflections and made claim to the genre as a clearly identified Jewish performer. In such songs as "Red Hot Mama" (1924), "I've Got a Cross-Eyed Papa (But He Looks OK to Me)" (1924), and "Nobody Knows What a Red Head Mama Can Do" (1925), we find Jewish references, vocal turns drawn from cantorial practices, and Yiddish inflections. She even recorded one mama song in Yiddish: "Mama Goes Where Papa Goes (or Papa Don't Go Out Tonight)" (1924).

In this sense, Tucker's ethnic mama was less strictly supervised than Smith's black mama. Where Smith's transgressions were limited to crossing boundaries of gender and sexuality, Tucker was also able to cross lines of racial and ethnic difference. She could do so, of course, because she was white, and she was inclined to do so, in part, because she was Jewish. While Tucker could perform in blackface so as to reveal herself to be at once white and ethnic, Bessie Smith had no equivalent options of empowerment. If she had performed in blackface, as did many blacks on the minstrel show circuit, she would only have emphasized the inseparability of mask from "essential" blackness.

But if Tucker's red hot mama was free to explore dimensions of subjectivity denied to Smith, her artistry was equally formed around her embodiment as a woman and an ethnic. As with Smith, Tucker's physical presence as a red hot mama was specifically associated with the volume of her voice and domination of the stage. Like Smith, the focus of commentary was often on size, and the issue of size was often associated with maternal excess and ethnic and racial identity. Tucker, who stated openly that "My embonpoint is my fortune," was described throughout her career as "a broad and buxom vocalist," "the fat lady who sings." Her voice, in fact, seemed to grow in size during her career: in 1909 it was described as a "40-horse power voice," in 1915, the metaphor had been adjusted upward to a "250 h.p. voice," and by 1922, the height of her career, she was said to be "vocally hitting on all cylinders – twin sixes in her case."

As in Smith's case, these attempts to measure and fix the size of body and voice revealed anxiety about the threat of indeterminacy. "Although she has a 'big voice,'" one review noted, "she has sufficiently learned the science of repression to prevent it from being strident." Each description of her bigness was accompanied either by an eager notice of that science of repression, that is, her femininity – her "little pink fingers" and "charming smile" – or an agitated critique of misplaced masculinity:

---

[18] From the Tucker scrapbooks in the Locke Collection, 10,833 (n.d.), n.p., and 10,834 (1909), n.p.

"And speaking of elephants and ladies," a 1914 review of a Chicago performance began, "there is Sophie Tucker . . . She has a voice – well, if [female impersonator] Julian Eltinge's singing voice was as virile as Miss Tucker's he would be executing a long overdue male impersonation."[19]

The multifaceted art that Tucker developed within, and despite, these conditions is apparent in her recording of *You've Got to See Mama Ev'ry Night, Or You Can't See Mama at All* (1923; words and music by Billy Rose and Con Conrad). The contours of the mama become particularly apparent in a comparison between the original sheet music and its revision in Tucker's voice, body, and musical performance:

(Sheet music version)	(Tucker version)
Daddy dear, listen here,	Daddy dear, listen here,
Mamma's feeling blue	Your mama's feelin' blue.
I don't see much of you,	I don't see much of you,
And that will never do.	That will never do.
Once a week Mamma's cheek	Once a week your mama's cheek
Gets a kiss or two,	Gets a kiss or two.
I'm not showing you the door,	Now I'm not showing you the door,
But I must lay down the law.	I'm just layin' down the law.
You've got to see Mamma ev'ry night,	You've got to see mama ev'ry night
Or you can't see Mamma at all,	Or you can't see mama at all.
You've got to kiss Mamma, treat her right,	You've got to kiss mama, treat her right,
Or she won't be home when you call.	Or she won't be home when you call.
If you want my company,	————
You can't "fifty fifty" me,	
or	
I don't want the kind of man	Now I don't care for the kind of a man
Who works on the installment plan	Who loves his mama on the installment plan.
You've got to see Mamma ev'ry night,	You've got to see mama ev'ry night,
Or you can't see Mamma at all.	Or you can't see mama at all.
Monday night, I sat alone,	For instance, Monday night, I sat alone,
Tuesday night, you didn't phone,	Tuesday night, you didn't phone,
Wednesday night, you didn't call,	Wednesday night, you didn't call,
And on Thursday night the same old stall.	Thursday night, the same old stall.

[19] All quotations in this and the preceding paragraph are from newspaper articles included in the Tucker scrapbooks; the specific locations, in order of reference, are as follows: Envelope 2391 (n.d.), p. 3; 10,833 (n.d.), n.p.; Envelope 2391, p. 3; 10,834 (1909); 10,842 (1915), n.p.; 10,850 (1922), n.p.; 10,834; 10,834; 10,833.

Friday night, you dodged my path,
Saturday night, you took your bath,
Sunday night, you called on me,
But you brought three girls for
   company.

You've got to see Mamma ev'ry
   night,
Or you can't see Mamma at all.
You've got to kiss Mamma, treat
her right,
Or she won't be home when you call.

Daddy dear, when you're near,
Ev'ry thing's O. K.,
But when you stay away,
I mope around all day.

I must know where you go
And what makes you gay.
I don't want to share my love
With another turtle dove.[20]

Friday night, you dodged my path,
Saturday night, you took your bath,
Sunday night, you called on me,
But you brought your wife and your
   family.

Dya da da da . . .
Now you've got to see mama ev'ry
   night,
Or you can't see mama at all.
You've got to kiss mama, treat her
   right,
Or she won't be home when you call.

—————

—————

Now I don't care for that kind of a sheik
Who does his sheiking once a week.

You've got to see mama ev'ry night,
Or you can't see mama at all.

Tucker's revision of the original lyrics offers our first glimpse of the presence of the mama. In essence, Tucker has shaped the narrative to be more directly oedipal even as she reassesses her role as a mama in that narrative. Her adding of "your" in the opening stanza intensifies the illusion, present in the sheet music version, that the lover here is really the mother – waiting at home for a kiss on the cheek. The "naughty" puncture of that illusion comes in Tucker's major revision, the line "But you brought your wife and your family." In Tucker's version the singer is the mistress rather than the girlfriend, a role with more complicated implications, less easily fixed, when placed in the context of mother-love. When seen in conjunction with the addition of "your" in the first stanza, this change is especially interesting: as she becomes the mistress, she also becomes *his* mama.

She is also insisting that she is not just a girlfriend (as represented in the original version); their relation is more intimate than that, and she is thus possessed of greater claims to his affection, as well as the

[20] The original lyrics of "You've Got to See Mama Ev'ry Night" are reprinted by permission of CPP Belwin, Inc.

prerogative to turn away from him altogether. But as we saw in Smith's "I Used to Be Your Sweet Mama," the singer's resistance to being fixed – indeed luxuriating in being unfixed – is somewhat countered by the overall narrative: the role of mistress is also a recognition of the forces that keep her in her room. At the same time, her elimination of the original version's last two stanzas suggests she will never be content to "mope around all day."

Tucker adds nuances to this complex positioning of the mama by emphasizing the racial and ethnic dimensions of the narrative. By changing numerous words into contraction form, she confirms what she says outright in her "sheik" reference toward the end: that she is an ethnic mama, an "other" in all sorts of ways, from her desirability to her capacity for desire. Her performance does not exactly specify the ethnicity with which she identifies. Some of her intonations evoke black minstrel forms, some the stylings of the classic blues singers, and some the ragtime exoticism of Jewish popular song. Consequently, she declares herself to be both ethnically identified and yet beyond the trappings of any discrete ethnic category. This red hot mama is black yet Jewish yet American, mother yet mistress.

Tucker communicates the artful interweaving of these various perspectives through her embodied voice. In the song's second line, for instance, Tucker sings "blue" as what I will call a Jewish blue note. Imitating, or perhaps satirizing, Al Jolson's plaintive call to "mammy," Tucker draws the word into a microtonally descending sweep, evoking a complex of emotions broader than any whole- or half-tone run could represent. One hears the note's black roots, its Jewish variation, and its possession in the female voice.[21] That self-proclaimed vocal authority is made even more explicit later on when, before the final verse, Tucker sings a scatting phrase ("dya da da da"). The phrase itself takes its inflections from Yiddish, and so once again associates the mama with her ethnic background. But one also hears the pure music of the voice. Tucker here shows that her red hot mama has authority as a singer,

---

[21] Where black culture used the blue note to "signify" upon the confines of white musical conventions, and thus to register both racism and the presence of a black selfhood that it could not articulate, Jewish culture used a similar wavering note, specifically a descending tone that was reminiscent enough of the blues note to make the same point, yet different enough to specify its Jewish intonations. In both cases, the notes represented the relation between indigenous musical forms – African and Middle-Eastern microtonal movements – and the musical conventions of the dominant culture. Insofar as this note can ultimately be traced back to cantorial vocal style, one might argue that Tucker's appropriation is a reclaiming also of Jewish patriarchal musical traditions. Strikingly, those traditions stand behind Jolson not only as a singer but as a popular figure: the character he played in the film *The Jazz Singer* (1927) was a cantor's son. And while that character's dilemma over assimilation is represented as an oedipal battle over voice, he never finally rejects the tradition itself.

and takes a pleasure in that authority. That is the real artistry of the red hot mama.

As can be seen from this brief exploration of Bessie Smith's and Sophie Tucker's careers, their art cannot be adequately defined by the extremes of either co-optation or liberation. On the one hand, the mama precisely embodied the stereotype of the racial or ethnic mother-lover, while on the other hand she resisted being fixed in body, role, language, or voice. Typically, as demonstrated in Tucker's performance, she preferred being mistress to wife, insisting not only on her desirability but her desire as well, and her ability to direct it where she chose or not direct it at all. She preferred double-entendre to direct address, demonstrating her possession of her own language by revealing that the language of popular song was incapable of naming, containing, or possessing her.

The flexibility of this art is evident in the extraordinary range of responses and desires found in mama songs and performances. Some mama performers used the oedipal-ethnic narrative to enhance their own attractiveness, some to identify with their oppressors, some to identify the source of their oppression, some to attack those oppressions and those oppressors, some to turn the tables on the oppressors, some simply to opt out of the narrative altogether. In many of the red hot mama's songs – and this is especially characteristic of the classic blues – we find a number of these attitudes expressed in succession, and sometimes many at once. In one song Bessie Smith might sing, "Daddy, daddy, please come back to me / Your mama's lonesome as she can be" ("Midnight Blues," 1923), and in another song, "If you see me settin' on another daddy's knee / Don't bother me, I'm as mean as can be" ("Mistreating Daddy," 1923), and in consecutive lines in the same song, "I love my man better than I love myself / And if he don't have me, he won't have nobody else" ("Any Woman's Blues," 1923). Ethel Waters can declare her independence in "I'm No Man's Mama Now" (1925), Ma Rainey can declare her preference for women in "Prove It On Me" (1928), and Hattie Hart can declare her preference for herself above all in "Coldest Stuff in Town" (1934): "When I go out singing: I goes out all alone."[22] There were, in other words, many mamas with many voices.

And these voices continue to be heard. While the figure of the red hot mama had largely disappeared by the 1930s, the influence of her art can been felt in a long line of artists of song and film, from Mae West to Bette Middler and Madonna, from Big Mama (Willie Mae) Thornton to Queen Latifah. Here are women who have endowed the embodied voice with a complex subjectivity, and have transformed that "liveable embodiment" into art.

[22] Taft, *Blues Lyric Poetry*, p. 103.

14

Maternalism and the material girl

NANCY J. VICKERS

When I was just a little girl, I asked my mother, "What would I be? Would I be pretty? Would I be rich?" Here's what she said to me . . .   Doris Day[1]

On March 2, 1989 the National Broadcasting Company (NBC) aired mid-*Cosby Show*, which is to say mid-primetime family television, a ten million dollar Pepsi Cola commercial directed by Joe Pytka and starring Madonna. It represented the "world's most famous woman" in the privacy of her home ostensibly sipping a Pepsi while watching home movies;[2] its soundtrack was almost entirely drawn from the title song of her then soon-to-be-released album, *Like a Prayer*. Promoted by a teaser commercial ("No matter where you are in the world on March 2, get to a TV and see Pepsi present Madonna") and viewed on the same night in forty countries by an estimated 250 million, this event constituted "the single largest one-day media buy in the history of advertising."[3] *Advertising Age* observed that "from Turkey to El Salvador to Anytown USA, 500 million eyes [were] glued to the screen."[4] Calculated to be a triumph of joint promotion, this two-minute spot (entitled "Make A Wish") qualifies as a hymn to the global capabilities of the age of electronic reproduction; it celebrates "the pancultural ambitions of both soda pop and pop star."[5]

For their collective contributions to this essay I am grateful to audiences at the Harvard Center for Literary and Cultural Studies, the Lyrica Society, Northwestern University, the University of Pennsylvania, the University of Southern California (USC), and the Yale Institute of Sacred Music. I have also benefited greatly from the participation of my students in lyric seminars at Dartmouth, Harvard, the University of Pennsylvania, and USC.

1   The 1956 hit, "Whatever Will Be, Will Be," is cited as in the epigraph to Sandra Bernhard's *Confessions of a Pretty Lady* (New York: Harper and Row, 1988).
2   Bill Zehme, "Madonna: The *Rolling Stone* Interview," *Rolling Stone*, March 23, 1989, 50.
3   Leslie Savan, "Desperately Selling Soda," *Village Voice*, March 14, 1989, 47.
4   Bob Garfield, "Pepsi Should Offer Prayer to Madonna," *Advertising Age*, March 6, 1989, 76.
5   Savan, "Desperately Selling Soda," 46.

On March 3, 1989 – one day later – Music Television (MTV) aired a radically different video directed by Mary Lambert, again starring Madonna, and promoting the same song, "Like A Prayer." Italian national television (RAI), under pressure from Catholic groups, reportedly censored it as blasphemous. After a month's hesitation, Pepsi bowed to fundamentalists (principally Donald Wildmon and his American Family Association) claiming consumer "confusion between the ad and a Madonna music video which depicts the singer kissing a saint and coming away with stigmata."[6] They then definitively withdrew the advertisement. In these very weeks the Vatican took pains to instruct American cardinals and bishops that it was "essential" to follow the Church's teachings on sexuality and the family. Specifically targeted for criticism were the combined influences of "planned parenthood, the entertainment business, and feminism."[7] In the heat of a controversy that was itself arguably more media event than true protest, the cola advertisement was even accused of unacceptable innocence. Since its star was a tainted woman, its "sweet" and "sentimental" cast (to invoke Madonna's own descriptive adjectives[8]) was deemed a dangerous and calculated deception.

"Make a Wish" thus constitutes a fascinating case of guilt by association; it demonstrates the operative power (be it consciously planned or unconsciously enacted) of one Madonna production to silence another. For, if considered as paired self-stagings, the combined effect of the advertisement and the video is patently ironic: our first perception of a domesticated, relatively de-eroticized, vulnerable, little girl Madonna (suitable for selling Pepsi) is immediately challenged by our confrontation with overpowering images of a highly sexualized adult moving through a narrative studied to push racial and religious buttons.[9] Given

6   Peter Waldman, "This Madonna Isn't What the Reverend Really Had in Mind," *Wall Street Journal*, April 7, 1989: A1(E). On the cancellation of the advertisement, see Richard Morgan, "In Being a Good Corporate Citizen, Pepsi Came to the Wrong Conclusion," in Adam Sexton, ed., *Desperately Seeking Madonna* (New York: Dell, 1993), pp. 93–95; on the possibility that Madonna sought to "deliberately undermine Pepsi's effort," see Matthew Schifrin (with Peter Newcomb), "A Brain for Sin and a Bod for Business," in Sexton, ed., *Desperately Seeking Madonna*, p. 159.

7   *ABC World News Tonight*, March 10, 1989.

8   As cited by Becky Johnston, "Confessions of a Catholic Girl," *Interview*, May 1989, 56.

9   In *Truth or Dare* (Propaganda Films/Boy Toy Productions, 1991), Madonna asserts: "I'm interested in pushing people's buttons, in being provocative and being political." For a parallel relating of the video to the commercial, see Ramona Curry, "Madonna from Marilyn to Marlene – Pastiche and/or Parody?" *Journal of Film and Video* 42, 2 (Summer 1990), 26. On the video, see Carla Freccero, "Our Lady of MTV: Madonna's 'Like A Prayer,'" *boundary 2* 19, 2 (1992): 174–183; Andrew M. Greeley, "Like a Catholic: Madonna's Challenge to her Church," *America*, May 13, 1989, 447; and Ronald B. Scott, "Images of Race and Religion in Madonna's Video *Like A Prayer*: Prayer and Praise," in Cathy Schwichtenberg, ed., *The Madonna Connection: Representational Politics, Subcultural Identities, and Cultural Theory* (Boulder: Westview, 1993), pp. 57–77.

that they share the same score, the video and the commercial constitute video variations on a musical theme; in tandem they serve to contradict the notion that visualizing lyric necessarily shuts down meaning (a standard criticism of music video) by dramatically producing two alternative meanings within twenty-four hours. Though shown only once to American viewers, Pepsi's "lovely music video/cola ad" nevertheless swept industry awards and won high praise from media critics.[10] "But the ad itself," judged *The Village Voice*, "if viewed as video, is so canny it cooks."[11]

This essay will retrieve Madonna's "censored" Pepsi Cola commercial to argue that it adumbrates – in two minutes – some of the broad terms of a two-year creative cycle of albums, videos, films, interviews, and performances that range from "Make A Wish" (1989) to *Truth or Dare* (1991).[12] That cycle will further be understood to center on the explicitly autobiographical album *Like A Prayer*. As Madonna's most critically acclaimed lyric sequence,[13] *Like A Prayer* self-consciously seeks to locate her within the tradition of women's creativity; it represents her most credible bid to join the company of those "serious" women "artists" who clearly fascinate her (Frida Kahlo and Tamara de Lempicka in the plastic arts; Martha Graham in dance; Ann Sexton – who, she maintains, looks like her mother – in poetry). Though always available to multiple interpretations ("Everything I do is meant to have several meanings, to be ambiguous"[14]), Madonna nonetheless sees herself as a singer-songwriter whose work "tends to be confessional and semi-autobiographical."[15] The commercial thus constitutes an initiation into

[10] Garfield, "Pepsi Should Offer Prayer," 76. Barbara Lippert described the piece as a "beautifully filmed, directed and edited music video with a few gentle Pepsi references," in "Pepsi's Prayer Answered by Madonna's Pop Imagery," *Adweek*, March 6, 1989, 21.

[11] Savan, "Desperately Selling Soda," 47.

[12] On the one- to two-year creative cycle represented by any given pop album, see Will Straw, "Music Video in its contexts: Popular Music and Post-modernism in the 1980s," *Popular Music* 7 (1988), 250. Curry discusses the importance of reading Madonna as a "composite image, which is an intertextual conglomerate" of films, videos, commercials, and publicity ("Madonna from Marilyn to Marlene," 16). With the exception of "Make A Wish," all texts cited from this cycle are available on the album *Like a Prayer*, Sire Records 25844, 1989; on the videocassettes *Madonna: The Immaculate Collection*, Warner Reprise Video 38195, 1990, and *Madonna: Truth or Dare*, Live Home Video 69021, 1991; or on the laser disc *Madonna: Blond Ambition World Tour Live*, Pioneer Artists Laser Disc 13023 24646, 1990.

[13] On the melding of autobiography and lyric with specific reference to women's writing, see Celeste Schenck, "All of a Piece: Women's Poetry and Autobiography," in Bella Brodski and Celeste Schenck, eds., *Life/Lines: Theorizing Women's Autobiography* (Ithaca: Cornell University Press, 1988), pp. 281–305.

[14] As quoted by David Ansen, "Madonna: Magnificent Maverick," *Cosmopolitan* (USA), May 1990, 310.

[15] As quoted by Carrie Fisher, "True Confessions: The *Rolling Stone* Interview with

a cycle of self-representation; it is a collectively "authored" autobiographical fiction – one in which Madonna "participated closely"[16] – that challenges hierarchies of "high" and "low" cultural production by its very existence. As a study of the roots of stardom through a representation of personal history, it muses upon the not trivial question of the coming to voice of the world's most famous woman. A pivotal moment tellingly shapes that authorizing process: "It was the single most . . . the greatest event in my life, my mother dying."[17] In such a context, "Make A Wish" stages Madonna's global resonance by ventriloquizing maternal speech, by dramatizing a fantasy of empowerment in which a daughter (of necessity) talks "like a mother" to herself.[18]

To characterize "Make A Wish" as "autobiographical fiction" is, of course, not to deny its commercial function. For, clearly, it also enacts strategies developed by Pepsi Cola in the 1980s to produce "the most popular advertising on television": first, the use of teen idols to capture the youth market; and second, the appeal to consumer emotions through

Madonna, Part One," *Rolling Stone*, June 13, 1991, 36. E. Ann Kaplan considers that "her whole corpus is constructed as a thinly disguised public confession or autobiography," in "Madonna Politics: Perversion, Repression, or Subversion. Or Masks and/as Master-y," in Schwichtenberg, ed., *The Madonna Connection*, p. 162. On the role of autobiography in Madonna's self-construction as a star, see Greg Seigworth, "The Distance Between me and You: Madonna and Celestial Navigation (or You Can Be My *Lucky Star*)," in *The Madonna Connection*, pp. 291–318. Michael Musto notes that "she brings her deepest secrets into our homes with diary-like immediacy," in "Immaculate Connection," *Outweek*, March 20, 1991, 36.

16 See Johnston, "Confessions of a Catholic Girl," 56. Madonna (who suggested using "her" song) collaborated with creative teams from Pepsi and its advertising agency, BBDO, to produce "Make a Wish." See Betsy Sharkey, "Making a 'Wish': Pytka Directs Madonna for Pepsi," *Adweek*, March 6, 1989, 30–31. Though all of Madonna's work is done in collaboration with an extended range of directors, composers, producers, designers, and photographers, it nonetheless bears a single signature. On the persistence of the fiction of the author in popular music, see Andrew Goodwin, "Sample and Hold: Pop Music in the Digital Age of Reproduction," in Simon Frith and Andrew Goodwin, eds., *On Record: Rock, Pop, and the Written Word* (New York: Pantheon, 1990), p. 272.

17 As quoted by Adrian Deevoy, "If You're Going to Reveal Yourself, Reveal Yourself!" US June 13, 1991, 20. For Madonna's representation of her coming to terms with her mother's death, see Kevin Sessums, "White Heat," *Vanity Fair*, April 1990, 208; and Patrick Goldstein, "It's Not Easy Being Notorious," *Los Angeles Times*, May 5, 1991: Calendar 31.

18 This essay refers to, but does not repeat, theories of the role played by maternal voice in the construction of the subject. For extended summary and critique, see Kaja Silverman, *The Acoustic Mirror: The Female Voice in Psychoanalysis and Cinema* (Bloomington: Indiana University Press, 1988). For the absent mother as "pre-text for the daughter's autobiographical project," see Bella Brodzki, "Mothers, Displacement, and Language in the Autobiographies of Nathalie Sarraute and Christa Wolf," in Brodski and Schenck, eds., *Life/Lines*, pp. 243–59. Barbara Johnson asks, "Is autobiography somehow always in the process of symbolically killing the mother off by telling her the lie that we have given birth to ourselves?" in *A World of Difference* (Baltimore: The Johns Hopkins University Press, 1987), p. 147.

a category of mini-narrative that creative director Alan Pottasch labeled "papa, puppies, and ponies."[19] This telling identification of three paradigmatic Pepsi commercials (a New World family greets an Old World father; a boy plays with puppies; a father gives his son a birthday pony) underscores the challenge to normative masculinity performed by "Make A Wish." Barbara Lippert of *Adweek* explains: "It's hard to believe that telling a younger self to 'make a wish' could have so much meaning, but the female version hasn't been done. Did Mean Joe Greene ever throw his jersey to a girl?"[20] Here, under the sign "Madonna," a classic feel-good birthday narrative undeniably renegotiates Pepsi's pitch to consumers along lines aimed at the cola's largest market, women. The result is a strikingly feminocentric vision of a founding "human" relationship. To unpack the mother/daughter plot inscribed both in this initial text and in the broad cycle of subsequent production which – by temporal accident or design – it informs, I will read each of the three parts of "Make A Wish" in sequence.[21]

As the commercial opens we hear a projector and we see a darkened interior. Within blue-black shadow, the projector's light serves to reveal an isolated figure in an armchair watching a home movie of children at a birthday party. Our gaze moves between the color of the spectator's space and the black and white of the movie screen. Eventually we recognize Madonna in the armchair, while on the screen we see a child party-goer displaying a sign to the camera, "Madonna's eighth birthday." A sudden chord introduces music: it is, in the terms musicologist Susan McClary uses to describe "Like A Prayer," the audio "halo of a wordless (heavenly) choir," "an invocation of stereotyped mystical Catholicism."[22] The child has received a doll and that too is held up to the camera. The receiving of this gift is singled out by the very fact of the dramatic musical intervention; it focuses the piece on a mother/daughter (girl/doll) configuration that will be "at play" throughout.[23] In close-up and medium-shot we (all 300 million of us)

[19] See Mark Landler and Walecia Konrad, "Pepsi: Memorable Ads, Forgettable Sales," *Business Week*, October 21, 1991, 36. Pottasch is quoted by Alan Wolf, "Pottasch, Take Two," *Beverage World*, April 1991, 22ff.

[20] Lippert, "Pepsi's Prayer Answered," 21. This comment alludes to a famous Coca Cola advertisement in which an exhausted football player, Joe Greene, is given a Coke by a boy while walking alone through a stadium tunnel. Ignoring the child, Greene keeps walking, has a second thought, turns back, shouts "Hey kid!" and throws him his jersey. Also see Morgan, "In Being a Good Corporate Citizen," p. 94.

[21] My phrasing clearly echoes that of Marianne Hirsch, *The Mother/Daughter Plot: Narrative, Psychoanalysis, Feminism* (Bloomington: Indiana University Press, 1989).

[22] Susan McClary, "Living to Tell: Madonna's Resurrection of the Fleshly," *Genders 7* (Spring 1990), 14; reprinted in *Feminine Endings: Music, Gender, and Sexuality* (Minneapolis: University of Minnesota Press, 1991), p. 164.

[23] In relation to the madonna-child-doll configuration of the commercial, see Silverman

watch Madonna enjoy watching Madonna. Alone, relaxed, at home in a room of her own – she holds a Pepsi can and smiles. In shot/reverse shot, young Madonna's pleasure in her doll parallels adult Madonna's autoerotic pleasure in herself as a child, in "feeling like a little girl again."[24] Looks are exchanged across generations: the child of 1966 looks at her doll; she also looks beyond a foregrounded Pepsi bottle at the camera, and, presumably, at the parent who operates it. Her look fosters the illusion that she also sees through the apparatus to the adult superstar of 1989, to her future self. As their gazes move slightly to an angle, their mutual smiles fade; their expressions mirror and freeze.[25] Madonna's face pales from color to black and white, and her frozen image crosses from the TV room onto the screen. Since the introduction of the music, her disembodied voice has been heard singing the D minor prelude to "Like a Prayer": "Life is a mystery / Everyone must stand alone / I hear you call my name / And it feels like home."[26] On the prelude's final word, "home," child Madonna emerges, surprised, from within the armchair. As the thirty-year-old is displaced to the black and white "screen" space of the mid-sixties, so the eight-year-old is displaced to the color "real" space of the late eighties. She still wears her birthday-girl crown;[27] her anachronistic Pepsi bottle is now in her left hand; but she no longer holds her doll in her right. Clearly "home" – the familial "then" and the solitary "now" – is at issue: the double (but single) protagonist-dreamers have switched.[28]

on why "the *choric* [maternal voice] fantasy . . . invariably projects a three-generational community of women," *The Acoustic Mirror*, p. 153.

24 Madonna describes the pleasure of returning home in these terms, in Lynn Hirschberg, "The Misfit," *Vanity Fair*, April 1991, 198.

25 The merging of these gazes (with related implications of separation or loss) could be argued to stage a Kristevan "fantasy" of pre-oedipal oneness of mother and child. For extensive analysis, see Silverman, *The Acoustic Mirror*; in specific relation to music video, see E. Ann Kaplan, *Rocking Around the Clock: Music Television, Postmodernism, & Consumer Culture* (New York: Methuen, 1987), pp. 89–100.

26 "LIKE A PRAYER," performed by Madonna and The Andrae Crouch Choir; written by Madonna Ciccone and Patrick Leonard. Copyright © 1989 WB MUSIC CORP., BLEU DISQUE MUSIC CO., INC., WEBO GIRL PUBLISHING, INC. & JOHNNY YUMA MUSIC. All rights on behalf of BLEU DISQUE MUSIC DO., INC. & WEBO GIRL PUBLISHING, INC. administered by WB MUSIC CORP. All rights on behalf of JOHNNY YUMA MUSIC for the world, excluding the US and Canada, administered by WARNER-TAMERLANE PUBLISHING CORP. All rights reserved. Quoted throughout by permission.

27 For the use of the Virgin's crown on the cover of *Like A Prayer*, see Freccero, "Our Lady of MTV," 169.

28 On the centrality of "home" to the mythos of Italian-American immigrant communities as related to "Like A Prayer," see Freccero, "Our Lady of MTV," 175. On relating music video to dream, see Marsha Kinder, "Music Video and the Spectator: Television, Ideology and Dream," *Film Quarterly* 38, 1 (1985), 2–15. Doubling is a consistent feature of Madonna's "self-representation" in video: see Kaplan, *Rocking Around the Clock*, p. 132; Lisa A. Lewis, *Gender Politics and MTV: Voicing the Difference* (Philadelphia: Temple University Press, 1990), pp. 137–38; and McClary, *Feminine Endings*, p. 163.

In the commercial's second part we are immersed in the musical core, the "bath of sounds," of "Make A Wish."[29] Here, and only here, do we encounter verse and chorus (including the critical hook) of "Like A Prayer." This formal break is further accentuated through harmonic contrast, through a shift from one musical register (signaling the Catholic tradition) to another (signaling the African American): "What seems to be a struggle between mystical timelessness on D minor and exuberant, physical celebration on F major ensues."[30] Rapid-fire editing – a visually percussive instant of rhythmic imaging – shifts the piece out of the Catholicizing prelude into the idiom of ecstatic, funky, gospel pop. Though the shot sequence follows the child and the adult in alternating montage, I will treat each independently.

The adult Madonna literalizes the urge implicit in her armchair retrospection; she returns "home" to Detroit in 1966.[31] Her switch with her child self, however, is not literal; she does not find herself surrounded by eight-year-olds at a birthday party. Rather a narrative maneuver consistent with the selective autobiographical drive of both the advertisement and the album takes over. Elements of Madonna's past retrospectively deemed constitutive of her present become "home": first, a corner drugstore and its adjacent street; then, a Catholic girls' school; and finally an African American church. All three are notably traditional adolescent spaces (school, street, and church), "homes" where one goes to get away from home. As in the case of the studied interracialism of the piece, the combined locales direct the commercial's appeal to a broad audience. They prompt a "natural" identification with three distinct age markets: children, in the school; teenagers, in the drugstore – street sequence; and adults, in the church.

In the drugstore and in the street, teens in sixties' dress dance with abandon. Madonna dances with them, though clearly marked by her eighties' style as a singular other, as a time traveler. In the store window a pale red, white and blue Pepsi sign breaks the black and white definition of the space; its pinkish and bluish cast stylizes the Pepsi colors that inform the full piece. In the street, Motown cars are parked and Motown dance moves performed. These specific images are underscored by the song's upbeat chorus; only within this context –

---

29 I refer here to the "theoretical commonplace" that characterizes maternal voice as a "blanket of sound," "a sonorous envelope," "a bath of sounds," or "music." See Silverman, *The Acoustic Mirror*, p. 72.

30 McClary, *Feminine Endings*, pp. 164–65.

31 The return "home" to Detroit repeatedly figures in Madonna's production. For example, in her first tour video, *Madonna: The Virgin Tour* (Warner Music video 38105, 1985), an adoring home crowd is calling her name when she interrupts the flow of the concert to shout: "There's no place *like home* [a sentence repeated years later when *The Blond Ambition Tour* goes to Detroit] . . . I was never elected *homecoming* queen or anything, but I sure feel *like* one now" (my emphasis).

a teenage dance culture – will the act of performance be "at home," will Madonna embody her voice through intermittent lip syncing of her own song. The period setting points to the apogee of Detroit production; classic Chevrolets and classic Motown hits. A visual/verbal pun suggests "Dancing in the Streets" (Martha and the Vandellas, 1964); the chorus repeatedly invokes "In the Midnight Hour" (Wilson Pickett, 1965): both Martha Reeves and Pickett are Detroit-based crossover artists schooled in the gospel tradition.[32] Even the vintage dances (jitterbug, madison, stroll) are melded with moves that quote the style of Motown choreographer Cholly Atkins. The sequence thus capitalizes on the Motown nostalgia of the late 1980s, a nostalgia that is at once personal (in terms of Madonna's Detroit history) and cultural (in terms of its resonance for baby boomers also known as the Pepsi Generation).

As the music shifts out of chorus into verse, as it re-invokes the D minor McClary identifies with "stereotyped mystical Catholicism,"[33] the spectator/camera moves to the classroom of a Catholic girls' school. Sitting in perfect rows, attentive students slowly dissolve into a solitary, pensive Madonna. She looks out of a window and is lost again in nostalgic reverie, as in the earlier invocation of this key. Here, too, we hear her disembodied voice. The camera cuts to a hallway where students march with military discipline, only to have that discipline disrupted as the chorus returns and as Madonna, appealing to pre-adolescent fantasies of schoolhouse rebellion, instigates unruly dance. Montage unites the schoolgirls with the teens of the previous sequence, interspersing the dancers in the hallway with those in the street.

The culminating sequence of the second part transports the spectator/camera to an African American church where the performance of a gospel choir underlines gospel's role in defining the Motown sound. Gospel has, moreover, long been an idiom of compelling female voices: Patti Labelle, Aretha Franklin, Anita Baker, Oleta Adams to name only a few crossover successes. It is a tradition specifically invoked in the commercial by vocal and visual insistence on female choir members and on a "maternalized" African American soloist.[34] As the music reaches its high point, only the choir is given voice as it lip syncs a phrase ("Like a prayer / I'll take you there") familiar to gospel audiences from

---

[32] To be precise, Reeves recorded with Motown, and Pickett did not, though he lived and worked in Detroit.

[33] McClary, *Feminine Endings*, p. 164.

[34] On a parallel figure in the "Like A Prayer" video, see Freccero, "Our Lady of MTV," 180–82; bell hooks (who sees a stereotypical "casting of the black female as Mammy"), *Black Looks: Race and Representation* (Boston: South End Press, 1992), p. 162; McClary, *Feminine Endings*, p. 153; and Scott (who considers that the "fact that Madonna, unlike the divas before her, is a white female is irrelevant"), "Images of Race and Religion," p. 62.

a 1972 Staple Singers' hit, "I'll Take You There."[35] The movement of the choir parallels the movement of the young street dancers, but it is Madonna who enjoys the spotlight as she "strolls" up the church aisle to appropriate the choir (visually, if not vocally) as her back-up. Her patent tribute to her gospel "mothers" flirts with exploitation; it is an affirmation of creative origins that simultaneously displays a cultural theft at the core of white dance pop. As we shall see, the racial dynamics of this maternalized moment, evolving from the popular-catholicism-meets-gospel tension of the music, will be reproduced at least three times: in Lambert's video variation on the song, in the staging of *The Blond Ambition Tour*, and in *Truth or Dare*, the documentary chronicle of that tour.[36]

While the adult explores her past, the child explores her future – the adult Madonna's "home." Immersed in art deco style as well as in a color palate that connotes contemporary Los Angeles, she initially watches the adult sing and dance her new hit on a screen now transformed into a video monitor. The "document" has technologically shifted with the decade from the 8 mm home movie of the sixties to the home video of the eighties. Platinum records decorate the wall. As she crosses the room, she passes a piano and takes a dance step: hers will be a career in song and dance. She then looks at a glamorous Madonna poster; fascinated, her future as a sexy pop icon displayed before her, she sips her Pepsi. Finally, the alternating narratives graphically intersect to close the second sequence: adult Madonna turns in front of the gospel choir; the projector reel turns on the mantelpiece; and child Madonna looks at that same mantelpiece only to find the doll she got for her eighth birthday. Having cut in with the initial discovery of the doll as gift, the music cuts out at the instant of rediscovery.

Puzzled, the child turns and interrogates the screen only to find herself at "home" in Detroit again, holding her Pepsi bottle and her birthday doll. The adult too returns – Pepsi can in hand – to her armchair. Thus, in the commercial's third part, we ostensibly return to where we began . . . but not really. For now in shot/reverse shot both adult and child are still more firmly constituted as looking subjects; communication is established between them; and, smiling broadly at one another, they share a toast that would eradicate loss, time, distance, and even the apparatus (as well as Dad, the person who runs it?). Moving out of the musical "bath of sounds" that marked nostalgic reverie, the adult Madonna enunciates the only words spoken in the commercial:

[35] I am indebted to Kim Hall for calling "I'll Take You There" to my attention.

[36] Hooks reads such appropriations as "attempts to mask her acts of racist aggression as affirmation," *Black Looks*, p. 159; Scott disagrees, "Images of Race and Religion," p.73. See also Curry, "Madonna from Marilyn to Marlene," 26–27; and Freccero, "Our Lady of MTV," 180–82.

"Go ahead. Make a wish." The child Madonna then blows out the candles; the screen fades to black and then reads, in a canny twist on an old tag, "Pepsi. A Generation Ahead."

"Make A Wish" is an unusual advertisement. No Pepsi jingles are sung; precious little Pepsi is consumed – and none of it by Madonna as we know her. It is highly effective in performing its promotional function – a Pepsi can, bottle, or sign is discernible at least eleven times – though always in the mode of the "soft sell."[37] Pepsi, in fact, is constructed as glamourous, festive, intimate, nostalgic, and satisfying; Madonna's promotional hook, "like a prayer," is etched in consumer memory through insistent, catchy repetition. But this "lovely cola ad/video" reads also as something other. Indeed, when asked if she agreed to the commercial only for the money, Madonna rehearses familiar terms: "No, but I consider it a challenge to make a commercial that has some sort of artistic value. I like the challenge of merging art and commerce."[38] And indeed "Make A Wish" holds its own, in the spirit of the album it introduces, as self-conscious and self-serving (though none the less corporate-serving) mini-autobiography. From the point of view of the adult "retro-spectator," it is selective, even revisionary, in terms of the past it represents; it is an explanatory recasting of experience. From the point of view of the child "pro-spectator," it invests prophecy with proof (the doll that traverses boundaries to be equally "at home" in both spaces): it is a dream, a fantasy, a wish that *will be* fulfilled.

Let me turn briefly to the lyrics of "Like A Prayer" as heard in "Make a Wish," for they too are selective. The choices required to produce even a long version of the short form we know as "the advertisement" reduce a five-and-a-half-minute song to under two minutes. The resulting textual density necessarily privileges selected passages of the full piece. The prelude and the chorus are quoted in full; the verses, to which I will return, are radically truncated:

[Prelude]   Life is a mystery
                Everyone must stand alone
                I hear you call my name
                And it feels like home

[Chorus]   When you call my name
                It's like a little prayer
                I'm down on my knees
                I wanna take you there
                In the midnight hour

---

37 Garfield, "Pepsi Should Offer Prayer," 76.
38 As quoted by Zehme, "Madonna," 180.

> I can feel your power
> Just like a prayer
> You know I'll take you there
> (Variant: "Your voice can take me there")

Across these two passages, "I" slips into "You," and "You" into "I" around an act of naming – a traditional trope of granting authority, of ascent into voice. And the name in question, Madonna, is that which is "like a little prayer." Indeed, if we read the song's lyric "you" as addressing Madonna's mother,[39] a slippage between subject and object is virtually guaranteed by the name since it identifies both mother and daughter. Madonna thus calls Madonna by name; address moves in both directions; "*I* will take *you* there" and "*Your* voice can take *me* there" (my emphasis).[40] This overdetermining attribution of the name "Madonna" to both mother and daughter – a name standing for "one of the most potent imaginary constructs known to any civilization"[41] – is enacted consistently and in depth thoughout Madonna's multiple production: "I sometimes think," she observes, "I was born to live up to my name."[42]

At the center of *Truth or Dare*, we see Madonna "down on [her] knees" at a gravestone marked with a variation on her own name, "Madonna Fortin Ciccone: 1933–1963." Madonna Ciccone died at the age of thirty when her daughter Madonna (born the day after Assumption Day, 1958) was only five. And when that namesake daughter reached thirty, she participated in the production of an extravagantly public event ("the single largest one-day media buy in the history of advertising"), one that was staged in the form of a private commemorative gesture, a remembering of the "birth day" that bound mother and daughter: "When I turned thirty, which was the age my mother was when she died . . . I kept thinking 'I'm now outliving my mother.' I thought something horrible was going to happen to me."[43] Indeed, Madonna's most ambitious album, *Like A Prayer*, belongs to her mother: "This album is dedicated to my mother who taught me how to pray." As Stephen Holden notes, "Its songs intertwine [Madonna's] search for faith with

---

[39] The identification of the "you" addressed in "Like A Prayer" as Madonna's lost mother is determined here by the specific context of "Make A Wish." Madonna's aggressive recontextualizations of the song's structure of address will radically alter its subsequent meanings.

[40] Silverman describes the "endless reversibility" of the mother/daughter positions, *The Acoustic Mirror*, p. 153.

[41] Julia Kristeva, "Stabat Mater," in *The Female Body in Western Culture: Contemporary Perspectives*, ed. Susan Suleiman (Cambridge, MA: Harvard University Press, 1985), p. 101.

[42] As quoted by Hirschberg, "The Misfit," 200.

[43] As quoted by Sessums, "White Heat," 142.

her search for her mother."[44] Its lyric voice would speak across the divide that figures repeatedly in the works associated with it.

Another *Like A Prayer* song, "Promise To Try," specifically asks "Does she hear my voice in the night when I call?"[45] Later, in that same song, an adult seems to admonish a child: "Little girl, don't you forget her face"; "Don't let memory play games with your mind / She's a faded smile frozen in time." Indeed, the Pepsi Cola commercial's visual fix on the mirroring of mother–daughter faces, as well as its transition into the memory-driven dream sequence by way of the literal "freeze" of a faded smile, imagistically "echoes" these verses. "Promise To Try" (for which no video was produced) is further remotivated in David Fincher's direction of Madonna's storyline for the different, but equally familial, "Oh Father" – her self-proclaimed "most autobiographical" work.[46] Here, as in the Cola commercial, the Madonna persona is split into a child and an adult who repeatedly fuse and separate. As the narrative opens, for example, the camera focuses on a child, "Madonna," playing in a snowscape; it then moves inward through a window to a room where a priest and a husband–father attend the death of a young wife–mother, "Madonna." A fatherly (Fatherly?) hand pulls a white sheet over the dead "Madonna's" face and then extends his gesture to unveil the return to the snowscape. There the solitary child-turned-adult "Madonna" finally takes voice; she can now break into song. "I think," she notes in an observation pertinent to this moment, "the biggest reason I was able to express myself and not be intimidated was not having a mother."[47] As the narrative develops, the child Madonna will "sing," but the adult Madonna's voice will be heard; the adult will appear, but her shadow will be that of the child; two couples – her father and her mother? her husband and herself? – will repeatedly dissolve into one another. And at her mother's open coffin, in one of the most troubling shots in mainstream music video, the child will tremble before lips sewn shut (a sealed, lost kiss; a silenced, lost voice; a faded, frozen smile) and enact a verse from "Promise to Try": "Can't kiss her goodbye – but I promise to try." In addition, Fincher and Madonna

---

[44] Stephen Holden, "Madonna Re-creates Herself – Again," *New York Times*, March 19, 1989, H12.

[45] "PROMISE TO TRY" (Madonna Ciccone, Patrick Leonard) Copyright © 1989 WB MUSIC CORP., BLEU DISQUE MUSIC CO., INC., WEBO GIRL PUBLISHING, INC. & JOHNNY YUMA MUSIC. All rights on behalf of BLEU DISQUE MUSIC CO., INC. & WEBO GIRL PUBLISHING, INC. administered by WB MUSIC CORP. All rights on behalf of JOHNNY YUMA MUSIC for the world, excluding the US and Canada, administered by WARNER-TAMERLANE PUBLISHING CORP. All rights reserved. Quoted throughout by permission.

[46] As cited by Ansen, "Madonna: Magnificent Maverick," 310.

[47] Cited by Goldstein, "It's Not Easy," 30. This reading of "Oh Father" owes much to Giuliana Lund.

work to situate "Oh Father" in direct relation to a dominant cinematic model in which a narrative of maternal loss founds a comic/tragic narrative of megalomaniacal success. Repeatedly citing *Citizen Kane*,[48] the video ominously recasts and rethinks the formative trauma of a now canonical boyhood as the formative trauma of an aspiring girlhood.

In the commemorative staging of "Madonna's eighth birthday," then, we witness a party for a motherless child, a child shown to be standing alone, confronting the irreparable loss of a parent who is now "like an angel" – "the closest thing to God."[49] And the gap implicit in such a loss may well reveal itself in the obsessive return to the bittersweet figure of simile that overruns "Like a Prayer": "like an angel sighing," "like flying," "like a muse," "like a dream," "like home," "like a child," "like a prayer." For simile is sweet in terms of the empowering promise of imitation, of approximation of an absolute; yet bitter, in the impossibility of gaining (or regaining) that absolute. It is a "wannabe" figure. Consider, as example, the only fragment of the song's extended verses selected for use in the Pepsi commercial, the chiastic lines that may well have generated the creative team's "concept" and that musically reintroduce the strain that McClary terms a jarring audio "halo":[50]

> Like a child
> You whisper softly to me
> You're in control
> Just like a child.

In a paralleling visual chiasmus, while we hear the phrase "like a child," the child passes the adult's piano and takes her dance step; "you whisper softly to me" sounds under the image of the schoolgirls seated in the classroom who slowly dissolve into the solitary, remembering adult; "you're in control" next underscores the Catholic girls marching in the hallway; "just like a child" returns to the child studying the poster of Madonna. In this brief sequence, the constituent elements of the career – song, dance, image – are all adumbrated as a voice, like that of a child, whispers the message that enables that career: "You're in control."

And the tension of the piece resides precisely in the ambiguity of that phrase. Does "You're in control" mean "You're in line, in uniform, and under control" like a schoolgirl; or rather, "You're in charge,

---

48 On this video in relation to *Citizen Kane*, see Kaplan, "Madonna Politics," p. 162. On maternal loss and "the maternal voice fantasy" in *Citizen Kane*, see Silverman, *The Acoustic Mirror*, pp. 86–87.

49 In *Truth or Dare*, Madonna states that in death her mother seemed "like an angel"; earlier, a friend commented: "I remember praying to Madonna . . . her mother Madonna. She was the closest thing to God."

50 McClary, *Feminine Endings*, p. 164.

standing alone, doing well, being the boss, and in control" like a pop superstar? For it is in these double terms that Madonna repeatedly articulates the ambiguity inherent in her multiple self-constructions: "And while it might have seemed like I was behaving in a stereotypical way, at the same time I was masterminding it. I was in control of everything I was doing"; "I'm definitely compulsive, but I'm compulsive about being in control."[51] Madonna's response, her fictions would tell us, to the loss of her mother's "sweet voice" of "real advice and solace"[52] – a voice that, given more time, might have taught her to behave "like a girl," accept the "typical constraints of blue-collar, big-Catholic-family upbringing," and never become "Madonna"[53] – was the formulation of a compensating American dream of autonomy: "I went to New York. I had a dream. I wanted to be a big star. I didn't know anybody. I wanted to dance. I wanted to sing . . . I worked really hard. And my dream came true."[54] In pursuit of that dream, she tells us, she took with her only two remembrances of home: "a giant baby doll and a photo of my mother who died when I was very young."[55] At thirty she then reclaims her mother's voice within herself and for herself by speaking a variant of "You're in control" in chorus with birthday-party mothers everywhere: "Go ahead. Make a wish." Such a wish – like a dream, like a prayer – would empower self-realization through maternal sanction. Here the will to wish takes the form of a childlike whisper from beyond the grave, voiced by an idealized mother, a mother idealizable precisely because lost.

The Pepsi Cola commercial sets in place a maternal discourse that moves across the *Like A Prayer* cycle to reach its culmination in Alek Keshiashian's documentary rendering of the *Blond Ambition Tour*. For *Truth or Dare*, like "Make A Wish," invokes "childhood games" in its title and conjures the label "home movie."[56] Striking in its foregrounding at

---

51 As cited by McClary, *Feminine Endings*, p. 149; and by Carrie Fisher, "True Confessions: The *Rolling Stone* Interview with Madonna, Part Two," *Rolling Stone*, June 27, 1991, 45.

52 The phrase is taken from an interview of an Italian-American woman who invokes her fantasy of parental behavior in contrast to her experience of the patriarchal "authoritarianism of the [Italian-American] domus." cited by Robert Orsi, *The Madonna of 115th Street: Faith and Community in Italian Harlem 1880–1950* (New Haven: Yale University Press, 1985), p. 115.

53 Madonna is quoted by Goldstein, "It's Not Easy," 8 and 30. See also Maureen Orth, "Madonna in Wonderland," *Vanity Fair*, October 1992, 306.

54 This is the ironized opening speech of *The Virgin Tour*.

55 Quoted by John Sachs and Piers Morgan, *Private Files of the Stars* (London: Angus and Robertson, 1991), p. 11.

56 The descriptive phrase "childhood games" is Madonna's, as quoted by Deevoy, "If You're Going to Reveal Yourself," 19. On revealing one's "true" self as "game," see E. Deidre Pribram, "Seduction, Control, & the Search for Authenticity: Madonna's *Truth or Dare*," in Schwichtenberg, ed., *The Madonna Connection*, p. 203. Madonna notes of Warren

all levels of its subject's (and executive producer's) control, the documentary relies heavily on a strategic deployment of matriarchal family fictions: "I didn't realize how matriarchal I am, how maternal I am, until I watched this movie."[57] Appropriating in studied detail the family structure of the houses of New York's ball circuit,[58] Madonna's mimetic casting of herself as a drag queen "mother," and of her dancers (predominantly gay men of color) as her "children," stands in tense relation to the repeated invocations of "real" mothering throughout the film. We see the backstage visits of the dancers' mothers on Mother's Day. We meet Moira, a childhood friend about to become a mother (again), who asks Madonna to act as godmother of a baby girl to be named Madonna. On film, only Moira will weep openly over the death of Madonna's mother, Madonna, to whom she tells us she prayed as a child; she even gives Madonna a "Madonna and Child" that she has painted. And we witness an overdramatic, chilling visit to a mother's grave where a daughter imagines being buried: "I'm gonna fit in right here. You're gonna bury me sideways." The documentary's central graveside sequence is notably scored to the song "Promise to Try" and narratively framed by the crisis of the superstar's loss of voice, of her literal inability to sing. Even the archetypal family event that demands home-movie documentation – the birthday party – is restaged as thousands of concert-goers sing "Happy Birthday" to Madonna's father or as Madonna recites a birthday poem to her personal assistant.

Thus the film disruptively centers on an ambivalent maternalism that is variously represented as highminded, or campy, or cruel, but that is always pragmatic. For it serves above all to bind together a complexly articulated performance troupe for the duration of a demanding promotional tour. Similarly, the maternal empowerment imagined in "Make A Wish" nonetheless casts Pepsi Cola as a nurturer that never goes away, one that even transcends generations; it also sells *Like A Prayer* to a researched market of "wannabes" programmed to identify with its sweet dreamer. Indeed, a failure to recognize the pragmatics of Madonna's maternalist fictions may have helped fuel the lawsuit

(56 contd.) Beatty's resistance to the filming: "He just thought I was fucking around, making a home movie," as quoted by Don Shewey, "The Saint, The Slut, The Sensation ... Madonna," *Advocate*, May 7, 1991, 44. On home movies and women's autobiography, see B. Ruby Rich and Linda Williams, "The Right of Re-vision: Michelle Citron's *Daughter Rite*," in Bill Nichols, ed., *Movies and Methods*, vol. II (Berkeley: University of California Press, 1985), pp. 359–69.

57 As quoted by Shewey, "The Saint, The Slut," 44.

58 On this appropriation of the role of "house mother," see Joan Buck's review in *Vogue*, July 1991, 76. On the ambivalence of the appropriated subculture ("should we feel grateful or raped?" "an exploitation we enjoy"), see Musto, "Immaculate Connection," 37 and 41; and Lisa Henderson, "Justify Our Love: Madonna and the Politics of Queer Sex," in Schwichtenberg, ed., *The Madonna Connection*, pp. 122–24.

brought against "mommie dearest" by "children" Oliver Crumes, Kevin Stea, and Gabriel Trupin.[59] Following Madonna's lead in conflating matriarchy conceived as the mirror image of patriarchy with matriarchy conceived as a utopian site of boundless maternal nurture, Trupin, for instance, maintained that he and his fellow litigants believed Keshiashian was shooting only "for Madonna's private home movies": "She claimed to be a friend. A friend is someone you can ask something from. We asked. She didn't care."[60] By contrast, "children" Jose Guitierez and Luis Camacho celebrate being offered contracts by Madonna's record company. They observe that "Madonna is part girlfriend, part mother, but always in charge"; critic Jonathan Van Meter adds, "What seems to fuel their motivation is the desire not to let Momma down. After all, she has her own dreams for them. Dreams, perhaps, that they don't even have for themselves."[61]

Always a consummate business woman, Madonna would seem to dispense "matronage" selectively and on grounds other than those of unconditional, even-handed mother love: "I'm sorry," she observes of the workplace she enables, "this is not a democracy."[62] Her ambivalent status as the denying/nurturing sovereign mother of an "x-rated Partridge family,"[63] is, of course, amply enacted in the final sequences of the film itself. Over the repeated verse "Keep people together, forever, and ever," her children are dismissed one by one until she alone is left in the spotlight. As the credits come up her "maternal voice" is heard teaching them a goodnight prayer. She then prefaces a goodnight kiss by calling the name of each child, though she forgets Carlton's. She tells them to close their eyes and "dream some dreams." She says "Goodnight," like a mother, only to demand repeatedly that they "shut up." Silence fills the theater, or the TV room, until Madonna reappears sitting alone on a sofa. She brandishes a remote control as if she were back at home in front of a screen – not on one – and says: "I'm gonna press POWER, and when I press it, the camera's gonna go off instantly." And it does go off. But it does so reluctantly, resistantly. The closing moments of *Truth or Dare* recast the opening autobiographical gesture represented by "Make A Wish" in patently parodic terms; they return us, in the context of another "home movie," to Madonna ventriloquizing maternal voice. *Like A Prayer* was, after all, "dedicated to [her] mother who taught [her] how to pray." Thus the documentary gives pause to

---

59 In Julie Brown's parody, *Medusa: Dare to Be Truthful*, a banner at the tour's farewell party reads "Goodbye, Mommie Dearest," Just Julie Productions, 1991.

60 As interviewed by *Hardcopy*, January 22, 1992; and as cited by Chris Morris, "'Truth' Consequences: Dancers Sue Madonna," *Billboard*, February 1, 1992, 90.

61 "Madonna's Boyz Make Good," *NYQ*, January 26, 1992, 43 and 69.

62 As quoted by Orth, "Madonna in Wonderland," 306.

63 *Hardcopy*, January 22, 1992.

Pepsi's feel-good appropriation of the rescue fantasy of an enabling maternal voice, of a call to "dream some dreams."

Claire Kahane reminds us that feminists have been seeking "to construct empowering representations of a mother precisely by dreaming; dreaming, however, not in the privacy of an interior space, but in a public discourse that asserts the power of the dream."[64] Madonna's Pepsi commercial would seem a textbook enactment of that fantasy, albeit one that lasts only for the instant sanctioned by its multinational patron. But already within "Make A Wish" the power of the dream seems inextricably bound to a dream of power.[65] And that political double bind is in turn played out when the *Like A Prayer* cycle culminates in a re-vision of maternal control so problematic as to beg resistance.

[64] Claire Kahane, "Questioning the Maternal Voice," *Genders* 3 (1988), 82. Both Kahane (83) and Silverman (*The Acoustic Mirror*, p. 125) acknowledge the theoretical impasses as well as the political advantages of the "maternal voice fantasy."

[65] On the distance (specifically on the issue of power or control) between Madonna and feminists, see hooks, "Desperately Seeking Madonna, the Feminist," *On the Issues* 26 (Spring 1993), 5–6; Lynne Layton, "Like A Virgin: Madonna's Version of the Feminine," in Sexton, ed., *Desperately Seeking Madonna*, pp. 190–91; and Roseann M. Mandziuk, "Feminist Politics and Postmodern Seductions: Madonna and the Struggle for Political Articulation," in Schwichtenberg, ed., *The Madonna Connection*, pp. 167–87.

Index

Index

Cato, 41
Cephisus (Boeotia), shrine of, 32
Chapman, George
  The Gentleman Usher, 87
Chevalier, Maurice, 105, 106, 111, 115, 116
Children of Paul's, 94
chora, 66n2, 74, 78
Chorley, Henry
  Thirty Years' Musical Recollections, 143,
    147n24
Christiansen, Rupert, 145
Chrysaor, 20, 23
cinéma vérité, 176
Circe, 18, 38, 130–31, 134
Cixous, Hélène, 4, 12, 55
Cixous, Hélène and Catherine Clément
  The Newly Born Woman, 4, 65n1
Clément, Catherine, 3, 4, 6, 10, 55, 62, 139, 149
Coleridge, Samuel Taylor, 67
  "Lines Composed in a Concert-Room,"
    78–79
Colet, Louise, 152–54, 163–64
  La Servante, 11, 152–64
community, 198–99, 200, 203, 207
Conrad, Peter, 142n10, 149
"coon" songs, 213, 222, 223, 224–25
  "coon shouting," 224
Coryat, Thomas, 93
cross-dressing, 88–89, 92–93, 150, 223
Cullen, Countee
  "Heritage," 203

Danae, 22, 26–28
Dante Alighieri, 7, 8, 35–49
  the pilgrim, 8, 35, 36, 39, 41, 46, 49
  the poet, 36, 37, 40, 46
  Amor che ne la mente mi ragiona, 41
  Convivio, 41
  De vulgari eloquentia, 41
  Divine Comedy, 35
  Inferno, 38, 39, 44
  Paradiso, 35, 36
  Purgatorio XIX, 8, 37–49
Daphne, 160–61
David, as Psalmist, 49
de Beauvoir, Simone, 129
Dekker, Thomas
  Blurt, Master-Constable, 92–97
Delacroix, Eugene, 160
Delphi, 21
Demetrakopoulos, Stephanie, 198, 200,
    202n8

De Quincey, Thomas
  Confessions of an English Opium-Eater,
    69n13
Despoina, 24
diaspora, black, 197, 198
direct address, in film, 167–78
  and embodiment, 175–78
diva, 3, 5, 8–9, 10, 113, 139–40, 145–51
Doane, Mary Ann, 5
documentary, in film, 167, 168, 173–78
dolce stil nuovo, 40
Du Bois, W. E. B.
  Souls of Black Folk, 202–3
Du Maurier, George, 140
Dumont, Margaret, 113
Dunn, Leslie C., 8, 9

Eddy, Nelson, 9, 103–19
  see also MacDonald, Jeanette
Edison, Thomas Alva, 123–24
effeminacy, 57, 61, 85, 86, 90, 92, 93
Eliot, George, 7, 10, 139–51
  Armgart, 7, 10, 139, 140, 145–51
  Daniel Deronda, 148, 149
  Middlemarch, 140, 151
  "Mr. Gilfil's Love Story," 145
Engh, Barbara, 7, 9
epistolary form, in film, 169–70
Erichthonius, 23
Eumenides, 23
Euripides
  Heracles Mad, 18
  Ion, 26

family romance, 157–59
Farnell, Lewis, 23
father, 77, 174
  as language giver, 158
  and *nom du père*, 158
  and paternal order, 158–59
Feldman, Thalia, *see* Phillies-Howe, Thalia
feminism, 1, 84, 246
feminist theory, 1, 4, 12, 120, 129–30
  and film studies, 4
  and musicology, 5–6
  see also maternal voice; psychoanalytic
    theory; voice
film musical, 103, 104–108, 109, 113–14,
    118, 119
Fincher, David, 241–42
Finnish Karelia, 11, 179–94
Fitz-Lyon, April, 144

Index